Understanding
FRANZ WERFEL

Understanding

Franz Werfel

by
Hans Wagener

University of South Carolina Press

Published in Columbia, South Carolina, by the
University of South Carolina Press

Manufactured in the United States of America

Library of Congress Cataloging-in-Publication Data

Wagener, Hans, 1940–
    Understanding Franz Werfel / by Hans Wagener.
        p.   cm.
    Includes bibliographical references and index.
    ISBN 0–87249–883–2 (alk. paper)
    1. Werfel, Franz, 1890–1945—Criticism and interpretation.
I. Title.
PT2647.E77Z84   1993
833'.912—dc20   92–41141

Contents

EDITOR'S PREFACE

*U*nderstanding *Modern European and Latin American Literature* has been planned as a series of guides for undergraduate and graduate students and nonacademic readers. Like its companion series, *Understanding Contemporary American Literature,* the aim of the books is to provide an introduction to the life and writings of prominent modern authors and to explicate their most important works.

Modern literature makes special demands, and this is particularly true of foreign literature in which the reader must contend not only with unfamiliar, often arcane artistic conventions and philosophical concepts, but also with the handicap of reading the literature in translation. It is a truism that the nuances of one language can be rendered in another only imperfectly (and this problem is especially acute in fiction), but the fact that the works of European and Latin American writers are situated in a historical and cultural setting quite different from our own can be as great a hindrance to the understanding of these works as the linguistic barrier. For this reason, the UMELL series will emphasize the sociological and historical background of the writers treated. The peculiar philosophical and cultural traditions of a given culture may be particularly important for an understanding of certain authors, and these will be taken up in the introductory chapter and also in the discussion of those works to which this information is relevant. Beyond this, the books treat the specifically literary aspects of the author under discussion and attempt to explain the complexities of contemporary literature lucidly. They are conceived as introductions to the authors covered, not as comprehensive analyses. Nor do they provide detailed summaries of plot since they are meant to be used in conjunction with the books they discuss, not as a substitute for the study of the original works. The purpose of the books is to provide information and judicious literary assessment of the major works in the most compact, readable form. It is our hope that the UMELL series will help to increase our knowledge and understanding of the European and Latin American cultures and will serve to make the literature of those cultures more accessible.

Professor Wagener's book is a thorough and well-balanced appreciation of the considerable achievements of a talented and—in his day—successful writer. To follow Werfel is to trace not only the literary life of the first half of the twentieth century but also its tragic historical development, from the pathos-laden, hymnic Expressionist poetry of the famous collection of poems *Wir sind* (We Are, 1913) through the emotionalism of Expressionist drama to the novel of New Objectivity, from the optimism and utopian yearnings of the pre-World War I period to the life of the near destitute exile fleeing the Nazi regime. Although the reputation of this productive and great-hearted Austrian writer has declined in the last two decades, he is still a fascinating figure in the history of Expressionism and German exile literature. Beyond that, it may be argued that several of his works are literary masterpieces that still deserve our attention and analysis. Wagener succeeds in analyzing the entire oeuvre of Werfel and in concentrating on those works that have best withstood the test of time.

J. H.

ABBREVIATIONS

Book titles cited in the text are abbreviated as shown below. Unless stated otherwise, the page numbers following these abbreviations refer to the original American editions listed in the Bibliography.

BHE   *Between Heaven and Earth*
C   *Cella, or, The Survivors*
DLW   *Gesammelte Werke: Das lyrische Werk.* Ed. Adolf D. Klarmann. Frankfurt am Main: S. Fischer, 1967.
EH   *Embezzled Heaven*
ER   *The Eternal Road*
FD   *The Forty Days of Musa Dagh*
HV   *Hearken unto the Voice*
JC   *Jacobowsky and the Colonel*
JM   *Juarez and Maximilian*
P   *Poems*
PF   *The Pascarella Family*
PH   *The Pure in Heart*
SB   *The Song of Bernadette*
SU   *Star of the Unborn*
TW   *Twilight of a World*
V   *Verdi: A Novel of the Opera*

CHRONOLOGY

1890   10 September 1890: Franz Werfel born in Prague, the son of Rudolf Werfel, the owner of a glove factory, and his wife Albine, née Kussi.

1896   Attends private Catholic elementary school of the Piarist order in Prague.

1904   September: Attends public high school, the Royal and Imperial German Gymnasium, Stefansgymnasium, in Prague. First attempts at writing.

1909–10 Attends lectures on philosophy and law at the German University of Prague (Karlsuniversität), without choosing a major.

1910–11 Fall 1910–May 1911: In Hamburg; is employed for the first few weeks as a business apprentice at the shipping agency Brasch and Rothenstein.

1911–12 Fall 1911–September 1912: In the army as a one-year volunteer at Hradcany Castle in Prague.

1911   December: First collection of poems, *Der Weltfreund* (The Philanthropist), published by Axel Juncker Verlag.

1912   Fall: Moves to Leipzig and works as editor for Kurt Wolff Verlag (until July 1914).

1913   One-act play *Die Versuchung: Ein Gespräch des Dichters mit dem Erzengel und Luzifer* (The Temptation: A Conversation of the Poet with the Archangel and Lucifer) and the collection of poetry *Wir sind* (We Are) published by Kurt Wolff Verlag.

1914   End of August: Called up to serve in the First World War. On furlough November 1914–April 1915. Then works in a military office and, from Spring 1916 on, as telephone operator of an artillery regiment at the Eastern front (Galicia). August 1917–November 1918 works in the Military Press Bureau in Vienna.

1915   Reworks version of Euripides' *The Trojan Women;* collection of poetry *Einander* (Each Other) published.

1915ff. Correspondence with the nurse Gertrud Spirk whom he intends to marry after the war.

1917	November: Meets Alma Mahler-Gropius. On 2 August 1918 she has a son by Werfel, Martin Carl Johannes, who dies June 1919.
1918	January 18–April 15: Presents about ten lectures on behalf of the Austrian Military Press Bureau in Switzerland. Due to their pacifist nature, Werfel is ordered back to Vienna.
1918	Fall: Joins his friend Egon Erwin Kisch in the "Red Guard," a small socialist faction, which calls on the masses to storm the banks.
1919	Collection of poetry *Der Gerichtstag* (The Day of Judgment) published.
1920	Drama *Spiegelmensch: Magische Trilogy* (Mirror Man: Magic Trilogy), *Spielhof: Eine Phantasie* (Spielhof: A Phantasy), and novella *Nicht der Mörder, der Ermordete ist schuldig* ("Not the Murderer") published.
1921	Drama *Bocksgesang* (*Goat Song*) published.
1922	Drama *Schweiger* published.
1923	Collection of poetry *Beschwörungen* (Conjurations) published.
1924	1 April: *Verdi: Roman der Oper* (*Verdi: A Novel of the Opera*) published and, during the same year, drama *Juarez und Maximilian* (*Juarez and Maximilian*); both published by Paul Zsolnay, Werfel's new publisher.
1925	Travels with Alma to Egypt and Palestine.
1926	15 January: Grillparzer Prize for *Juarez and Maximilian*. End of August: Drama *Paulus unter den Juden* (*Paul among the Jews*) published. Fall: Member of the Prussian Academy of the Arts.
1927	Novella *Der Tod des Kleinbürgers* (*The Man Who Conquered Death*) and collection of novellas, *Geheimnis eines Menschen* ("Saverio's Secret"), published. State Prize of Czechoslovakia.
1928	Novel *Der Abituriententag: Geschichte einer Jugendschuld* (*Class Reunion*) published.
1929	8 July: Marries Alma Mahler. Fall: Novel *Barbara oder Die Frömmigkeit* (*The Pure in Heart*) published.
1930	Second trip with Alma to Egypt and Palestine. In Damascus encounter with young Armenian refugees. Drama *Das Reich Gottes in Böhmen* (The Kingdom of God in Bohemia) published.
1931	Speech *Realismus und Innerlichkeit* ("Realism and Inwardness"), novella *Kleine Verhältnisse* ("Poor People") and novel *Die Geschwister von Neapel* (*The Pascarella Family*) published.

1932   Speech *Können wir ohne Gottesglauben leben* ("Can We Live Without Faith in God") published.

1933   Werfel signs declaration of loyalty; is expelled from the Prussian Academy of the Arts. End of November: Novel *Die vierzig Tage des Musa Dagh* (*The Forty Days of Musa Dagh*) published. December: Attempts to become a member of the Reich Association of German Writers.

1934   February: *The Forty Days of Musa Dagh* banned in Germany.

1935   Stepdaughter, Manon Gropius, dies from polio. Drama *Der Weg der Verheißung: Ein Bibelspiel* (*The Eternal Road*), *Schlaf und Erwachen: Neue Gedichte* (Sleep and Awakening: New Poems), and drama *In einer Nacht* (During One Night) published.

1935   November 1935–January 1936: Werfel travels with Alma for the first time to the United States to attend the rehearsals of *The Eternal Road* under the direction of Max Reinhardt, music by Kurt Weill, at the Manhattan Opera House in New York. First performance delayed until 7 January 1937.

1937   19 March: The Austrian government bestows the Order of Merit for Art and Science upon Werfel. Fall: Novel *Höret die Stimme* (*Hearken unto the Voice*) published; also an American anthology of prose, *Twilight of a World.*

1938   March: After the annexation of Austria by Nazi Germany, Werfel does not return from Italy but meets Alma in Zurich. After a trip to Paris, Amsterdam, and London, he chooses to reside in Paris. End of July: Werfel suffers his first heart attack at Sanary-sur-Mer on the Côte-d'Azur. Speech *Von der reinsten Glückseligkeit des Menschen* ("Of Man's True Happiness") published.

1939   Fall: Novel *Der veruntreute Himmel* (*Embezzled Heaven*) published by exile publisher Bermann-Fischer, Werfel's new publisher, in Stockholm.

1940   Summer: After German invasion of France, Werfel unsuccessfully attempts to flee across the border into Spain. During his stay in Lourdes, he vows to write a novel about St. Bernadette, should he be saved from the Nazis. 13 September: Werfel and Alma flee with Heinrich Mann and his wife on foot across the Pyrenees to Spain. They proceed to Madrid and Lisbon and to the United States. 13 October: Arrival on the "Nea Hellas" in Hoboken, N.J. After a stay in New York, the Werfels journey to Los Angeles on 26 December.

1941 Novella *Eine blaßblaue Frauenschrift* (A Pale Blue Woman's Writing) published in Buenos Aires. 13 July: Death of Werfel's father in Marseilles. December: German edition of novel *Das Lied von Bernadette* (*The Song of Bernadette*) published in Stockholm; 11 May 1942 American edition published.

1943 9 June: Receives honorary doctorate (Doctor of Law) from the University of California, Los Angeles (UCLA). 11 September: Suffers severe heart attack from which he never fully recovers.

1944 December: Essays and "Theologumena" *Between Heaven and Earth* (*Zwischen oben und unten*) and drama *Jacobowsky und der Oberst: Komödie einer Tragödie* (*Jacobowsky and the Colonel*) published (first performance on 14 March 1944 in New York).

1945 *Poems*, first English translation of selection of poems, published. 17 August: Manuscript of novel *Stern der Ungeborenen* (*Star of the Unborn*) completed. 26 August: Dies at his desk in his home in Beverly Hills, Calif.

1946 Fall: Novel *Star of the Unborn* and *Gedichte aus den Jahren 1908–1945* (Poems from the Years 1908–1945) published.

1982 Novel fragment *Cella oder Die Überwinder* (*Cella, or, The Survivors*) published.

Understanding
FRANZ WERFEL

INTRODUCTION

"You know," Kafka wrote in December 1912 to his fiancée Felice Bauer, "Werfel is really a miracle; when I read his book *Der Weltfreund* (The Philanthropist) for the first time, I thought that the enthusiasm for him would drive me crazy. That man is capable of tremendous things." Another Prague poet, Rainer Maria Rilke, sent encouraging letters to his youthful fan, Franz Werfel, in the summer of 1913, and later wrote in his essay "On the Young Poet": "For the author [Rilke] the generally happy occupation with Franz Werfel's poems was in some way the prerequisite for this work." Werfel's first collections of poetry, *Der Weltfreund* (The Philanthropist; 1911), *Wir sind* (We Are; 1913), *Einander* (Each Other; 1915), and *Der Gerichtstag* (The Day of Judgment; 1919) were hailed as the beginning of a new era in literature, known today as Expressionism. It is not surprising that the most famous trend-setting contemporary anthology of German Expressionist poetry, Kurt Pinthus's *Menschheitsdämmerung* (Twilight of Mankind; 1920), contains more poems by Werfel than by anyone else. During the 1920s Werfel also attained success as a dramatist and even more success as a novelist. When he came to the United States as an exile in 1940 his fame was already firmly established in this country on the basis of his novels *Barbara oder Die Frömmigkeit* (*The Pure in Heart;* 1929) and particularly the bestseller *Die vierzig Tage des Musa Dagh* (*The Forty Days of Musa Dagh;* 1933). His novel *Das Lied von Bernadette* (*The Song of Bernadette;* 1941) was one of the greatest American bestsellers of all time; millions read the book, and the 1943 cinematic version became a major box office success. But by 1946, only a year after Werfel's death, the popularity of his work began to decline. His last novel, the posthumously published *Stern der Ungeborenen* (*Star of the Unborn;* 1946) was a critical disaster. Today Werfel is little read in the United States, with the exception of *Musa Dagh*—the national epic of the Armenians—and it is only through the movies *The Song of Bernadette* and *Me and the Colonel* (1948; based on *Jacobowsky und der Oberst* [*Jacobowsky and the Colonel;* 1944]) that Americans are familiar with his work. It is unlikely that there will ever be a Werfel Renaissance in this country, even if long-standing plans are realized to film *Musa Dagh*. Yet Werfel's avant-garde poetry made him a very important figure of German Expressionism, and his great novels of the 1930s and 1940s once received the enthusiasm of millions. Rereading these novels can be extremely entertaining. Understanding them critically, on the basis of Werfel's philosophy and his personal credo, provides us with a deeper understanding not only of the author but also of the unique spirit of the 1930s and 1940s, both in the German-speaking countries and in the United States.

Franz Werfel was born on 10 September 1890 in the city of Prague, today the capital of Czechoslovakia, then the district capital of Bohemia, part of the Austro-Hungarian Empire. He was the oldest of three children, being followed by sisters Hanna (born 1896) and Marianne Amalie (born 1899). Werfel's forefathers were German-Bohemian Jews, and a great-grandfather on his father's side of the family had participated in Napoleon's campaign against Russia as a staff courier. In the middle of the nineteenth century his grandfather had moved to Prague where he acquired considerable wealth, but left his son, Werfel's father, Rudolf, considerable debts when he died. Rudolf Werfel attained wealth in the manufacturing of gloves and other leather goods. Franz's mother, Albine, née Kussi, came from a well-to-do family of mill owners. The Werfels resided in an elegant house in Prague's Marienstraße next to the municipal park in the new part of the city. The children were cared for by a Czech, Catholic maid named Babi whom young Franz often accompanied to Catholic mass in the nearby Heinrich's Church—visits that left a lasting impression on him. Regular attendance at the Maisel Synagogue, where Werfel was bar-mitzvahed in mid-September 1903, seemed to have influenced him less, as his parents were assimilated Jews for whom religion was little more than a matter of form. Another important childhood influence were the frequent visits to the theater and the opera. He accompanied his parents to the Prague Festival in May, which regularly featured the most famous opera singers in performances of Italian operas, most notably in the works of Verdi. In 1904 Werfel attended a performance of Verdi's *Rigoletto* performed by the great tenor, Enrico Caruso. Werfel came to know many Verdi arias by heart and used to sing them in the company of friends, earning him the nickname "Caruso."

In 1896 Werfel was sent to the private Catholic elementary school of the Piarist order in Prague's Herrengasse which Rainer Maria Rilke had also attended a few years earlier. Most of the students of this monastery school came from Jewish homes, a situation which was normal in Prague at that time. From the start Franz was not a good student, something that did not change when he was sent to the *Grabengymnasium,* where he was forced to repeat one class.[1] In September 1904 he was sent to public high school, the

2

German Royal and Imperial *Stefansgymnasium,* at the Stefansgasse in Prague, where Willy Haas and Paul Kornfeld, who later on also became important literary figures, were his fellow students. From the age of fourteen on he began writing poetry, dramas, and novellas. Werfel's lifelong friend, Willy Haas, brought him into contact with the already successful writer Max Brod who was six years older than Werfel, and who sent some of the young poet's poems to the Vienna daily *Die Zeit.* Consequently, a poem by Werfel, "Die Gärten der Stadt Prague" (The Gardens of the City of Prague) was the first of his poems to be published in the newspaper's Sunday supplement of 23 February 1908.

Werfel and a group of friends who were interested in literature engaged in literary and philosophical discussions, staged theater performances, and spiritistic seances, avoiding school to visit places of entertainment, including brothels. The students favored an establishment named "Gogo" in the Gemsengasse where a prostitute, Angela, held forth on literature. This is where the students would sit together with half-naked girls, discussing Kierkegaard, Augustinus, and the latest theater performances.[2] These experiences would, much later, provide the basis for his *Der Abituriententag (Class Reunion;* 1928). Werfel's love for a girl his own age, Maria Glaser, was not returned by her; she treated him condescendingly. He would write of her in his dramatic poem "Der Besuch aus dem Elysium" (The Visit from Elysium), written in 1910, as well as in many early poems.

In 1909–10 Werfel enrolled at the German University of Prague (Karlsuniversität), where he attended lectures on law and philosophy without being able to decide on a major. He wanted to become a writer, to the consternation of his father. Rudolf Werfel considered his son's interest in literature and writing a pleasant pastime but intended to make him into a businessman able to take over the family company. Thus in the fall of 1910 he sent his son as an apprentice to the shipping agency Brasch and Rothenstein in Hamburg, with whose owner he had become friendly, in order for Franz to gain business acumen. But within a few weeks it became clear that young Werfel had no interest in business and was sabotaging the attempt to turn him into a businessman: when he was supposed to audit some ocean bills of lading, he became so frustrated that he disposed of them by flushing them down the toilet. This episode effectively ended his business career. Nevertheless, Werfel stayed in Hamburg until May 1911, enjoying the free life of a large German city. From the fall of 1911 to September 1912 he served his obligatory year in the Royal and Imperial Army with an artillery regiment which was stationed at the Hradcany Castle in Prague. He hated the strict discipline of boot camp and consequently often managed to get into trouble with his superiors, thus repeatedly having to serve time in confinement. During these years as a student and a soldier in Prague, Werfel was friendly with many other young Prague literati—apart from Willy Haas and Max Brod—including Franz Kafka, Karl Brand, Franz Janowitz, Johannes Urzidil, the actor Ernst Deutsch, and the journalist Egon Erwin Kisch. They met at the elegant Café Arco where Werfel recited his poems and where they had heated discussions about literature and philosophy. During his student days Werfel also participated in a number of spiritistic seances, together with Kafka, Brod, and others. This period is also incorporated into his later novel *Class Reunion.*

In 1911 Werfel's first collection of poems, *Der Weltfreund* (The Philanthropist), appeared from the publishing house of Axel Juncker, which had accepted it only after Max Brod had threatened that he himself would no longer publish his works with Juncker. This first book made him famous overnight: the first edition of 4,000 copies was immediately sold out and several new editions had to be quickly printed. With his first book Werfel had become the mouthpiece of the new generation whose literary loyalty was Expressionism. Karl Kraus, the famous editor of the Viennese literary magazine *Die Fackel* (The Torch), printed several of the poems from *Der Weltfreund* even before the book came out and he recommended it to his readers. Unfortunately, the good relationship between Werfel and Kraus soured because Werfel allegedly spread gossip about the editor. The result was a bitter literary feud that continued for a number of years.

In the fall of 1912 Werfel left Prague to settle in the city of Leipzig in Germany. He left his birthplace after having experienced its mystical heritage, its Jewish, German, and Czech (about 90 percent of the inhabitants were Czech) climate to the fullest. Looking back at this time he later said of Prague:

> In 1921, in the twenty-first year of my life, I left Prague for good. At that time it was an attempt to save myself which was only half conscious. It seems to me that this city has no reality for a non-Czech person, it is a daydream for him which does not render him any experience; a paralyzing ghetto without having even the poor relations of the ghetto, a musty world from which no or only false activity emanates. You can bear Prague only as an intoxication, as a fata morgana of life, and that is the reason why so many artists did not flee. The German citizen of Prague who left in time is expatriated quickly and radically and yet he loves his home city whose life appears to him like a distant illusion; he loves it with a mysterious love. For the healthy, simple strong race which is now in charge of the

country, Prague signifies life, capital, culture, culmination—the homeless person has a better understanding of the secret of the city when he is abroad.[3]

That Prague left an indelible impression on Werfel is apparent from the fact that time and again he incorporated experiences and people from his childhood in his short narratives and in his novels, as he did with his Catholic childhood nurse Babi in *The Pure in Heart*.

In Leipzig he became an editor of the newly founded Kurt Wolff publishing house, which published Expressionist authors as well as the works of Franz Kafka and Karl Kraus. Rudolf Werfel signed the contract for his son since the writer was still a minor. As an editor Werfel had a good life, having little work to do since his publisher expected him to write his own works rather than to perform office duties. As a result Werfel was extremely productive in the next few years, writing the one-act play *Die Versuchung* (The Temptation; 1913), the collections of poetry *Wir sind* (We Are; 1913) and *Einander* (Each Other; 1915), and producing a reworked version of Euripides' *The Trojan Women* (*Die Troerinnen des Euripides;* 1915) which was first performed on 22 April 1916 in Berlin's Lessing Theater. Together with Walter Hasenclever and Kurt Pinthus, the publisher's first editor whom he had also befriended, he edited a book series entitled *Der jüngste Tag* (The Youngest Day), a most important collection for German Expressionism, the first volume of which was Werfel's *Die Versuchung*. His contacts with members of the young generation added a number of important authors to the publisher's list, including the Austrian poet Georg Trakl. In Leipzig Werfel shared an apartment with two of his colleagues at Kurt Wolff, his friend Willy Haas and the dramatist Walter Hasenclever, and he was active in literary circles, presenting readings from his works in Prague as well as in various German cities.

As a consequence of the mobilization of the Habsburg army in July 1914, Werfel was called to arms and had to leave Leipzig at the end of August 1914. He successfully faked illness and so was excused from serving until November 1914. During the early months of the First World War he wrote antiwar poems, which he would follow with frequent attempts to escape from frontline service. While vacationing in the city of Bozen in Tirol at the end of April 1915, he suffered a serious cable car accident, hurting his leg. After his recovery in a military hospital, he was sent for a short time to his old unit, an artillery regiment, and then was released again. In Spring 1916 he was drafted once again, and sent to the heavy artillery regiment near Prague. From Spring 1916 to August 1917 he worked as a telephone operator at the

Eastern front in Galicia, which allowed him time to read and write poetry and letters to a nurse from Prague, Gertrud Spirk, whom he had met in 1912 and whom he intended to marry after the war. During this time Werfel was supposedly involved—together with the philosophers Gustav Landauer, Martin Buber, and Max Scheler—in founding a secret order against militarism.

In 1917, with the help of Harry Count Kessler, a famous sociopolitical writer and peace activist, Werfel succeeded in being transferred to the Military Press Bureau in Vienna where other famous Austrian writers, including Rilke, Hugo von Hofmannsthal, Robert Musil, Peter Altenberg, and Franz Blei, were also able to survive the war. Werfel stayed there from August 1917 until November 1918.

Franz Blei introduced him to Alma Mahler, Werfel's future wife. She was the beautiful and intelligent daughter of the Austrian landscape painter Emil Jacob Schindler and the widow of the renowned composer Gustav Mahler, who had died in 1911. Since 18 August 1915 she had been married to the architect Walter Gropius. Alma was already familiar with Werfel's poetry; herself a musician and composer of great ability, she had even set one poem to music. Their relationship developed quickly, although Alma was eleven years older than Werfel. There is no doubt that this mature woman had a stimulating and stabilizing effect on the youthful Werfel and that throughout his life—she survived him by nineteen years—she was also his friend, his critic, and his muse who spurred him on to create new works. She encouraged him when he was tempted to yield to his natural indolence, and her political conservatism prevented him from becoming more deeply involved in the revolutionary activities of 1918. Alma was also an important figure in the artistic and social life of Austria, and her circle of friends included many distinguished personalities in the fields of literature, music, art, and science. Clearly, Werfel profited from the inspiring company of her many notable friends.

In January 1918 Werfel was sent to Zurich where, on behalf of the Austrian Military Press Bureau, he was to give lectures supporting Austrian patriotism by spreading Austrian culture. Instead he made provocative pacifistic statements: in his "Rede an die Arbeiter von Davos" (Speech to the Workers of Davos) he addresses the workers as "Genossen" (Comrades) and ends by expressing his hope that his poetry might be "a contribution to the dissolution of the bourgeois world and the renewal of socialism." Between January 18 and April 15 Werfel presented approximately ten such public lectures and readings. Given the spirit of these lectures, it is no surprise that he was ordered back to Vienna under the threat of punishment and threatened to be released from his duties. In November 1918, when the war had come to an end and the collapse of the Austro-Hungarian Monarchy was imminent, Werfel joined his friend, the journalist Egon Erwin Kisch, in becoming a member of the "Rote Garde" (Red Guard), a small socialist faction. In a public speech Werfel even called on the masses to storm the banks. However, when questioned by the police, he declared himself to be a pacifist and an enemy of the use of any kind of force. When at night he returned to Alma, she refused to let him enter her home. It was due to her conservative convictions that Werfel quickly gave up all socialist revolutionary ideas. In her country home in Breitenstein and, later, in a house she had bought in Venice in 1922, Werfel found the undisturbed time to work. But Alma's country house in Breitenstein also offered Alma and her children a place to spend the summer and it became a social center frequented by such luminaries as Arthur Schnitzler, Hugo von Hofmannsthal, Sinclair Lewis and his wife Dorothy Thompson, Gordon Shepherd, Gerhart Hauptmann, Arnold Schoenberg, and Carl Zuckmayer. The composer Alban Berg and his wife, with whom Alma and Franz had close contacts, were neighbors in this rural setting.

On 2 August 1918 Alma, who at that time was still married to Walter Gropius, gave birth to Werfel's son. Unfortunately, the child, christened Martin Carl Johannes, was sickly and died in June 1919. Werfel blamed himself for this death and considered it God's judgment because of his relationship with Alma. He gave all his paternal love to his stepdaughter Manon Gropius, who unfortunately died from polio on 22 April 1935 at the age of twenty. The novel *The Song of Bernadette* is dedicated to her memory. Following Manon's death, Alma sold her house in Venice.

In 1919 Werfel's new collection of poetry, *Der Gerichtstag* (The Day of Judgment) appeared, followed in 1920 by the Expressionist drama *Spiegelmensch* (Mirror Man), *Spielhof: Eine Phantasie* (Spielhof: A Phantasy) in which he treats the generation conflict in positive terms, and *Nicht der Mörder, der Ermordete ist schuldig* ("Not the Murderer"), a novella in which the typically Expressionist theme of the battle of the generations, the son against the father, is treated in violent form. At this time Werfel still felt somewhat uncomfortable writing prose. He viewed himself primarily as a dramatist, a fact that seems to be confirmed by his literary production of the following years. The year 1921 saw the appearance of the drama *Bocksgesang* (*Goat Song*), and in 1922 Werfel's last drama that may be termed Expressionist, the psychological drama *Schweiger*, was published. As is obvious from these titles, Werfel, who had started out as the author of poetry, had become more and more a dramatist. Yet at this point he also turned to prose

7

which was to be his ultimate genre. His first novel, *Verdi,* which pitted his beloved Verdi against Richard Wagner, Italian against German opera, was published on 1 April 1924.

Verdi was the first of Werfel's works to be released by the newly founded, Vienna-based publishing house of Paul Zsolnay. Werfel had left his old publisher, Kurt Wolff, on friendly terms. Because of the runaway inflation in Germany the royalties he had received from Wolff were practically worthless, whereas the young Baron Paul von Zsolnay was able to pay Werfel in hard Swiss currency. *Verdi* was the first publication of the Zsolnay Verlag and, until the Anschluss of Austria to the Third Reich on 13 March 1938, all of Werfel's works continued to appear in this house. Other Kurt Wolff authors, including Max Brod and, in 1925, Heinrich Mann, defected to Paul Zsolnay, who was also the German language publisher of John Galsworthy, H. G. Wells, and Theodore Dreiser.

On 9 September 1924 Werfel completed his drama *Juarez und Maximilian* (*Juarez and Maximilian;* 1924), which was first performed in Magdeburg in April 1925 but only later became a big success via Max Reinhardt's staging in Vienna and Berlin later that year.

On 15 January 1925 in Trieste, Alma and Werfel embarked on a sea voyage that took them to Egypt and Palestine. Under the influence of the impressions he received on this journey, Werfel wrote his drama, published at the end of 1926, *Paulus unter den Juden* (*Paul among the Jews*), dealing with the emergence of Christianity from Judaism. Soon honors were bestowed on the now famous dramatist: on 15 January 1926 he received the Grillparzer Prize for his drama *Juarez and Maximilian,* and on 27 October he was made a member of the Preußische Akademie der Künste (Prussian Academy of the Arts) as one of the twenty founding members of the section on literature. In 1927 he not only received the Schiller Prize but also the Czech State Prize. Werfel was now one of the most recognized writers of the German language. When the literary magazine *Die schöne Literatur* took a poll on 7 July 1927 among its readers, Werfel received more votes than Gerhart Hauptmann, Stefan George, or Rainer Maria Rilke. Moreover, Werfel also continued his efforts to regain the German stage for his favorite composer of operas, Verdi, by reworking the libretto of Verdi's *La forza del destino.* By making the action less confusing and by subdividing the opera into a prologue, overture, and three acts, he in fact modernized it. After 1945, however, Werfel's version was eventually forgotten by the German opera houses, and they returned to the original libretto by Francesco Maria Piave. In 1928, together with the Viennese director Lothar Wallerstein, he reworked Verdi's opera *Simone Boc-*

canegra, and in 1932, again with Lothar Wallerstein, he worked on a new version of the libretto for Verdi's opera *Don Carlos.*

In 1927 Werfel not only published his novella *Der Tod des Kleinbürgers* (*The Man Who Conquered Death*), but also the collection of novellas *Geheimnis eines Menschen* (Saverio's Secret) which also contained the stories "Die Entfremdung" ("Estrangement"), "Das Trauerhaus" ("The House of Mourning"), and "Die Hoteltreppe" ("The Staircase"). These novellas, all of which were included in the 1937 American anthology *Twilight of a World,* translated into English, have as a background Werfel's Austrian homeland and its unique atmosphere. The short novel *Class Reunion* of 1928 was also suitably included in this American anthology. Werfel's voluminous novel *The Pure in Heart* (1929) continued his preoccupation with recent Austrian history in its description of the hero's experiences in the First World War and during the revolution of 1918 and made use of the author's own personal experiences during that time. Werfel's popularity was so great that 50,000 copies were printed for the first German edition alone.

On 8 July 1929 Alma and Franz were married after Werfel had hesitatingly left organized Jewish religion on 27 June, thus fulfilling Alma's sole condition for the marriage. Later on Werfel stressed that this step did not mean that he had stopped being a Jew and that he did not intend to deny his heritage. In 1930 they went on a second trip to the Middle East. It was particularly on these trips that Werfel was confronted with his Jewish roots and with the relationship between Judaism and Christianity, which he addressed in his dramas and his prose. While in Damascus Werfel was so moved by seeing half-starved Armenian refugee children working in a carpet mill that he became obsessed with the fate of the Armenian people. The result was his novel *The Forty Days of Musa Dagh* (1933), in which he describes the last stand of a small number of Armenian villagers against an overwhelming force of Turks. But a number of other works were written by the productive Werfel prior to this masterwork: the drama on the Hussite wars, *Das Reich Gottes in Böhmen* (The Kingdom of God in Bohemia; 1930), and the novel *Die Geschwister von Neapel* (*The Pascarella Family;* 1931) which continues and brings to an end the theme of the conflict of generations, this time in an operatic Italian atmosphere under the rule of fascism. Tina Orchard, a lady whom the Werfels had met at the Imperial Palace Hotel in Santa Margherita Ligure, had given the impetus to write this novel by telling them the story of her life.

In March 1931 Alma and Franz moved from their apartment in Vienna's Elisabethstraße 37 into a large home in Steinfeldgasse 2, in the exclusive Hohe Warte district. Here Werfel had a huge study of which he hardly made any use as he preferred to work in hotel rooms—close to Vienna, in Italy—and also in Alma's country home in Breitenstein. One of the reasons for his discomfort was Alma's entertaining. Her salon was the frequent setting for famous parties attended by Vienna's political and artistic elite.

During the early 1930s Werfel formulated his philosophical and religious ideas in several important speeches, published as essays. Their spirit is at the basis of most of his mature works, and they include *Realismus und Inner-lichkeit* ("Realism and Inwardness"; 1931) and *Können wir ohne Gottes-glauben leben* ("Can We Live Without Faith in God"; 1932). He gave these speeches not only in Vienna but also in various German cities before the rise of national socialism. In November 1932 he went on his last lecture tour through Germany and read from the fifth chapter of his still unpublished *Musa Dagh,* which contains a conversation between a German pastor, Johannes Lepsius, and the unmovable advocate of persecution and nationalism, Enver Pascha. In February 1934 the novel was forbidden in Germany, having already been banned from public advertisement and display. Werfel had, of course, taken notice of the political changes in Germany but he did not seem willing to face reality. This is evident from his wish to continue his member-ship in the Prussian Academy of the Arts by joining his friends and col-leagues Georg Kaiser, Fritz von Unruh, Alfred Mombert, and Bernhard Kellermann in signing a declaration of loyalty to the new national socialist philosophy of the association. Thomas Mann, Jakob Wassermann, and Alfred Döblin took this opportunity to resign their membership, and on 5 May 1933 Werfel was excluded. Several of his books were burned in public in Germany in May 1933, and they were removed from all public libraries. Nevertheless, on 11 December 1933 Werfel applied for membership in the Reichsverband deutscher Schriftsteller (Reich Association of German Writers), possibly out of fear of losing his German market. An official answer to this degrading ini-tiative has not been preserved.

In response to the events in Germany, in particular to the early persecution of the Jews, Werfel began working on a biblical drama, *Der Weg der Ver-heißung (The Eternal Road;* 1935) for which Kurt Weill composed the music. The American theater manager Meyer W. Weisgal had suggested such a play to Max Reinhardt who in turn encouraged Werfel to undertake the project. The play required much adaptation and rewriting for the New York perfor-mance. On 12 November 1935 Alma and Franz arrived in New York in order to watch the rehearsals and to attend the opening performance. The planned opening on 23 December did not materialize, however, and the production went bankrupt in February 1936. As a result of Weisgal's untiring energy, the play finally opened on 7 January 1937 at the Manhattan Opera House. Werfel had unfortunately given up and had long since returned to Europe (in January 1936). But the journey had not been entirely in vain. Werfel received an enthusiastic reception from the Armenian community, whose national epic he had created with *Musa Dagh*.

Werfel continued his occupation with biblical themes by writing a new novel, *Höret die Stimme* (*Hearken unto the Voice;* 1937), on the Old Testament prophet Jeremiah. During the same year he received the Austrian Order of Merit for Art and Science, which was personally presented to him by Chancellor Kurt von Schuschnigg of Austria. In June 1937 Werfel attended a meeting of the World Association of Writers—the Poets, Essayists, Novelists (PEN) Club—in Paris where he engaged in angry discussions with the writer Lion Feuchtwanger who had visited the Soviet Union and returned enthusiastic about the accomplishments of communism. Werfel condemned communism as he did national socialism, and when Feuchtwanger made an anti-Hitler speech, Werfel reproached him for having been received by Stalin during his trip to the Soviet Union. Evenings in Paris were spent in the company of James Joyce. Due to the language barrier, they had difficulty conversing but went barhopping together, singing Verdi arias. On 5 October 1937 Werfel's last play to be performed in Austria before his exile, *In einer Nacht* (During One Night), opened in Vienna under the direction of Max Reinhardt and was successful in spite of mixed reviews and the increasing anti-Semitic atmosphere.

Franz and Alma spent the month of February 1938 on Capri. When the Austrian chancellor Schuschnigg was summoned by Hitler to Berchtesgaden in Bavaria, Alma became so worried about the political situation that she returned to Austria and succeeded in saving some money and valuables and in persuading her daughter Anna to escape. Werfel had stayed on Capri because he was suffering from a severe throat infection, and thus missed the fateful events in Austria—to which he was never to return.

Schuschnigg had tried to avoid Austria's capitulation by calling for a referendum in which the Austrian people were to decide whether to live in an independent Austria or to be annexed by Germany. Hitler did not wait for the outcome of this referendum. On 12 March 1938 his troops marched into Austria—welcomed by many—and on 13 March Austria ceased to exist as an independent state. Alma and her daughter left Austria on 13 March 1938 and went to Italy by way of Prague and Budapest. They met Franz in Milan, from where they proceeded to the home of Werfel's younger sister, Marianne Rieser, who lived in Zurich together with her husband Ferdinand, the director of the Zurich theater. Since Alma found the atmosphere in Zurich—the first stop for many emigrants—intolerable, she and Franz went on to Paris. In actuality, Alma had precipitated the negative atmosphere as, even then, she continued to make anti-Semitic remarks in her in-laws' house. In May 1938 Alma and Werfel went together to a Mahler festival in Amsterdam and continued their journey to London. There Werfel entered into an agreement with the publisher Gottfried Bermann-Fischer who had just moved his publishing activities from Germany to Stockholm. As a result of the Anschluss, Paul Zsolnay no longer owned his publishing house. Thus the essay *Von der reinsten Glückseligkeit des Menschen* ("Of Man's True Happiness"; 1938) was Werfel's first work to be published by Bermann-Fischer in the series *Ausblicke* (Prospects). After a few weeks Alma and Franz returned to Paris. Werfel, for whom Alma had rented a roomy study in St. Germain-en-Laye, wrote poems and various essays of a more or less political nature for exile publications, but his main effort was devoted to the novel *Der veruntreute Himmel* (*Embezzled Heaven;* 1939).

In the spring of 1938 Werfel suffered his first serious heart attack. The Werfels left Paris and settled in Sanary-sur-Mer on the French Riviera where he recovered quickly from his illness. There they lived in an old tower, "Le Moulin Gris," which had been renovated by a French painter. Sanary-sur-Mer had a large colony of German exiles who were writers, among them Lion Feuchtwanger, Ludwig Marcuse, Robert Neumann, and Arnold Zweig. Life was inexpensive and Werfel often went on short trips to Paris. In September 1938 he began working on his novel *Cella oder Die Überwinder* (*Cella, or, The Survivors;* 1982), a novel about Hitler's annexation of Austria and the persecution of Jews. In March 1939 Werfel stopped working on it, apparently because events had outstripped fiction. The endeavor thus remains a fragment, one of the few works, however, in which the author dealt directly with the political events of the day.

Werfel obviously did not take the threat of national socialism seriously enough. He wanted to stay in France and rejected his father's fears that he might be shot by the Gestapo. Thus Franz and Alma Werfel did not make use of the U.S. visas they had obtained on 14 October 1938. On 15 March 1939 the German army marched into Prague. Hitler established the protectorate Bohemia-Moravia and the former state of Czechoslovakia ceased to exist. At the beginning of June 1939 Werfel had said goodbye to his old friend Willy Haas who went to India. On 1 September 1939 German armies attacked Poland, and on 3 September England and France declared war on Germany. Suddenly Werfel and many other German emigrants in France were viewed with suspicion as possible collaborators with the enemy and were rounded up and detained in internment camps. Fortunately, Werfel's parents had managed to escape to France. They now lived in Vichy, where Franz and Alma were able to visit them.

In 1940 Werfel wrote his novella *Eine blaßblaue Frauenschrift* (A Pale Blue Woman's Writing)—which was going to appear in 1941 in Argentina—dealing with the theme of exile and anti-Semitism. On 10 May 1940 the German attack on the Western front began. After the capitulation of Belgium on 28 May and the ensuing invasion of France by German troops, Alma and Franz decided to try and leave. In May they first attempted in vain to renew their expired U.S. visas of 1938. Then in June 1940 they left Sanary-sur-Mer just ahead of the advancing German troops and tried to reach Spain and Portugal without valid visas. In rented cars they frantically crisscrossed southern France, first to Bordeaux, then to the Spanish border, then, by way of Pau, to Lourdes where they arrived on 27 June and stayed for seven weeks. Lourdes was the site of a now famous pilgrimage where St. Bernadette had had visions of the Virgin Mary in the second half of the nineteenth century. Werfel used his time to familiarize himself with the background of the events, and he vowed to "sing the song of Bernadette" should he be able to escape to America. On 16 July 1940 the *New York Post* erroneously reported that, according to a BBC broadcast, Werfel had been apprehended and shot by the Nazis. Indeed, the Werfels had attempted to obtain Spanish and Portuguese visas without success. Unable to cross the border without valid visas, they continued an adventurous flight that took them back to Marseilles. There they were finally able to obtain the necessary visas with the help of Varian Fry, the emissary of the American Emergency Rescue Committee. They went by train through southern France and, in the company of the aging Heinrich Mann—brother of Thomas Mann—his wife Nelly, and Thomas Mann's son, Golo Mann, they crossed the Pyrenees on foot on 13 September 1940. Varian Fry followed them with their twelve suitcases which contained Werfel's manuscripts as well as original compositions by Mahler and Anton Bruckner. A train took the Werfels to Madrid; from there they traveled by airplane to Lisbon where, after a wait of two weeks, they boarded a ship, the *Nea Hellas*, which took them to the United States. On 13 October 1940 at 9:00 A.M. they arrived in Hoboken, N.J.—together with the Heinrich Manns and Golo Mann—where they were welcomed by a representative of the Emergency Rescue Committee. They remained in New York for about ten weeks, meeting with Werfel's old friends, Franz Blei, Hermann Broch, and Anton Kuh, as well as Alfred Döblin and George Grosz. On 26 December 1940 they proceeded to Los Angeles. Friends there had rented a large home for them in the Hollywood hills—at 6900 Los Tilos Road, close to the Hollywood Bowl—so that they were able to settle down immediately. In a short while Alma's salon also reestablished itself in its new Los Angeles setting. On 22 March 1941 the Werfels officially emigrated to the United States from Nogales, Mexico, a requirement of emigrants without an immigrant visa. Werfel never became an American citizen, dying before he was eligible to apply for such status.

In the summer of 1941 Werfel's father suffered a stroke and died on 31 July 1941 in Marseilles. His mother succeeded in leaving France shortly thereafter and she settled in New York.

Despite the Werfels' hardships, Franz did not have to worry about financial matters: *Embezzled Heaven* had appeared in English in November 1940 and was enjoying excellent sales—in December it had already sold 150,000 copies. It made Werfel one of the wealthiest writers in the German refugee colony in the United States. True to his promise at Lourdes, he began immediate work on *The Song of Bernadette.*

One night he beguiled some friends about the adventures of a banker from Stuttgart by the name of Stefan S. Jakobowicz whom he had met in Lourdes, and who had told him about his flight from Paris in the company of a Polish colonel.[4] Max Reinhardt, also in exile in the United States, became so enthusiastic about the story that he immediately asked Werfel to turn it into a drama, resulting in Werfel's 1945 comedy hit, *Jacobowsky und der Oberst* (*Jacobowsky and the Colonel;* 1944). Werfel wrote most of the work in Santa Barbara where he had rented a bungalow at the Biltmore Hotel.

After Sanary-sur-Mer and Paris, New York and Los Angeles were the places to where most of the German exile writers had fled. This was not so much due to the attractive climate as to the fact that the film industry extended to many of them at least a one-year contract—thus offering brief financial support. In Los Angeles Werfel had stayed in close contact with Bruno Frank, Gottfried Reinhard, Lion Feuchtwanger, Oskar Homolka, Thomas and Heinrich Mann, Erich Maria Remarque, Arnold Schoenberg, Friedrich Torberg, Bruno Walter, and Lotte Lehmann. His closest friend became the American Germanist Gustave O. Arlt of the University of California, Los Angeles (UCLA), who also was the translator of his final works. On 9 June 1943 the University of California, Los Angeles, bestowed upon Werfel the honorary degree of Doctor of Law. Franz Werfel was, as we see, one of the few German exile writers who managed to translate his previous success, both in literary and financial terms, into a similar degree of success in the United States. *The Forty Days of Musa Dagh* had established Werfel's American fame. The sales of *Embezzled Heaven* had also been excellent, and *The Song of Bernadette* was a world bestseller. The book and the resulting film were appreciated by millions. The opening night of the movie was on 21 December 1943 at the Cathay Circle Theater in Hollywood. Unfortunately, Werfel himself was unable to attend since he had suffered two severe heart attacks during the previous months.

With the possible exceptions of Vicki Baum and Erich Maria Remarque, no other German exile writer, not even Lion Feuchtwanger or Thomas Mann, could rival Werfel's immediate success. But apart from his rented hotel bungalows in Santa Barbara which he used for writing, Werfel lived in a modest home on 610 North Bedford Drive in Beverly Hills which he and Alma had moved into on 25 September 1942. While Werfel was busy working on *Star of the Unborn* (since May 1942) he also reworked *Jacobowsky and the Colonel*. He found the adaptation by Samuel N. Behrman to be a sentimentalized shadow of this original play. The resulting long phone calls and telegrams between Werfel and the Theatre Guild in New York were in vain, however. Behrman's version was performed on Broadway on 14 March 1944 and was a great success. In December 1944 a collection of essays from the early 1930s, as well as new aphorisms and thoughts—most of them of a religious nature—"Theologumena," appeared under the title *Between Heaven and Earth* (*Zwischen oben und unten*). The main theme of the "Theologumena" is the position of the Jewish people versus Christianity: Werfel believed that their function in God's plan of salvation is to serve as incarnate witnesses of the Revelation. He thus gave a detailed, theoretical reasoning for his insistence on remaining a Jew and not being baptized, despite his strong feelings favoring the Catholic faith. On 17 August 1945 Werfel was able to complete the manuscript of *Star of the Unborn*. He died at his desk while editing a selection of his poems for the Los Angeles Pacific Press on 26 August and was buried at the Rosendale Cemetery in Los Angeles. The eulogy was given by Father Georg Moenius, who spoke not only as the representative of the Catholic Church but as a personal friend of the Werfels. Franz Werfel's body was exhumed and reburied in Vienna after the war.

NOTES

1. See Norbert Abels, *Franz Werfel: Mit Selbstzeugnissen und Bilddokumenten* (Reinbek bei Hamburg: Rowohlt, 1990) 17.

2. Abels 19.

3. *Prager Tageblatt* 3 June 1922: 6. Quote taken from Lore B. Foltin, *Franz Werfel* (Stuttgart: Metzler, 1972) 24, from which many of the biographical facts reported here are taken.

Many other facts go back to *Franz Werfel: 1890–1945. Katalog,* ed. Heinz Lunzer and Victoria Lunzer-Talos (Vienna: Zirkular, 1990), the catalogue of an exhibition, jointly arranged by the Foreign Office of the Republic of Austria and the Dokumentationsstelle für Neuere Österreichische Literatur in Vienna; Peter Stephan Jungk, *Franz Werfel: A Life in Prague, Vienna, and Hollywood,* trans. Anselm Hollo (New York: Grove Weidenfeld, 1990); as well as the Werfel biography by Norbert Abels (see n. 1).

4. According to Samuel N. Behrman's memoirs, Werfel told the story at a dinner party at Max Reinhardt's house. See Lore B. Foltin and John M. Spalek, "Franz Werfel," in *Deutsche Exilliteratur seit 1933,* ed. John M. Spalek and Joseph Strelka, vol. 1, *Kalifornien* (Berne: Francke, 1976) 651.

CHAPTER ONE

Between Heaven and Earth: Essays and Aphorisms

Although the majority of Werfel's essays were not written until the early 1930s, I would like to discuss them before turning to his major works. The first reason is simply that nowhere else does Werfel's worldview, his position in contemporary thinking, become as clear as in these theoretical writings. The second reason is that, having considered Werfel's philosophy at the onset, our interpretation of his works will be greatly facilitated. In discussing his works we shall see that Werfel already formulated his basic ideas at an early stage and incorporated them in those fictional works which were written before the major essays. Furthermore, he published his most important essays from the early 1930s in English translation for the first time in his book *Between Heaven and Earth* (1944; *Zwischen oben und unten;* 1946),[1] thus clearly demonstrating that he adhered to his basic views until he died. One additional essay, available only in English translation, served as an introduction to his collection of novellas and short novels, *Twilight of a World* (1937),[2] "An Essay upon the Meaning of Imperial Austria." We will concentrate on these essays here because they are readily available to the American reader and they most clearly express Werfel's thinking. The shorter pieces, particular those on literature and music, are less important for the overall understanding of his writings.[3]

The essays contained in *Between Heaven and Earth* were philosophical in nature, not only defending a belief in God but also justifying a metaphysical worldview. As in his fictional works, Werfel makes clear his religious orientation, his quest for metaphysical values, and his belief in the mission of Christians and Jews.

Very early in his career Werfel had defended the Christian religion and rejected political activism, which he was to resort to very briefly in 1918 in his essay "Die christliche Sendung" (The Christian Mission; 1916). Werfel's main objection to activism is that every action (*Tat*) has two opposite effects, helping one individual and simultaneously harming another. Furthermore, activism is aimed at the acquisition of power, an evil force in Werfel's view. He labels activism with one of his favorite terms, "abstraction" which implies disregarding the (concrete) individual by espousing the case of (abstract) humanity—merely substituting one system for another. Abstraction, or the process by which human consciousness moves away from consciousness of the immediate world, from individuality, is equated with sin itself. The opposite of abstraction and activism is Christianity, which leads humankind back to reality, to individuality. In Werfel's opinion Christianity is life- and self-affirming, teaching by example and not by abstract political manifestos. It is by no means ascetic, but the only true hedonism, embodying those humanistic values which the activists believe can only be attained through revolutionary action. As Lionel B. Steiman has pointed out: "In developing this conception of Christianity, Werfel ignored the mystery of the Incarnation and concentrated instead on the individualism he thought was the core of the Christian religion."[4] By rejecting any kind of activism because it involved abstraction, the hidden political stance Werfel took in "Die christliche Sendung" was extremely conservative, if not to say reactionary.

In 1928 Werfel published an essay entitled "Der Snobismus als geistige Weltmacht" (Snobbism as a Spiritual World Power) which was planned as a chapter of a book to be entitled "Die Krisis der Ideale" (The Crisis of Ideals). In this chapter, the only one published, he analyses society at a time of instability and confusion. Werfel shows society to have lost its old beliefs and to have fallen victim to pseudo-ideals, the embodiment of which is the snob. A snob has no spiritual roots and he adheres to these pseudo-ideals not because he believes in them but only because they are fashionable. In this essay Werfel already attacks national socialism and communism as related phenomena.

Although Werfel repeated the basic ideas of the above essays later on, only his next three essays finally became part of *Between Heaven and Earth*. They were originally all delivered as lectures in Vienna and published separately thereafter. The first one, "Realismus und Innerlichkeit" ("Realism and Inwardness"; 1931) deals with the conflict between the spiritual nature of man and the spirit of our age which he terms "radical realism." Werfel defines realism "in its broadest, cultural sense" as "man's direct attitude toward the things of life, his most unbiased relationship to nature, unclouded by religious, political or other abstractions" (BHE 47). But, in his opinion, contemporary radical realism no longer corresponds to this definition. Repeating and further elaborating ideas from "Die christliche Sendung," he instead concludes that "History scarcely knows a more unreal, a more abstract age than the present one which considers itself fairly bursting with reality" (BHE 48). "The enemy, the object of hatred of the realistic conviction, is man's inwardness, his soul, his creative spirit" (BHE 50). This modern attitude, he felt, originated with the French Revolution which had done away with a highly intellectualized world and created the bourgeoisie. Instead of the ideals of the past—the heroic ideal of chivalry and the ascetic ideal of religion—the bourgeoisie created the ideal of work and the morality of achievement, which entail economic activity and money-making. This led to an unexpected advance in technology, while it produced an industrial proletariat and ultimately a proletariat of the unemployed. During the first decade following the First World War, it had accomplished "the intimidation and suppression of human inwardness and the devaluation of the human spirit. It deprived our soul of faith, and particularly of faith in the soul itself" (BHE 56f.). This new kind of radical realism prevails in the Soviet Union just as much as in the United States, "the Russian State is the one and only pan-capitalist" (BHE 57). Both communism and capitalism negate the individual. In Werfel's view the failure of the modern age is that objects and symbols have become the sole measure of man. To be sure, Werfel admits that "radical realism" has "alleviated the material misery of the masses" (BHE 60) and he recognizes the merits of European social democracy in this respect; but happiness is more than the state of nonsuffering, it is rather "the wealth of a reality transfused into inwardness. . . . The Kingdom of Heaven and the chance of salvation lie only within ourselves" (BHE 61). Happiness is spiritual.

In Werfel's spiritualism creative inwardness reveals itself in three spheres: religion and morality, science and speculation, art and imagination. The churches defend themselves against the forces of antimetaphysics; modern science is in the camp of the realistic outlook; the human intellect has been deified, something that is most radically represented by psychoanalysis. In order to counter this adoration of intellectualism, Werfel modifies a sentence by Einstein and concludes: "The spirit is so constituted that it is impossible intellectually and deductively to determine its truths. . . . This means that man's fixed frame of reference is determined not rationally but esthetically" (BHE 64). Consequently, radical realism can be successfully fought only by the third sphere, that of the muses: "only the man favored by the muses can rebuild the inwardness that has been destroyed by the belief in things" (BHE 65). By that Werfel means "the man who is moved by the soul and spirit, the man of sympathetic emotion, capable of rapture, full of imagination, receptive to the world, infused with sympathy and holy grace, the man who, in the widest sense, is musical" (BHE 65). The realistic outlook can only be struck in its unreality and inner emptiness. Werfel thus advocates revolution, "the revolution of life against abstract regimentation" (BHE 68), "this secular desolation of the inner life" (BHE 69). To achieve this goal we must believe "that, in spite of all material misery, the supreme goal of our happiness and existence is the unfolding and the intensification of the inner life'' (BHE 74). It is amazing that Werfel was able to diagnose the desolate state of the world at this time of the Great Depression without any reference to social or economic facts.

In his next essay, ''Können wir ohne Gottesglauben leben?'' (''Can We Live Without Faith in God?''; 1932), written a year later, ''radical realism'' gives way to the perhaps more accurate term ''naturalistic nihilism.'' It embodies the state of modern consciousness for which

> all life, including personal life, is a pleasurable and unpleasurable interruption of the unconscious void. Nature, as far as we comprehend it, represents a soulless mechanism of forces which either balance or destroy each other, a sort of permanent catastrophe held in balance. . . . Culture is a constant war of position against the brute forces of nature outside and inside of man, with technology its main weapon. There is no possibility of approaching a higher meaning of the universe by knowledge or sensation. . . . As for the so-called religious feelings, they have long ago been exposed by our extremely smug modern psychology as infantile residues, both in the individual and in society. (BHE 88f.)

According to Werfel this is the worldview that is held by modern man, by the metropolitan populations of Europe, the Soviet Union, and the United States. Man has been severed from his metaphysical ties. Science, in particular, is responsible for this blindness to God which resulted in the First World War. This war, which demonstrated to common man that he possesses nothing in the world but his poor, beloved ego, has also shown him that things could no longer go on as they had. The two—hypothetical—sons of this common man have turned to communism or national socialism, both of which Werfel reveals as substitute religions or substitutes for religion. Both are outgrowths of naturalistic nihilism, steps away from the helpless ego. Communism ''represents a substitute for religion with a scientific mask of reason, a primitive heresy in the guise of political economy'' (BHE 96). But communism at least is ''vibrant with the thought of justice for the deliverance of mankind. By contrast, nationalism is nothing but a reaction of feeling, a dark impulse, a powerful upheaval, and does not pretend to be anything else.'' It ''raises biological membership to a value'' (BHE 99). Related phenomena that have contributed to the current crisis, the rise of naturalistic nihilism, are technology, the apotheosis of the state, and the crowding together of millions in large cities. Man has forgotten that there is an Above and a Below, that is, a spiritual realm transcending our materialistic, earthly one. Werfel's reply is thus: "When all paths are blocked then only the path to heaven remains" (BHE 106). Humanity must be made aware that there can be no human life without a relationship to the transcendental sphere. Werfel counters the claims of psychologists and atheists, insisting that a human soul possesses a "perception of the Divine" (BHE 109). As he points out, even eminent physicists have arrived at the conclusion that there must be a higher being. But the existence of God cannot and need not be proven by science. Rather, humanity by its very nature is capable of religious experiences. Man must go deep inside his inner self, into his loneliness, and must transform his consciousness in order to renew himself. "Everyone to whom it is granted to awake out of the practical soddenness of mere vegetative existence can become a servant in the renewal of the general consciousness. Only one thing is demanded of him, that he decide for and against the Divine, and that he should not evade the central question of existence" (BHE 119). By focusing our attention onto the perception of the divine, we have already taken the first step toward conquering the modern state of consciousness. Although a Jew himself, Werfel then goes on to say that the world can be spiritually healed only if it finds its way back to true Christianity.

> The road is clear. It begins here, directly before us. And a very troublesome road it is. It demands work, study, criticism, struggle, solitude, pangs of conscience, decision and renunciation. The void still clings to us with a thousand tentacles. It is inconceivably difficult to convert oneself to divine affinity out of nihilistic nonaffinity and in the face of temporal opinion. But we must hope that the procedure will be of benefit to us. All who are in despair should set forth upon this road. Its goal is the goal of all the world: Joy. (BHE 123)

The text of the lecture is followed by "A Summary of Some Principal Reasons Why Faith in God Appears Necessary and Unavoidable."

When this essay is analyzed carefully, one realizes that in spite of his theological terminology and frequent use of terms such as "metaphysical," Werfel actually advocates pure humanism. Furthermore, as Steiman observes, "Werfel argued not so much in favour of God and religion as on behalf of the individual with the latter emerging ever more clearly as Werfel's own subjective orientation. As the world seemed increasingly to cast doubt on the integrity of individual subjectivity, Werfel sought to give it supernatural confirmation and metaphysical support."[5] The implicit denial of social and historical forces again shows the inherent conservative and politically abstinent spirit of Werfel's thinking. This, in particular, mars the possibility of using the two speeches in the fight against national socialism, which he attempted by reading them on a lecture tour through Germany in the summer of 1932. Rejecting all contemporary political systems by viewing them as pseudo-religions which must be fought with spiritual means, he "left the field open to the strongest of them."[6]

Werfel's last lecture in *Between Heaven and Earth* is entitled "Von der reinsten Glückseligkeit des Menschen" ("Of Man's True Happiness"; 1938). In contrast to the previous ones, this one deals with art and its significance for man in finding his true self. "Art is the opposite of 'killing time.' It is the 'arresting of time.' It is the 'killing of death' " (BHE 16). In our time man has turned to the exterior things in life and, in his desperation, he has suppressed his inner happiness. This happiness in ancient times was insight that there is no death. It was and is the role of art to imbue in us in certain moments the mystical consciousness of the nonexistence of death. In a golden age, in Atlantis, Lemuria, or somewhere in Mesopotamia, man may have attained a cosmic knowledge lost to us now, he argues. These lost powers of the soul, this creativity and spirituality, are buried in us but they can be released again through the power of art. Art "is the most merciful reflection of the ancient powers of the soul in exile, wandering in the diaspora of modern life. Each time that almost incommunicable ecstasy touches us at the experience of some work of art, the sundering spiritual powers of the Golden Age are once more brought together in us for an instant" (BHE 31). In contrast to the age of myth which saw supernatural meanings everywhere in nature, our age is characterized by realism. Realism, however, "is the defiant will to insignificance, to meaninglessness. The realist with his enfeebled soul fears and denies the mystery created in things although it had been the first and foremost meaning of all art to sing of this mystery" (BHE 32). With the help of the prophesy and poetry of art, man will be able to wake up from the materialistic delusion of the present. It is ironically characteristic for Werfel's political abstinence that he would publish this kind of escapist philosophy in 1938, after the Anschluss of Austria, in the exile publishing house of Bermann-Fischer in Stockholm.

The aphoristic "Theologumena," modeled after Blaise Pascal's *Pensées,* make up the remainder, approximately one-half of *Between Heaven and Earth,* repeating many ideas contained in the above essays. For example, Werfel again deals extensively with the implications of the "naturalistic-nihilistic mentality" (BHE 158ff.). But since the majority of these mostly short aphoristic essays, which often consist of a few paragraphs only, were written in the early 1940s at the time when Werfel was working on *The Song of Bernadette* and *Star of the Unborn,* a great number of the "Theologumena" deal with religious matters, specifically with Christianity and Judaism and their relation to each other. In this respect the section "On Christ and Israel" states most clearly Werfel's view which is based on the belief that Christ was God incarnate. The Jews, however, must necessarily reject this doctrine of incarnation and live separately through the course of history as negative witnesses to the truth of Christianity: "If Christ is Truth and Life, then the Jews are the everlasting witnesses in the flesh, of this Truth. Without this living witness, that wanders, persecuted and scourged through the whole world, Christ would sink down into a mere myth, like Apollo or Dionysos" (BHE 193). The Jews cannot be healed by virtue of baptism alone, but they must remain separate among Christians and other nations. They cannot be Christians because their separateness as a people constitutes repentance for the rejection of Christ as the Messiah. Israel was condemned by divine providence to reject God himself for the salvation of the whole world. Its relation to Christ is that of a mother-of-pearl to the pearl. Israel was preserved as a separate entity for the purpose of bearing witness. "Israel, bearing negative witness to Christ on earth through its suffering of persecution and dispersal, will be the positive state's witness in that last trial beyond history when the infinite Father-and-Son love of God will be ultimately revealed, for the promise made to Abraham is still valid" (BHE 202f.). The "Theologumena" thus not only contain Werfel's reasons for remaining a Jew in spite of his belief in Christ but also a religious philosophy accusing and justifying Judaism.

As Steiman has pointed out, the position Werfel has taken here is neither historically accurate nor logically consistent:

> He was well aware that Paul had hoped to inspire the Jews to convert by his own work among the heathen, and it likely occurred to him that any 'negative witnessing' to the reality of Christ loses its point if the witnesses know in advance that Christ is real and true. There is no explanation valid on theological or logical grounds for Werfel's failure to convert to Christianity; that he persisted in his paradoxical position in spite of his awareness of its many contradictions confirms the view that his ultimate source and sanction was mystical.[7]

Werfel's "An Essay upon the Meaning of Imperial Austria" which constitutes the prologue to his collection of novellas and short novels, *Twilight of a World,* bears the date of Locarno, April 1936, and thus actually predates the last essays dealt with here. It attempts to provide a unifying bond for the novellas and short novels of the volume by demonstrating that imperial Austria and its downfall provide the background for all of them. Werfel feels

Empires have been, and will be, founded in the sign of a higher idea. . . . [T]rue empires arise only when a supranatural, divine element is mingled with the daemonic, "natural" entities, to lift them above themselves: a revelation, or a lofty idea. For every true empire is an unrealized effort to establish the kingdom of God upon earth. At least at the hour of birth it is that. Now our child of old Austria believes that his dead and gone world, the Austrian imperial state, was such an empire. (TW 7)

In accordance with this definition, the United States is a genuine empire, too, "not a natural, daemonic unity, but the result of an effort to give shape to a higher, a transcendent idea" (TW 11), the idea of the "highest possible personal freedom within a highly responsible community" (TW 11). "America the seething smelting-oven, and Austria the slowly absorbing and digesting soil. One process is mechanical, the other organic" (TW 14).

Werfel at this point was clearly looking increasingly toward the United States as the fulfillment of an idea then in decline in old Europe. But in describing the process of the formation of empires he relies very much on metaphors taken from nature and physics, without basing his statements on empirical data and without presenting a sharply focused intellectual analysis. As Steiman points out, "These desiderata are lacking in Werfel's presentation, in which the process of historical development is seen either as natural or mechanical *tout court*. What is natural and good is organic; what is natural but bad is daemonic. Empires are thus organic, but nations are daemonic. The United States is neither organic nor daemonic, but is a conscious creation consciously directed."[8]

Specifically regarding Austria, Werfel continues using this sort of inexact language which is part and parcel of European conservative, historical, and political thinking: in old Austria several racial stocks and many nations have been unified. They have been recreated and resmelted, sacrificing some part of their national identity, their own traditions to become new human beings—Austrians. This mission began when Charlemagne "laid the foundation-stone of the so-called Ostmark" (TW 14). It was to protect the West from barbaric assault and to

control and civilize these same barbarians, turn them from bloodbound, daemonic, "natural" men into western Christians. This mission of Austria has not, in the whole course of history, changed an iota. Logically then, it was doomed when daemonic, "natural" humanity in the shape of modern nationalism and its scientific theories overshadowed the imperial idea of occidental Christianity. (TW 14)

In the old "Holy Roman Empire of the German Nation" secular and spiritual power, Caesar and Christ—the earthly horizontal and the supernatural vertical elements—were ideally fused. In contrast to the Habsburg Empire, Prussia was "at the . . . best only a national state, a daemonic entity, as opposed to an empire of peoples bound together by an over-arching idea" (TW 16). Their rulers, the Hohenzollern family, "usurped an empty imperial title, out of hatred for the legitimate Caesars of the house of Habsburg" (TW 16). They attacked Austria and France after deliberately whipping up the demons of pan-German nationalism. Nations and nationalism are seen by Werfel as the archenemies of empires which are based on a higher idea. The historic conflict between Prussia and Austria is the conflict between these forces that has led to the contemporary catastrophe in European history.

In light of his other essays it becomes clear, then, that the Austrian Empire in Werfel's view was an ideal state, its downfall marking the regrettable split between political and spiritual powers. In the final analysis it was this lack of recognizing the spiritual element inherent in the idea of the empire, the false self-deification of nationalism, that was responsible for the empire's downfall: "For the common enemy was the passionate opponent of that old Austrian idea of universal humanity: the daemonic hatred, the vain exaltation of the part above the whole, the impudent self-deification—in a word, the fanatic nationalism displayed by the aroused middle classes of the peoples in general" (TW 21). These words clearly show the connection between Werfel's religious essays and his historical thinking. History for him was based on his theological ideas, just as were his socioeconomic ones.[9] In Emperor Franz Joseph he saw the idea of the empire personified to the very end. With him it also perished.

Werfel is, as we see, no systematic thinker, and many of his ideas are assailable from as well as a Jewish and a Christian point of view. They grew out of the rich experiences of his life and they are ideas that he has also embodied and exemplified in his fictional writings. Thus W. A. Willibrand states at the end of his survey: "These lectures constitute a valuable aid for the interpretation of the novels and plays Werfel published after the late twenties."[10] The following interpretations of Werfel's works intend to do precisely that: demonstrate this point and how Werfel has incorporated his theoretical ideas in his fictional writings.

NOTES

1. *Between Heaven and Earth,* trans. Maxim Newmark (New York: Philosophical Library, 1944); *Zwischen oben und unten* (Stockholm: Bermann-Fischer, 1946).

2. *Twilight of a World,* trans. H. T. Lowe-Porter (New York: Viking, 1937).

3. The best overview of Werfel's essays is provided by Lore B. Foltin and John M. Spalek, "Franz Werfel's Essays: A Survey" *The German Quarterly* 42 (1969): 172–203; and the best critical discussion, which includes many of Werfel's other occasional pieces, by Lionel B. Steiman, *Franz Werfel: The Faith of an Exile. From Prague to Beverly Hills* (Waterloo, Ontario: Wilfrid Laurier University Press, 1985). A summary of content is provided by W. A. Willibrand, "The Sermon-Lectures Of Franz Werfel," *Books Abroad* 19 (1945): 350–55.

4. Steiman 27.

5. Steiman 93.

6. Steiman 95.

7. Steiman 168.

8. Steiman 129.

9. As Steiman 134 states: "Werfel reduces the whole socioeconomic process to a cycle whose fundamental dynamic is theological. War, totalitarianism, capitalism—all are part of a vicious cycle that began with the fall from God."

10. Willibrand 355.

CHAPTER TWO

Speaking for the Young Generation: Poetry

We might discuss Werfel's work in two different ways: either strictly chronologically, with the advantage of always being able to show the inter-relationship of the various works regardless of their genre; or according to genre, then proceeding chronologically within each genre. I have decided to choose the second path for the following reasons: Werfel began his literary career as a writer of poetry, then turned to drama, and finally to prose, so that characterizing his works according to genre automatically means proceeding in chronological order. Admittedly, the chronological caesuras between the genres are not always quite clear. Werfel wrote poetry during his entire lit-erary career; he wrote his most successful drama, *Jacobowsky and the Colo-nel,* at the very end of his life, and his first successful novels while at the same time writing his great historical dramas. But, apart from these excep-tions, the sequence poetry—drama—prose is also a chronological one, and the advantages of looking at all works belonging to one genre by far outweigh the disadvantage of chronological overlapping.

This chapter on poetry is going to be briefer in comparison to those on drama and prose because Werfel's poetry in the United States had virtually no impact. It was not until 1945, shortly after his death, that a small anthology of his poems was first published in the United States, both in the original German and in English translation, under the simple title *Poems.* In his fore-word to this collection, dated "Beverly Hills, California, July 1945," Werfel explicitly points out that for him poetry is that part of his lifework which he regards as the most important. Edith Abercrombie Snow, his translator, is also convinced that "Mr. Werfel was a great novelist and playwright, but it is as a poet that he will live longest" (P ix). The poems in this collection are, with one exception, all taken from Werfel's collection *Gedichte aus dreißig Jahren* (Poems from Thirty Years) (Stockholm: Behrmann-Fischer, 1939). The result is that many famous poems of his early collections are not included and proportionally more are from the section "Neue Gedichte, 1925–1938" (New Poems, 1925–1938), particularly from the part "Gedichte 1938" (Po-ems 1938). It is understandable that the author considered his most recent production more valuable than much of what he had written at age twenty

Most scholars today feel differently and believe that Werfel was not only most productive but that he also wrote his most original poems as a young man.[1]

Werfel's first collection of poetry, *Der Weltfreund* (The Philanthropist), which appeared in December 1911, was enthusiastically received by a generation of poets and readers. Werfel immediately became the spokesperson for the young generation of poets whom we refer to today as Expressionists and he contributed much to the poetic style and to the philosophical concerns of this movement, not only in his poetry, but also in his early dramas, *Spiegelmensch* (Mirror Man), *Goat Song,* and *Schweiger,* and in his first novel, "Not the Murderer." However, many of the poems contained in *Der Weltfreund* do not strike us today as particularly Expressionist. They appear to be traditional and conventional poems, "showing the influence of Impressionism, Symbolism and 'Jugendstil,' the competing artistic and literary trends at the beginning of the twentieth century. Yet a number of the poems sound a very different note and already contain those features of style and content which were to characterise his later poetry."[2] Thus it seems odd that Werfel's contemporaries should have been enraptured by the often sentimental and naive poetry on childhood or childhood memories in the first part of the collection. Here Werfel expressed "his dissatisfaction with a lonely present and a consequent desire for the far-off, happy time of childhood when inanimate things—his toys, his books, his bed—seemed to have a soul and to recognize him as their friend. He longs for play with his little sister and for the love of mother and nurse."[3] According to Detlev W. Schumann, the reason for this is that "the child has an imaginative, magical, not a rationalistic, mechanistic attitude towards its cosmos. It has naively that which the romantic mind longs for as lost."[4] Childhood is the time during which man still has a realistic relationship to his environment, an unbiased relationship to nature in contrast to the later, often bemoaned abstraction and radical realism of our age. But even in these poems about childhood a new voice is audible. Thus in the poem "Early Spring" ("Erster Frühling"), the experience of awakening nature conjures up early memories in the speaker who is able to relate the inside experience of the child to the outside experience of nature. Enumerating a number of objects, a feature which many poems of *Der Weltfreund* have in common, serves to bring a whole atmosphere to life. It is one of the few Werfel poems in which nature plays an important role:

Early Spring

If one walks in the park today, the straw from the
flower-beds is gone,

> And a touch of green here and there pricks up through
>   the brown of the lawn.
>
> On the path, not yet pebble-strewn, leaves, trash and
>   other things sprawl.
> You powerful sounds of the air! What is it that I
>   recall?
>
> When someone sat at the sewing machine in my childhood
>   room.
> Forgotten duet: The sewing-machine and the fizzling
>   gas-plume.
>
> Didn't there, just as today, lie leaves, trash and many
>   things more,
> Colored strips, ribbons, ruffles and silk scraps on the
>   floor? (P 3)

But in the theme of childhood memories, memories of the speaker's wearing his sailor's suit or of a Sunday excursion on a boat, enhanced by the child's imagination, the real message of *Der Weltfreund* is merely hidden: children are closest to the smallest facets of the world; they have the greatest imagination that enables them to transcend the surface impression of things; and they are able to identify with all kinds of existence. "In other words, the child is really the *Weltfreund par excellence*."[5] This is why in "The Fat Man in the Mirror" ("Der dicke Mann im Spiegel") the poet, who has made himself much older than he is, suffers from an attack of fear because he realizes the loss of his childhood, thus the loss of his direct and intense relation to the world.[6]

The really innovative aspect of this collection does not lie in formal innovation but rather the new relation of the poetic self to its world, the poet's loving attitude toward the world. Love and caring for one's fellow man is also expressed in poems such as "For I Have Done a Good and Kindly Deed" ("Ich habe eine gute Tat getan") which in its hymnic tone of the brotherhood found in good deeds, recalls Goethe's famous Storm and Stress hymns, such as "Mahomet's Song" ("Mahomets Gesang"):

> Many hands reach out toward me
> Many cool, green hands;
> Completely en-nested
> In love and loveliness
> I stand imprisoned.

For I have done a good and kindly deed,
I'm full of joy and kindness
And no more lonely,
No, no more lonely.
Rejoice, oh, my heart! (P 15)

Neither human footsteps nor human words are ever lost ("Wanderlied"; P 11) and man is so close to nature that they are practically one. The poet desires to be part of the earth in loving longing:

The Wayfarer Kneels

ONLY grant that I may weep . . .
That I be dissolved by feeling
That I like a limpid water,
Trickle over all thy edges
And through all thy meadows ripple,
Dearest earth! ("Der Wanderer kniet"; P 7)

A great number of the poems in *Der Weltfreund* are sonnets, the most famous being "The Noble Radiant Man" ("Der schöne strahlende Mensch") in which the affinity of man with the earth is connected with the joy of existence:

Upon the twilight grass I will sit down,
And with the earth into the evening ride.
Oh earth, oh Evening, Joy! Oh in the world to be. (P 9)

In "Dying in the Forest" ("Sterben im Walde") death itself—decomposition and reunion with nature—is overcome by the consciousness of the eternal existence of the soul:

And my soul joins in:
You are on this world,
And jubilantly spreads out in all directions. (DLW 24;
    trans. H.W.)

The all-embracing love of one's fellow man which is in the center of *Der Weltfreund* culminates in the wish expressed in the last poem of the collection, "To the Reader" ("An den Leser"):

My only wish is to be related to you, o Man!
. . .

Oh, if only it could happen once
That we, brother, might embrace each other! (DLW 63;
trans. H.W.)

At this point in his life Werfel and his contemporaries, whom we now refer
to as Expressionists, were convinced that this universal love, this overcoming
of individuation, could be accomplished. The enthusiastic tenor of such
lines was clearly written under the influence of the American poet Walt
Whitman and the biblical Psalms. After Dostoevsky, Walt Whitman's *Leaves
of Grass* became Werfel's greatest personal literary experience. The influence of Whitman's hymnic tone on German Expressionist poetry cannot
be overrated.

The prevalent idea of embracing all of mankind had led later generations to
refer to Expressionist lyrics as "O Mensch-Lyrik" ("O Mankind Poetry"),
testifying to the fact that Werfel had become the spokesperson for a generation of young poets. What is behind this opening up toward the other is a new
attitude toward the world, toward God's creation, *Frömmigkeit:* a new spiritual concern about the world and about man. It is a gospel of love that forms
the basis of Werfel's poetry, and it is this new attitude rather than formal in-
novations which constitutes the Expressionist character of *Der Weltfreund.*
But Werfel was not to remain the spokesperson of the young Expressionists
for long. He soon became tired of his role, rejected Expressionism as exaggerated, without, however, being able to divest himself of its characteristics completely.[7]

In his early poetry Werfel repeatedly refers to God, but in a very general,
nondenominational sense, neither as conscious Jew nor Christian, but just as
a human being toward the creator. This remains constant throughout Werfel's
work: he believed it to be "the writer's responsibility to transform human
existence with the help of the 'Creator spiritus' and this demands the overcoming of a sense of resignation."[8] He tries to achieve this overcoming of
resignation in *Wir sind* (We Are; 1913), by time and again proclaiming a consciousness of existence which would initiate a transformation in man. In none
of his other collections of poetry has Werfel repeated the idea that all men
are spiritually related. The idea of brotherly love that is coalesced in the title
is repeated frequently and so clearly. An example is "A Song of Life"
("Ein Lebenslied"):

31

> . . . Unexpressible
> In words and artistic expression
> We are far and close to each other
>
> . . .
> But above all words
> I am pronouncing, man, *We are!!* (DLW 108;
>   trans. H.W.)

This message is expressed with a pathos and self-effusion which is the hallmark of Expressionism in literature:

> All of you, all who I am
> Yes, joy, joy is the meaning! ("The Spirit" ["Der
>   Geist"]; DLW, 76; trans. H.W.)

In his afterword to *Wir sind* Werfel states programmatically:

> We who have been pushed in this confusion of earthly limits, into the hustle and bustle and into the inferior, perspicuous consistency, we forget only too quickly the unfathomable, enormous word: *We are.* I believe that everything humanly noble, goodness, joy, jubilation, pain, loneliness, the ideal can rise from this eternal, impenetrable, tremendous consciousness of existence. A human being who never broke down in face of the heavens has never been good either. (DLW 137; trans. H.W.)

But whereas in *Der Weltfreund* the goal seemed attainable, in *Wir sind* man is bound by his individuation, unable to reach out, to free himself.

> For I am thus shut in!
> And all cries out for love.
> I, too, cry out for love,
> And yet for no one care. ("Despair"
>   ["Verzweiflung"]; P 27)

Here, even those closest to us cannot really reach out in love. Being born in itself begins the process of individuation, and yet while we are still close to each other as children, this primary experience will soon be lost.

> Once there was brotherly love
> I was running with the girls across the paths
>
> . . .

And there was deep fear that the other would die
And sometimes one would cry deeply into the darkness,
Until, faithfully, the breath of the other would come. ("The
Heart Growing Cold" ["Das erkaltende Herz"], DLW 101;
trans. H.W.)

Man is not only bound by individuation, he is viewed as guilty from conception on: the guilt of existence. Thus Werfel says in "Balance of the World"
("Balance der Welt"):

Yes, guilt is the enormous word.
It keeps turning the old globes.
And before even our time begins,
We become guilty because we are. (DLW 96;
trans. H.W.)

This feeling of guilt penetrates his life, and the speaker cannot enjoy love because others live in despair and misery:

As Your Sweet Ways Enraptured Me to Death

WHILE by your being I was charmed to tears,
And I through you in space soared far away
Did not unhappy people live that day,
Millions oppressed and wretched all their years?

As your sweet ways enraptured me to death,
The earth was noisy, workers round us trod,
And there were wastes, and folk unwarmed of God.
Men lived and died unblest to their last breath.

As you inspired me till my senses whirled,
There were so many who in darkness fretted,
Crouched over desks and before boilers sweated.

I hear on street and stream their gasping yet!
If there's a balance in this life and world,
In what way will I have to pay this debt? ("Als mich dein
Wandeln an den Tod verzückte"; P 17)

Man is alone, brotherhood has not been realized, the consciousness of the
plight of others prevents us from enjoying life. Yet there is hope in a spiritual

feeling that can break this loneliness, a feeling which finds Werfel very close to Christianity. "There still exists behind all this incomplete reality of ours the complete reality of God to which we must break through; there is redemption. There are among us the poor in spirit who have retained their contact with the divine reality."[9] In "An Old Woman Passes" ("Eine alte Frau geht") Werfel writes about the existence of this otherworldly reality:

> But, man, remember what in her you see,
> A mighty presence in the world are we,
> Since our life in time and space was hurled!
> . . .
> This world is not the only world. (P 23)

He then shows that this simple woman is able to establish an immediate relationship to God:

> As to her tasks the shuffling ancient bends,
> Oh, perhaps her tired mind comprehends.
> Now vanishes her crumpled, withered face.
> She feels her life expand itself in all,
> And on her trembling knees begins to fall,
> As from a flickering light upon the wall,
> God's countenance looms vast in the small place. (P 25)

Not only simple people are this close to God, but everyone is challenged to open themselves up to God in love. Werfel thus does not simply proclaim the human and divine holiness which overcomes all earthly frailness, but the idea of a love in which all of humanity is united: "At the centre of the cycle stands the idea of a brotherly love, joining all humanity together. . . . It is this feeling of love for everybody else which constitutes our link with the universe and thus with the Divine. . . . Style and language have now lost most of the traditional features that were still evident in *Der Weltfreund,* and tend to the abstraction, hyperbole and metaphorical density which is so typical of German Expressionist poetry."[10] In its hymnic character many poems of *Wir sind* were able to become models for other poets of this literary movement.

The hymnic, Expressionist style is perfected in Werfel's next book of poetry, *Einander* (Each Other; 1915), which contains poems written in 1913 and 1914, including the first months of the First World War. But in contrast to the all-embracing attitude of the first two books, the basic tenor of Werfel's at-

titude has become much more gloomy. In "Supreme Kinship" ("Hohe Ge-
meinschaft") the one thing that man has in common with his fellow man is
the fact that he must die. This is the source of man's nobility for Werfel:

> And that to you is due what each one is due,
> And you are akin to all last days of life!
> You are not deprived of pain's nobleness.
> For because you exist you are equal. Be proud! (P 31)

Werfel has to remind man of his nobility because "all our empirical world,
with its forms and phenomena, with its principle of individuation, is defec-
tion from God's original pure and holy world of all-unity."[11] The poet questions God's creation by asking him why he created man the way he did, with
all his flaws and his guilt:

> Why, My Lord and God?
>
> WHY did'st Thou create me, Lord,
> I, who flared up, unwitting candle-flame,
> And flicker now in wind of my own guilt,
> Why did'st Thou create me, Lord,
> To words' futility,
> That I fit words together,
> And bear presumptuous pride,
> Endure in my heart's secret places
> Loneliness?
> Why did'st thou create me, Lord, for this? ("Warum
>   mein Gott"; P 37)

The poet tries to be closer to God, but in the final analysis he blames God for
earth's creation and thus for man's guilt, including for all evil, as the rhe-
torical questions of "An Evening Song" ("Ein Abendgesang") consider:

> That is the hour when everything wakes up and a final
>   amazement
> Falls into our confusedly overgrown hearts,
> That we are and that good and bad moods
> Of the incomprehensible one has placed us into the
>   world!
> Who wanted me that I turn over wickedness in my chest,

Who destined it that goodness sweetly overcame me?
Who gave me humility and pride and arrogance,
Who made it possible that I walk around so estranged
from myself? (DLW 172; trans. H.W.)

Yet there is a way out of man's predicament. Man is able to be accepted by
God if he does good deeds, thus helping God in his realization:

The Good Man

THE POWER is his, the regiment of stars,
He holds the world enfisted like a nut,
And laughter wreathes his face eternally,
War is his being, triumph is his gait.

And where he stands, extending wide his hands,
Where his tyrannic call goes thundering down,
There crash creation's gross injustices,
And all becomes as God, and one. ("Der gute Mensch"; P 33)

The poet calls upon the Holy Ghost to break the icy nature of man's aloofness
and reconcile him with his brother:

Veni Creator Spiritus

Come, Holy Ghost, you, creatively!
Break the marble of our form!
So that no more wall, sick and hard,
Stare around the well of this world,
So that we together and upwards
Rage like flames together!

. . .

So that someone who embraces his brother,
Holds your deep beating sweetly close to his heart,
So that someone who receives a poor dog's looking,
Receives the gift of your wise glance,
So that in the abundance of kissing
We only kiss your holy lip. (DLW 153f.; trans. H.W.)

Already for the Werfel of 1914 this absolute love is personified in Jesus, about
whom he writes in "Jesus and the Carrion-Path" ("Jesus und der
Äser-Weg"). Here Jesus chooses a path which leads him to a carrion-stream,

Where leprous rats were swimming in a nest
Of serpents, by corrosion half-consumed,
Putrescent deer and asses, measureless
Decay and flies above it shimmering loomed.

But Jesus is able to overcome his horror and disgust and turns with love and pity toward the carrion. At that point a light of glory plays around his face and a scent of roses develops around him:

But He His hair with little carrion bound,
A hundred corpses from His girdle hung,
His head with writhing wreath of serpents crowned,
Upon His shoulders bats and rodents clung.

And as He stood thus in the day's dark light,
The mountains opened up; about His knee
Lions came and wept, and wild geese formed for flight,
With beating wings rushed down unswervingly.

Four darkling suns danced softly up above,
Broad in the air an endless ray was limned.
The heavens burst. And in the great blue wind,
Enraptured, hovered there God's holy dove. (P 47ff.)

The Holy Ghost which is present in Jesus's absolute love is thus able to overcome the most repelling horrors, accepting all of God's creation and promising redemption to even the lowest of his creatures. In Werfel's view this love which is present in the Holy Ghost is the basis for man's redemption from separation, individuation, and guilt.

Although Werfel was one of the few poets who wrote about war while at the same time serving at the front line, the theme of war comes up in only a few of his poems. As W. E. Yeates points out: "By temperament Werfel did not fall into any of the categories of writer most productive of war poetry. He was not a polemicist concerned with the events of the day, whether in convinced patriotism or in satirical dissent; nor was he a sober recorder of factual detail. Despite his anticipation of themes developed by other poets, it is indicative that his most overt and direct inveighing against the whole basis of war was not sustained beyond August 1914."[12] Yeates is referring here to two poems written in August 1914 which are contained in *Einander,* and which both criticize the hollow war propaganda and the patriotic jingoism during the first months of the conflict. Thus "The War" ("Der Krieg") begins with the verses:

> On a storm of false words,
> The head wreathed by empty thunder,
> Sleepless from lies,
> Girded with deeds which only do themselves,
> Bragging with sacrifices,
> Unpleasing, terrible for Heaven—That's the way you are
> going down,
> Time,
> . . . (DLW 162; trans. H.W.)

And similarly the next poem, "The Propagandists of War" ("Die Wortemacher des Krieges") deplores that now "the house of the mind" has been shot to bits, and brotherhood has fallen prey to a plague of rats:

> The fools are babbling and the overambitious are
> croaking
> And they call manliness their old excrements.
> Just so that the fat women are yearning for them,
> The chest full of medals
> Is vaulting into dawn. (DLW 162; trans. H.W.)

The reality of war was brought home to Werfel when he saw the first casualties returning from the front line in 1914:

The First Transport of Wounded 1914

> CAREFUL! No outburst now! Tremble! Hush!
> You people, you folk, it is true! Yes, it is true!
> Do not sob out, you people!
> Hold the scream tight in your throat!
> Still! Lower your head
> That now is bowed down forever, you women!
> Your kerchief, your hand hold to your mouth! Hush!
> People, you folk, it is true!
> Not a word more, no more wailing!
> Quietly pass on the horror-stricken look,

> And touch each other, oppressed ones, with a gentle
> touch!
> Bow down lover, sleep-walkers, pain-begotten ones,
> You wretched, oh you lamentable age! ("Der erste
> Verwundeten-Transport 1914"; P 51)

It is characteristic that Werfel only describes people's reaction to the horror but not actually the horror itself. There is no graphic detail, not even in met-aphorical terms as in the poems of Georg Trakl. In Werfel's poem "The Wounded Soldier" ("Der Verwundete") he similarly does not describe any wounds, only the pantheistic love of the surrounding nature into which the wounded soldier sinks.

It is amazing that the poems Werfel wrote during the war, many of them at the front line, and published in *Der Gerichtstag* (The Day of Judgment; 1919), are so very abstract in their wording. The contemporary reality of war is reflected in these poems only indirectly, in their resigned attitude. As Fred Wagner points out, the experience of the war obviously "made it very difficult for the poet to continue proclaiming his optimistic gospel of the brotherhood of man and deprived belief in divine grace of some of its credibility."[13]

In comparison to *Einander,* the hymnic tone has now given way to brood-ing, heavy lines, an expression of the poet's own state of mind during the war: "The author fights an agonizing and almost hopeless battle with despair and heartbreak."[14] The very first poem, "Ballad of Delusion and Death" ("Ballade von Wahn und Tod") sets the tone by saying:

> The word that pierced me, the word with two syllables,
> the word was: hopeless. (DLW 200; trans. H.W.)

In *Der Gerichtstag* the world is tried and sentenced. The God who rules in this world is the judging and avenging God of the Old Testament and the Apocalypse, as seen in the poem "The Passionate Ones" ("Die Leiden-schaftlichen"), where the final judgment is anticipated:

> My God, to your right will be
> Not the truthful ones and the just alone! (DLW 230;
> trans. H.W.)

Just like in his contemporary drama *Spiegelmensch,* the poet feels split into two, feels that he has the enemy within, and he wrestles with God, asking him to make him one, to free him from his inner enemy:

Liberate me, purify me, Father, destroy this enemy who entwines me!
How blessed are the simple-hearted, the unknowing,
　blessed the simple good, blessed the simple bad,
But cursed, cursed the divided ones, the two-faced, the
　waxing and waning antagonists!
Oh holy Water, for the sake of Thy greatness and mine,
　help me! ("Prayer For Purity" ["Gebet um Reinheit"]; P 57)

What Werfel criticizes is the individuation of man, the dehumanization, mechanization of our world which has found its expression in a war hardly ever mentioned, but constantly present in his work. The main tenor of the collection is thus gloomy and negative. The theme of resignation announces itself; there does not seem to be any earthly redemption.[15] The reason for all the overriding negativity is a lack of love which Werfel illuminates in "Impotence of the Heart" ("Trägheit des Herzens"):

And the Arms remain always empty,
And I am turning away and walking my path.
Thus day by day breaking my cowardly heart
And full of misery, bribing God with alms. (DLW 249f.;
　trans. H.W.)

Moreover, God too must realize himself: "The double nature of man has led the poet to assume a dividedness in God. He speaks of the world as the night upon God's face, of man's breathing as the throbbing of God's wound. Because of his double nature God is not yet complete. The task which Werfel sees for the individual is not only that of redeeming and perfecting his fellow man, but also of helping God to realize himself."[16] Werfel also talks about this necessary uniting of God in typically Expressionist optimism in the last poem of *Der Gerichtstag,* "The Light and the Silence" ("Das Licht und das Schweigen"), which concludes:

Come, come, man! It is up to you, to conclude the
　silence
Out of the noise, to redeem the song!
Come, come, man! It is up to you to form,
Out of the forces of the decay of colors, the light!
Come, come, man! Only you will, through your holy
　deeds

Create the Godhead.
Out of this confusion, the delusion and out of
  appearances
You will unite diversity into One. (DLW 315; trans. H.W.)

Der Gerichtstag is Werfel's most sprawling collection of poetry. Yet he included only a few of its poems in his last selection of poetry, *Gedichte aus den Jahren 1908–1945* (Poems from the Years 1908–1945; 1946). In the opinion of Fred Wagner the collection demonstrates that there "are the two main reasons for the demise of much of Expressionism in general and of Werfel's own Expressionist writing in particular. First, there is the vagueness and indeterminacy of the ethical appeal. And second there is the impossibility of sustaining a hymnic and ecstatic mode of poetic expression for a prolonged period."[17]

The poetry Werfel published after *Der Gerichtstag* "shows little of the formal and spiritual boldness of his earlier work . . . The style and content of *Beschwörungen* [Conjurations; 1923] suggest a return to a more traditional type of poetry, reminiscent of his very early verse, composed under the influence of the literary trends that were dominant at the turn of the century."[18] In the poems of *Beschwörungen* the feeling of resignation, already audible in *Der Gerichtstag,* is intensified. Man can no longer rely on God; redemption is not primary and has been replaced by an acceptance of the human condition:

Night Rain

THE rain's dead rustle! Gloomy glistening!
The more you try, the more you hark,
The less you'll ever hear by listening.

The rain blabs on in witless strumming.
Tensely you turn your thoughts within.
From God you'll find no word forthcoming.

Cease then your striving, agonizing.
The song comes not to him who waits.
All greatness loves to be surprising. ("Nachtregen"; P 61)

Nature does play an extraordinarily large part in *Beschwörungen,* more so than in any other of Werfel's collections of poetry, but it is always the negative side of nature that Werfel deals with, as in autumn and winter, dusk and night. Nevertheless, he uses nature, as in the above poem, to indicate a certain hope, a consolation for man in spite of the atmosphere of gloominess and decline:

Autumn Song

Now wanes the day, now wanes the year, now wanes the
man.

The apples crowd together now
On the gnarly-muscled bough.
Up the street there jogs a stalwart span.
The horses nod in hazy light;
Over the hill's high hips a flight
Of the wind-drunk, chattering crows.
The seed-secretive cricket throng,
Summer's fiddles, have hushed their song.
An unknown call from forest sent,
Swells darkly up from sacred instrument.
Through me goes too, I know not what,
A consolation, word-forgot:
That I, to autumn's world akin,
Like bird and tree and disappearing span,
Breathing, am included in.

Now wanes the day, the year, the man. ("Herbstlied"; P 59)

Although *Beschwörungen* contains many poems of dark, mythical content—many enigmatic ballads dealing with animals—the basic outlook for man is still one of hopeful acceptance. This trend is continued in *Neue Gedichte* (New Poems; 1928) covering the years 1923–27, which are also part of his collected poems, *Gedichte* (Poems; 1927), and in the collection *Schlaf und Erwachen* (Sleep and Awakening; 1935). Despite its many poems dealing with sickness and death, this latter collection again displays calm acceptance of God's will. This is obvious in:

Tempora Mea in Manibus Tuis

TO WHOM do I belong? My kindred? No!
The mine I mean are really not my own.
My nearest kin is cold and strange as stone.

> To whom do I belong? A nation? No!
> Just drunkenness and fear to herd are prone,
> And among thousands I'm a thousand times alone.
>
> To whom do I belong? To myself? No!
> Who is myself? A gloomy flesh and bone
> Whose flickering lamp with light of death is blown.
>
> To whom do I belong? I am His own,
> For being is being His; and as I mean,
> Into His open Father-hand I've flown. (P 99)

In "Every Beauty" ("Jede Schönheit") nature itself becomes a theodicy for the poet:

> Early March unfolding of this park,
> Last white of the pond and path I trod,
> And the willow's mother-heavy arc,
> Thrill through me as purest proof of God. (P 97)

As Werfel increasingly turned to the production of dramas and prose, his lyrical production became far less prolific, but the poems in "Gedichte 1938" and "Kunde vom irdischen Leben" (Tidings from Life on Earth) which are contained in *Gedichte aus dreißig Jahren* (1939) and *Gedichte aus den Jahren 1908–1945* (1946), respectively, were all written during Werfel's exile. They deal less with metaphysical issues and more with sickness, prompted by the poet's worsening heart condition, and with the theme of exile itself, as in:

Dream-City of an Emigrant

> YES, I am right, it is the well-known street,
> I've lived here thirty years without a change . . .
> Is this the street? I'm driven by a strange
> Compelling force there with the mass to meet.
>
> A barrier looms . . . Before I can retreat
> My arm is roughly seized: "Please show your pass!"
> My pass? Where is my pass? In a morass
> Of scorn and hate I move with faltering feet.
>
> Can human soul endure such anxious fear?
> Steel scourges that will strike me whistle near.
> The last I know upon my knees I'm flung . . .

And while I'm spat on by an unseen crowd,
"I have done nothing wrong," I scream aloud,
"Except I spoke in your own tongue, *my* tongue." ("Traumstadt
    eines Emigranten"; P 113)

His fascination with the present should not detract from the understanding of Werfel as basically a religious poet. From his earliest poetry he struggled with the position of man in relation to God and went through periods of doubt and resignation, but rebounded with a trusting attitude, which during his exile also documented itself in his prose, above all in his novel *The Song of Bernadette*.

In Werfel's poetry this spiritualism is an unquestioned reality; its existence cannot be denied by what he terms radical realism or naturalistic nihilism in his essays. It is the basic theme of man's relationship to God that connects his poetry with his other works, particularly with the views expressed in his essays of the 1930s. Moreover, in poetry the inwardness Werfel advocates in his essays can openly find expression, and become—at least a poetic—reality. In poetry Werfel, the creative man of the muses, expresses his inwardness more than in any other genre, and he addresses others who are leaning in the same direction. Thus, through his poetry, Werfel helps establish a community of men favored by the muses who alone are able to fight the radical realism of the twentieth century. In poetry Werfel and his readers are forced to delve into their inner selves; thus his poems help man in transforming his consciousness toward self-realization, and thus closer to God.

NOTES

1. E.g., Adolf D. Klarmann in the preface to his edition of Franz Werfel, *Gesammelte Werke: Das lyrische Werk* (Frankfurt am Main: S. Fischer, 1967) 5.
2. Fred Wagner, " 'Das herrliche Verhängnis': The Poetry of Franz Werfel," in *Franz Werfel: An Austrian Writer Reassessed*, ed. Lothar Huber (Oxford: Berg, 1989) 39.
3. Wilma Brun Merlan, "Franz Werfel, Poet," in *Franz Werfel: 1890–1945*, ed. Lore B. Foltin (Pittsburgh: University of Pittsburgh Press, 1961) 27.
4. Detlev W. Schumann, "The Development of Werfel's 'Lebensgefühl' as Reflected in His Poetry," in *The Germanic Review* 6, 1 (1931): 29.
5. Schumann 30.
6. Schumann 30.
7. See Klarmann in Werfel, *Gesammelte Werke: Das lyrische Werk* 5.
8. Wagner 41.
9. Schumann 36.
10. Wagner 44.
11. Schumann 38.
12. W. E. Yeates, "Franz Werfel and Austrian Poetry of the First World War," in Huber 32.

13. Wagner 46.
14. Merlan 33.
15. See Klarmann in Werfel, *Gesammelte Werke: Das lyrische Werk* 7.
16. Klarmann in Werfel, *Gesammelte Werke: Das lyrische Werk* 34.
17. Wagner 47.
18. Wagner 47.

CHAPTER THREE

From Myth to History: Drama

Early Attempts at Drama and *Spiegelmensch* (Mirror Man)

Werfel's activity as a dramatist began with the short romantic drama *Der Besuch aus dem Elysium* (The Visit from Elysium; 1920), written in 1910 and first performed on 9 June 1918 at the Deutsches Theater, Berlin. In this one-act play a man named Lukas visits his formerly adored love, Hedwig, from beyond the grave. The model for the woman is obviously Werfel's first love, Maria Glaser, and just as she had later married an engineer Hedwig becomes a "provincial madonna," an unhappy matron and lonely mother who admires the seemingly adventurous revenant, who has been successful in all his ambitious endeavors. Death, Werfel seems to say, is the last, the highest form of such an ecstatic existence.

Hymnic in tone is the one-act play or conversation, *Die Versuchung: Ein Gespräch des Dichters mit dem Erzengel und Luzifer* (The Temptation: A Conversation of the Poet with the Archangel and Lucifer; 1913) which, in typical Expressionist fashion, deals with the mission of the poet, here presented as the mediator between God and the world. Rejecting all of Satan's temptations the poet accepts his fate and his mission, as he is close to the angels.

In the summer of 1913 Werfel reworked Euripides' *The Trojan Women. Die Troerinnen des Euripides* was first performed in the middle of the First World War, on 22 April 1916 at Berlin's Lessing Theater. It was Werfel's first great theatrical success. Euripides' warning cries, directed against the Athenians who were preparing a military expedition against Sicily which ended in disaster, were understood in Werfel's version as a pronouncement against the hateful spirit of the times and against those who had started war.

Several other attempts at drama in these early years remained fragments: the dramatic dialogue "Euripides oder Über den Krieg" (Euripides, or, On the War), "Esther, Kaiserin von Persien" (Esther, Empress of Persia), and "Klingsohr," on which he worked in the summer of 1919. In the meantime, in June 1917 or prior to the Russian Revolution, he had written the somewhat longer fragment "Stockleinen," the story of a bureaucrat and ideologist who tries to realize a communist type of society. After the birth of his son in 1918, he penned the short lyrical drama "Die Mittagsgöttin" (The Noon Goddess),

originally part of *Der Gerichtstag*. The *Landstreicher* (hobo) Laurentin encounters Mara, the heathen Goddess of Noon who incorporates the eternal
feminine principle—in both a real and metaphysical power—and who helps
him toward self-realization. Clearly, Werfel has given poetic expression to
his encounter with Alma Mahler.

Werfel's plans for his drama *Spiegelmensch: Magische Trilogie* (Mirror
Man: Dramatic Trilogy; 1920) go back as far as 1915, but he did not begin
working on it until February 1919, finishing it in March 1920. The drama
constitutes a kind of self-reckoning, thus marking a transition from youthful
exuberance to self-critical maturity in Werfel's life.

Against the advice of the abbot, the thirty-year-old Thamal requests to be
admitted to a Buddhist monastery because he wants to flee from the insuffi-
ciency of all earthly things, particularly from himself. During the first night
in his cell he shoots at his own mirror image, wounding himself instead of the
mirror man, whom he thereby liberates to life. The mirror man turns out to
be a great tempter who subjects Thamal to numerous temptations, to all of
which he succumbs: he kills his own father through the power of his own
thoughts; he cheats his friend whose wife he seduces and then leaves her after
she has become pregnant with his child; he becomes the liberator of the people of Cholshamba, defeating their oppressing god Ananthas (Satan), but allows himself to be proclaimed a god. Each time he fails, the Mirror Man
becomes bigger and stronger, whereas Thamal sinks deeper and deeper until
finally he becomes a galley slave. Again confronted with Mirror Man, who is
now the richest man on earth, he decides to give himself up to the courts.
Appointed judge over himself, he sentences himself to death, although all the
witnesses, who are his victims, find excuses for him. Even his father is ready
to forgive him. The only one who does not is his dead child who had been
born sick, unfit to live. When the sick child collapses attempting to speak,
Thamal also breaks down and admits his guilt. In the prison cell Mirror Man
appears once more in various guises and tries to seduce Thamal to life again,
but Thamal resists and drinks the goblet with poison, which has been handed
to him. He awakens in a monastery, admitted as someone who has been freed
of all self-reflection (mirroring).

It is not accidental that Werfel dedicated the play "To Alma Maria
Mahler." In a dedicatory poem he acknowledges that she is the woman who
has led him, the restless man, from restlessness, from delusion and vanity,
back to communion with himself, to inner certainty and nature.[1] Werfel characterizes man as someone who has been fleeing in a dance of lies from one
mirror image to another until he has been redeemed by love. It goes without

saying that the "man" is Werfel himself, just as Thamal is not just man but, above all, the author himself, who saw reflecting himself as one of his greatest personal problems. The main theme of the play is clearly the freeing of man from delusion and vanity.[2] Obviously, the child who was born unfit for life is a literary counterpart to Werfel's own son by Alma Mahler. In this respect the drama expresses Werfel's own guilt for fathering this child. One might also wonder whether Thamal's futile attempt to free the country of Cholshamba by the power of his mind alone does not represent Werfel's reckoning with his own revolutionary adventures.[3]

To write about this problem, Werfel had familiarized himself with Eastern philosophies and religions. In accordance with such thinking the abbot who greets Thamal at the opening of the play distinguishes three stages of human development. The initial stage features pure selfishness and a lack of self-consciousness and insight. Those living this type of life must live it over again. The person of the second stage is destined to fight during his entire life with his alter ego, with his enemy. But he gains insight and becomes one with himself; he gains inner peace; and he sees and loves. The third stage is reserved for those who are redeemers of mankind. When at this point Thamal pronounces that he belongs to the second group of men the entire action of the drama is anticipated. What follows is a kind of mystery play which, in a number of representative symbolic scenes, leads Thamal through the trials of this second stage of possible human life.

The critics of the first performances in Leipzig, Stuttgart, and Vienna had trouble understanding the play, but they pointed out a number of parallels to other dramas, such as Goethe's *Faust,* Ibsen's *Peer Gynt,* Wagner's *Parzifal,* Hofmannsthal's *Jedermann (Everyman),* Schikaneder's *Die Zauberflöte (The Magic Flute),* Calderon's *Life, a Dream,* Grillparzer's *Der Traum, ein Leben (The Dream, a Life),* and Strindberg's station dramas, in particular, *To Damascus.* Even the Viennese popular and magical plays of Ferdinand Raimund were compared to Werfel's work. There is no doubt that Werfel has utilized elements from all these,[4] but this is an important issue only for academics. More important is his fusing of all these influences into a very personal Expressionist *Wandlungsdrama* (drama of inner transformation). Thamal's journey is a road to himself. It is less of a *Passionsweg,* a Christian passion, than a journey from station to station, during which he becomes increasingly guilty because he inflicts suffering on others. At the end, however, there is redemption, rebirth, and resurrection in a truly Expressionist manner.

As Lothar Huber points out, the main themes of the play are thus typically Expressionist ones: "liberation, redemption, transformation, renewal, rebirth, ecstasy, vision, ultimate perfection, authenticity, the sense of a mission. Clearly recognisable in theme, but also in style, in dialogue, in the use of figures, in the sequence of a number of loosely connected scenes through which the protagonist proceeds as a 'Wanderer', and of course in the all-pervading messianic pathos."[5] At the end Thamal is a type of introspective character, the kind which marks Werfel's essays of the early 1930s.

In addition to being an Expressionist *Wandlungsdrama*, "Mirror Man" contains a number of satirical elements which are directed against Werfel's contemporary world. The most noteworthy is a tirade against his former friend and then prime enemy, Karl Kraus, which is inserted in prose. This portion was eliminated from the script for the first Austrian performance in the Vienna Burgtheater on 22 April 1922 for fear of a public scandal. Other satirical remarks about the spirit of 1920 were voiced by the Three Admirers. The result was that the aspect of the mystery play became secondary to the stylistic mixture which offered many facets of satirical social criticism.

With "Mirror Man" Werfel had set out on a career as a dramatist. In a letter to his publisher, Kurt Wolff, in 1920, he stated quite seriously: "I do not know whether I am a dramatist, but I know that today nobody is writing who has so much theater inside of himself as I do."[6]

Goat Song (Bocksgesang)

Goat Song: A Drama in Five Acts (*Bocksgesang: In fünf Akten;* 1921) is Werfel's first prose drama. The words "goat song" are a literal translation of the Greek "tragoedia," which in itself means "tragedy" but originally denotes a song about the male goat which was part of the Dionysian rites in honor of the Greek god of vegetation and wine. According to Frank Lambasa, "this intentional play on words with its twofold reference to a ritualistic catharsis (rite becoming drama), on the one hand, and a literal story of the life, escape and death of a monstrous goatlike freak on the other, suggests that the play itself can either be taken literally or understood as a huge dramatic symbol."[7]

Werfel first got the idea for the play when, at the occasion of a visit to a pathological institute in the Vyschehrad, a fortress in the southern part of Prague, he saw a monstrously deformed human being with horns. This upsetting experience made him aware of the infinite possibilities of man who bears the entire possibilities of nature inside of himself.

The action takes place at the turn of the nineteenth century in a Slavic landscape. Mirko, the son of the rich *Gospodar* (squire) Stevan Milic is going to be married to Stanja. It turns out that Stevan has another, older son, a monstrosity who resembles a goat, and has therefore been hidden in a little stall in his farm for over twenty years. After the enlightened physician, a disciple of Voltaire, forgets to lock the door, the monster escapes and joins a band of dissatisfied social outcasts who, under the leadership of Juvan, a student and son of a prostitute, ask the rich for land. When their demands are denied by Stevan, they burn and pillage the countryside until the rebellion is put down by the Turkish military. Stanja has sacrificed herself trying to tame the monster and will bear its child. Juvan, Stanja's secret love, will be hanged. Mirko has been killed trying to save her. Sitting on the remains of their devastated farm, Stevan and his wife have found each other in love once again.

The play was first performed simultaneously on 10 March 1922 in Vienna's Raimund Theater and in Frankfurt am Main. Critics did not know what to make of it, and considered it revolutionary, confusing, and ultimately incomprehensible. They did, however, praise the dramatic power of several scenes, as well as the lyrical qualities and the poetic beauty of the language. In the United States the play was first performed on 25 January 1926 by the Theatre Guild in New York. In altogether 58 performances it became *the* event of the theater season and a considerable commercial success. On four Sunday afternoons the Guild scheduled presentations and discussions by writers and journalists on the significance of the play, filling the 2,000-seat theater. Werfel's play was also hotly debated in the press. In a letter published on 7 March 1926 in the *New York Times,* Eugene O'Neill wrote: "Here is a play which really justifies all one can say by way of enthusiastic praise." Most importantly, Werfel was introduced to the American public as an important European writer.

The confusion about the play arises because it contains a number of different themes: first, there is the social theme of the rebellion of the poor, disenfranchised, and social outcasts against the conservative rich. Juvan, the son of the prostitute, is pitted against the rich *Gospodar* Stevan. Both of them, Werfel seems to say, are wrong: at the conclusion Juvan understands his own guilt, and Stevan is truly happy only after he has lost his riches. In this respect the play is a reflection of Werfel's own revolutionary interlude and his anarchist leanings at the end of the First World War. The rebel mob aligns itself with the monster, becoming aroused to a frenzy of bloodthirstiness and destructiveness. The spirit of rebellion is fueled by the feeling of a lack of social recognition and equal opportunities, by the contemptuous attitude of the rich who do not allow the underprivileged a chance to improve their existence. The evil is seen as the result of a lack of love, of the rule of egotism among men.

In addition to the sociopolitical statement, there is a strong mythical one. Werfel suggests that the beast, an incorporation of evil and of demonic, devilish powers, is always with us. The goat represents the irrational, the unconscious evil which is inside of all of us and is the opposite to order by striving toward chaos. We may hide it, we may lock it up, but it is always ready to escape and we run the danger of its winning over people who deify it. In other words, this play is a drama about the omnipresence of the mythical evil. Viewed in this manner, it addresses a theme that was popular in German Expressionism, a style that often created its own mythologies. The poetry of the German Expressionist Georg Heym serves as a prime example for this type of literature. Of course, such an interpretation also lends a kind of prophetic quality to the play, which seems to prophesy the adoration of the evil of the Third Reich under the leadership of the social outcast Adolf Hitler.

The distinctly utopian fifth act—Expressionist in spirit—is one in which two human beings, who have been living next to each other in quiet hate and reproach, discover each other in love, as human beings. They enact the type of love Werfel was advocating at this time in his poetry. Many other motifs of his collection of poetry *Beschwörungen* (Conjurations), such as the opposites of the concealed and the obvious or animal and man, are also repeated here. Distinctly Expressionist is also the self-sacrifice of Stanja who will bear the monster's child, which nevertheless promises hope for the future. This is an element linking the play with Georg Kaiser's famous dramatic trilogy *Gas* (1917, 1981, 1920). Werfel does not specifically indicate that through her sexual act with the monster she has been able to tame its mythical forces; the creature ultimately finds its death in the burning forest and is taken away by the Drunken Butcher (in German: a knacker). He does, however, point out that evil, if not recognized, will emerge in full strength and cause destruction in its course; but it may also ultimately have positive effects and leave behind calm and brotherhood among men. This theme of the taming of the beast through the love of a virgin would later be more fully realized in Jean Cocteau's classic film *La Belle et la Bête* (*The Beauty and the Beast;* 1945).

Schweiger

Schweiger (1921), a tragedy in three acts, is Werfel's last Expressionist drama. It was first produced in Germany in 1922, where it was immediately adopted by 83 different stages. In Berlin alone it was given 100 consecutive performances. Although the English translation is not currently in print, it must be mentioned that the play was produced in 1926 in New York and again had over 30 performances.[8] The often unfavorable evaluation by contemporary critics is based on the fact that the plot seems to be a hodgepodge of motifs and events, reminiscent of nineteenth-century melodrama.

The master watchmaker Franz Schweiger, together with his wife Anna, has been living for six years as a respected citizen in a small town in Austria. He had met his wife after a sickness of two years duration which had also wiped out his entire memory of the past. Anna becomes pregnant by him, and Schweiger is wooed by the town's Social Democrats to be their candidate. A psychiatrist, Professor Burckhart von Viereck, comes to Schweiger's house and tells him that he had once treated Schweiger and given him a new name and existence as a watchmaker. He now reveals to Schweiger that he is actually an independent scholar by the name of Dr. Forster who had, in a fit of madness, shot at a group of children, killing one of them. Von Viereck restores Schweiger's memory in order to prevent him from working for the Socialists whom he, an ardent German monarchist and anti-Semite, despises. After he has also revealed Schweiger's past to Anna, she leaves him and has an abortion without his knowledge. Schweiger tries to atone for his crime by leading the rescue of a large group of children from a burning ship. Anna returns to tell him what she has done and leaves him once again. When the parents and children form a procession to his house to express their gratitude, he lapses back into his old insanity and attempts to shoot into the crowd. However,his memory of Anna stops him and he kills himself by jumping out of the window.

In spite of this melodramatic plot all the characters and their motivations are quite believable. Not even von Viereck nor another of his patients, mad Dr. Ottokar Grund—modeled on the anarchistic psychiatrist Otto Groß, are caricatures. Just like his fellow Expressionist writers, "Werfel proclaims a new faith in life, man, and God, and urges a new spirit of communality and brotherhood."[9] A man of goodwill like Schweiger, Werfel believes, could have been saved and had a happy, productive life within his family if society had not attempted to promote their own interests in their dealings with him. In his union with his wife and in his unborn child, Schweiger seems to have found a reason for living. Rotter, a Catholic priest, approaches Schweiger with the possibility of becoming a monk in a monastery. Schweiger, who believes that he is going to be a father, rejects this offer, pointing out that the senseless evil responsible for his crime was loneliness: "My madness was loneliness, my deed was loneliness! But now I am not lonely any more. I love, I am bound."[10] Anna is not strong enough; her love not absolute enough to support Schweiger. When she finally returns, it is far too late—Schweiger is dying. Rotter chooses to promote the interests of his church with Schweiger, as von Viereck and the representatives of the Social Democratic Party promote their political creed with him. Dr. Grund wants to use him to participate in an anarchist revolt of the mad, sick, and disenfranchised against society. Mrs. Strohschneider, a neighbor, desires to use him as proof of the validity of her spiritualist ideas and visions. Man is here determined by egotism, which prevents the help one man would be able to lend another, and true brotherhood. Werfel thus indirectly promotes love and compassion, typical elements of his and his fellow writers' Expressionist creed: "The poet's message is clear: faith and unselfish brotherhood are necessary to bridge the tragic chasms in life." [11] In *Schweiger* Werfel seems to have painted a pessimistic picture of society, of the inability of man evolving toward humanity, a brother to his fellow men. [12]

One might argue that Anna is responsible for Schweiger's death because she was unable to live with him and have the child of a murderer. Yet, this would be too much to ask of her. She does not consciously violate the commandment of love, but she was simply too weak for such a superhuman demand. [13] Schweiger's own suicide, however, is a true self-sacrifice. He has failed in the material world but has atoned for his wrongdoing by saving the children. By killing himself he makes a moral decision, namely, to prevent any future possibility of committing a crime against humanity. [14] Thus in his death Schweiger becomes a true Expressionist hero of humanity and a near saint. For that reason, when Rotter says: "He is no longer," the spiritualist, Mrs. Strohschneider, can say: "He is," [15] an application of the sentiments expressed in Werfel's collection of poetry, *Wir sind* (We Are).

Juarez and Maximilian (*Juarez und Maximilian*)

Juarez and Maximilian: A Dramatic History in Three Phases and Thirteen Pictures (Juarez und Maximilian: Dramatische Historie in 3 Phasen und 13 Bildern; 1924) was the first of Werfel's historical dramas, which also include *Paul among the Jews (A Tragedy) (Paulus unter den Juden: Dramatische Legende in sechs Bildern;* 1926) and *Das Reich Gottes in Böhmen: Tragödie eines Führers.* (The Kingdom of God in Bohemia: Tragedy of a Leader; 1930). John Warren points out that "the three plays . . . fall into what we can conveniently call his [Werfel's] 'middle period' as dramatist, as, emerging from his fervent expressionistic beginnings, he turns to a more realistic and controlled form of writing." [16] The radical, mythical style of Werfel's Expressionist dramas gives way here to a more realistic style, the central characteristic of New Objectivity.[17] This change in style mirrors the sobering effect that the end of the First World War had on the young generation of poets. The revolutionary fervor of Expressionism and the belief in a renewal of mankind had ended in bitter disillusionment. As a result, a new sobriety of language and the attempt to describe reality took hold instead of abstract utopian ideas. This general change of attitude and poetic style is obvious in the realistic mode of Werfel's new dramas and in the historical study and collection of documentary material prior to creation. What Werfel is interested in, however, is not a close re-creation of history, but to give expression once again of his spiritual ideals: all three dramas purvey the Christian spirit of "love thine enemy"; the conflicts are nearly identical in all three; and the heroes do not remain pure, but promote blood guilt in all of them. According to John Warren, "all three, too, incur guilt at a deeper and more psychological level which affects their characters and if Werfel shows an interest in the indecisive, problematic hero he is also fascinated by the traitor (López in *Juarez and Maximilian* and Klenau in *Das Reich Gottes in Böhmen*)."[18] The change in the type and style of drama parallels Werfel's turning to the novel form (including the historical novel) during the same years.

On the basis of a considerable number of historical sources, Werfel wrote the dramatized history of the Habsburg Archduke Maximilian, the brother of Emperor Franz Joseph of Austria. In 1864, at the instigation of Emperor Napoleon III and his own wife Charlotte, Maximilian went to Mexico, believing that he was called to be its legitimate emperor. There he battles Mexico's democratically elected president, Benito Juarez, who engages and defeats him in guerilla warfare. After he has been abandoned by the French troops of Marshal Bazaine and betrayed by the Mexican Colonel López, he is taken prisoner at Querétaro, sentenced to death, and executed.

As the subtitle indicates, Werfel wishes to present this story as a series of historical pictures, as dramatized history, rather than as a play. Therefore, he avoids the conventional subdivision of acts and scenes. These pictures are to be viewed less as Expressionist stations and more as historical tableaux. In contrast to his Expressionist plays Werfel insists on historically accurate costumes, and his characters use the more realistic language of New Objectivity. In his notes to the drama Werfel stresses the historical accuracy of the work in spite of the necessity to reconcile it with the form of drama:

> In these pictures the historical truth has been strictly preserved. Only the more concentrated passing of dramatic time and the narrowness of the theatrical space demanded a concentration in the treatment of dates and per-

sons which falls under the term of poetic license. To be sure, the epic nature of history, if it is not to be violated, prescribes a certain sequence of events and motivations which often enough run counter to the inexorable law of tragedy. But from ancient times the *dramatic history* is a conscious form that wants to reconcile the conflict between drama and epic.[19]

It would be wrong to assume that "historical truth" means nothing beyond what can be supported by historical sources. Many elements, including a number of scenes, have obviously been included because they follow a long tradition of German and Austrian literature, particularly Grillparzer's historical dramas.[20] This epic element manifests itself in the detailed stage directions. The most striking formal feature of the drama remains the fact that Maximilian's adversary, Benito Juarez, never appears on stage. He is omnipresent, and in the first and in the final scene of the drama—a classical dramatic trick—he is seen by one of the characters but neither the audience nor Maximilian ever come face to face with him. Yet he is the driving force in the drama, the man who acts, whereas Maximilian can only react. Napoleon III, who also determines Maximilian's fate, never appears on stage either.

As in his other historical dramas, Werfel presents two conflicting ideas incorporated in the two title characters. But since Juarez never appears on stage, it is Maximilian on whom Werfel concentrates. Both must be seen as embodiments of the two types which Werfel discusses in his essay "Realism and Inwardness": whereas Maximilian is a man favored by the muses, an introspective man, Juarez is the modern, abstract man, a pragmatic rationalist who represents radical realism. He is described as one who has never had a dream; he is "dreamless reason" (JM 71). Juarez has no passions and "he does, not good, but right" (JM 137). For him, Maximilian represents the foreign intruder who wishes to violate newly established democracy in America. He thus believes his is a crusade against foreign and even traditional evil.[21]

Maximilian, on the other hand, is "a beautiful person in the holiest sense of the word" (JM 137). He did not come to Mexico as usurper or conqueror but in the firm belief that he had been called. He believes in the legitimacy of his Mexican crown and in the moral foundation of his mission. Wanting to atone for the cruelties committed by, Cortés, the general of his ancestor, Emperor Charles V, he states: "It was always our dream to atone for the guilt of his barbary" (JM 36). He believes in the legitimacy of his power and in its redeeming effect, but is not interested in personal power. Maximilian wants to destroy politics and thus employ his power for a specific spiritual and social revolution.[22] In his opinion the constitutional empires of Europe lack inner truth; they are decadent and decaying, in contrast to his Mexican imperial crown which is ennobled by such new ideas. He believes in his divine rights and attempts to serve man ("Good must be imposed" [JM 27]), improving the education and living standards of millions of Indians: "The tremendous masses must be woken up and won. An unequaled social deed."[23] He is filled with inner love for the people—yet fails because he did not realize that his empire was based on Napoleon's power politics and not on an honest choice on the part of the Mexican people: the supposed monarchist plebiscite was forced by the church, which had been expropriated by Juarez and by the French army. By supporting the secularization of church property initiated by Juarez, Maximilian loses the support of the church so that even Labatista, the Mexican archbishop, betrays him. He also fails because of his reactions to such personal insults. He sent his portrait with the words "The wisdom of enmity is reconciliation" (JM 10) to Juarez. "You cannot kill opposites, only reconcile them" (JM 40), Maximilian says. Juarez returned the portrait with the comment: "The man mirrors himself" (JM 10). Also, Maximilian had given up his resistance to signing the blood decree which stipulated that anyone found with a weapon in his hand would be executed. He had thus violated the spirit of his own mission, and thousands of Mexicans were subsequently executed, strengthening the moral and popular power of Juarez. Maximilian's own decree could then be used against him, justifying his execution. This betrayal of his own ideas becomes immediately obvious to Maximilian: "I betrayed my ideal. God's mouth spews me forth" (JM 66). He considers abdication, but his wife, Charlotte, desires death to a loss of her titles. When Juarez, through his emissary General Porfirio Diaz, demands the emperor's humiliation, Maximilian, in an expression of his repentance, makes his second mistake and orders the declaration of abdication to be torn up. Unwilling to humiliate himself, he goes to Querétaro, knowing that it is a trap from which he will not be able to escape.

It is ironic that the self-knowledge Juarez demands, and which Maximilian seems to reject, is precisely what the emperor displays at the end of his life. He knows "Guilt is not to be great enough for one's deeds. Failure is guilt. My idea of a radical monarchy was unreal" (JM 146).

Maximilian is not only a representative of the Habsburg dynasty but a ruler who is willing to give up politics and power in an effort to bring happiness to the masses. He is a man favored by the muses, desiring to establish a utopian realm of love on earth by the application of Christian ideals to politics, especially the Christian commandment of "love thine enemy." It is the tragedy of a well-meaning "beautiful man"—a ruler who wants to do good but who fails because history has surpassed him and his beliefs—and that of a man who meant well but who became guilty; who had betrayed his ideals out of personal weakness and hurt pride.[24]

The play was first performed on 25 April 1925 in Magdeburg, and on 26 May, directed by Max Reinhardt, in Vienna. In the United States it was first staged in 1926 by the Theatre Guild. It was filmed as a major production in the United States in 1939 (directed by William Dieterle, with Paul Muni, Bette Davis, and Brian Aherne) under a title which ultimately seemed to deny Maximilian the heroic status Werfel had accorded him: *Juarez.*

Paul among the Jews (*Paulus unter den Juden*)

Werfel wrote *Paulus unter den Juden: Dramatische Legende in sechs Bildern* (*Paul among the Jews [A Tragedy]*) in 1926 following his trip to Palestine in 1925. It was intended as the first part of a trilogy, but a second part, "Paul among the Heathens," and a third part, "Paul and Caesar," were never written. The events of the drama occur during the rule of Emperor Caligula of Rome (A.D. 37–41), when Marullus was governor of Judea. Marullus, who has a generally positive attitude toward the Jews and their faith, accepts their freedom not to venerate the Roman emperor as a god and their insistence that no non-Jew may enter the temple in Jerusalem. Paul—formerly the Rabbi Saul—who has been miraculously converted on his way to Damascus after persecuting the Nazarites, has returned after a long absence. He is greeted as Saul by the high priest's son, Chanan, a Zealot, who plans an uprising, and who wants to establish a new Israel together with his former teacher. Saul declines, confessing his allegiance to Christ. When he also confirms this allegiance before the members of the Sanhedrin in Jerusalem, pronouncing that the law has been fulfilled and that Jesus was the promised Messiah whom Israel has killed, he is sentenced and handed over to the Exorcist. At that point the Zealots start their uprising against the Romans. Rabban Gamaliel, the patriarch of Jewry, succeeds in restoring calm, but Marullus uses the rebellion to desecrate the Jewish temple by introducing the statue of Caesar to be venerated there. Chanan commits suicide. Gamaliel dies. In the opinion of Simon Peter, the Anti-Christ has come, every promise has arrived, the hour of Christ has come.

The center of the story is the confrontation between Gamaliel and Paul. In contrast to the conservative rabbis who only recognize the Torah as Law and consider everything else blasphemy, the more liberal Gamaliel, after long contemplation, is willing to recognize that Christ was a holy man, but only a man. Paul insists that he was the Messiah, God's son. When he wants to kill Paul for his blasphemy and desecration of the Temple with a sacrificial knife in order to avoid further bloodshed and divisiveness for Israel, God does not answer him and he lets Paul go.

Blind adherence to the Law, the Torah and the new faith is questioned as well as rational thinking and love in a man who is honestly trying to understand, but cannot, and the one who has been converted by God himself. In the character of Paul, Werfel has again put on stage a hero who is not innocent, but who has become guilty—by having Stephen stoned to death. It is thus a drama of conversion, and as such, it is the drama of Werfel's own inner conversion: as early as 1916 he had confessed his belief in Christ.

In the characters of the play Werfel clearly incorporates the types of people he discusses in his essays: Chanan is the political activist and as such he must fail. The members of the Sanhedrin are abstract men, ideologists who can only act according to a set of rules, the law—in this case the Torah—but not from within. Even Gamaliel, who at least makes an attempt to understand Paul, is in the final analysis unable to free himself from ideological constraints. Paul and all the others who believe in Christ are the only people who act from within. They have the type of inwardness Werfel would soon advocate in his essay "Realism and Inwardness" (1931).

In his afterword, which is not contained in the American edition, Werfel points out that he chose for his drama one of the most important turning points in history: the moment when Christianity was breaking away from the world of its origin. He sees incompatibility of history and religion as the main problem of writing a tragedy about religion:

It is the essential quality of the divine that it cannot be reconciled with the course of the world and that it suspends history in the very moment that it touches upon it. How is it that we know and do not doubt the history of Alexander, Caesar and even more distant heroes, and why do we only have myths about the life of Jesus and Buddha? But drama, tragedy cannot be anything but history because it does not present the miracle, but rather men, justified passions and actions. But it presents them removed and broken, just as water shows the objects under its surface in a broken manner. Just as the dream is the deeper reconstruction of personal life, tragedy is the reconstruction of world affairs. In this sense "Paul among the Jews" is a historical tragedy. It is not religion which is put on stage, but rather the people who suffer it.[25]

Das Reich Gottes in Böhmen (The Kingdom of God in Bohemia)

Werfel's drama *Das Reich Gottes in Böhmen: Tragödie eines Führers* (The Kingdom of God in Bohemia: Tragedy of a Leader; 1930) unfortunately has never been translated into English. The first draft of the drama dates back to 1926. It is in many respects similar to, in fact an intensification of *Juarez and Maximilian*. The drama deals with the final phase of the Hussite rebellion in Bohemia in 1431–34. Prokop is the leader of the Hussites; under his leadership the Hussite Wars have spread to Saxony, Bavaria, Silesia, and Austria. Prokop wants to create an evangelical kingdom of God on earth which is based on absolute brotherliness. In order to do that he orders a general land reform, distributing the land of the nobility among the poor farmers. The result is that the land is not properly farmed and a famine results, forcing the noblemen to unite in resistance against the Hussites. Secondly, Prokop fails to use a victory on the battlefield at Taus over the army of Julian Cesarini, the cardinal legate in matters of the Bohemian heresy. He thus gives his enemies the opportunity to regroup, grow in strength, and finally defeat him.

Prokop's counterpart is Julian. After he has been defeated by Prokop, Julian assumes the identity of a simple priest, Angelo, and seeks out Prokop in Bohemia in order to better understand him. At the Council of Basel, Julian tries to bring about a reconciliation between the Hussites and the Catholic Church, but when Prokop feels insulted by a speech of one of the other council members, he abandons his restraint and makes impossible demands. Prokop becomes more and more blind to reality and fanatical, eventually persecuting some of his own supporters.

Werfel demonstrates, as in the case of Maximilian, that Prokop's good intentions ultimately have the opposite effect. He becomes increasingly more absolute—neglecting his wife and losing her to one of his officers; he wants to introduce absolute moral behavior for his soldiers, and is forced to have a death sentence carried out even against his own sister Stascha for fear of being judged unjust. A German is innocently beaten and a German city set on fire shortly after Prokop has pointed out to Julian that the Germans may live in peace under the Hussites. Instead of being surrounded by God-fearing leaders, he becomes the instrument of ruffians and loses all control. The idealist has been turned into a totally distorted image of his former self, into a drunk utopian who has contempt for human beings, even as he pretends to love them. Since he wants to be just, he is contemptuous of life, violates the spirit, and establishes the rule of fright and terror.[26] The tragedy consists of the irony that the preacher of nonviolence is forced to resort to violence in order to fight for his goal.[27]

A utopia, Werfel seems to say, cannot be realized. In spite of his good intentions, Prokop's attempt to establish peace through love and social justice fails. He becomes, in Werfel's terms, an absolutely abstract man who, in his quest for a utopian ideal, loses sight of what can be attained in reality. In this distant abstract goal he ignores the value of the individual human being, and he unrealistically demands the same sacrifices in the service of this ideal from everyone else. Like Maximilian, he signs a blood decree—in this case decreeing capital punishment for all prostitutes caught in the vicinity of his army camps—which even destroys his own sister. He blinds himself to the true individual love he should have for his sister, and to the love Julian offers him. A kingdom of love cannot be established if the individual is sacrificed for it. Love begins with the individual and this is where the kingdom of God is realized, not in lofty utopian dreams.

Werfel has written about a specific historical incident, the Hussite Wars, which, having grown up in Bohemia, was a personal chapter of history for him. Nevertheless, we may very well look at this play as his judgment upon all kinds of utopian political thinking that ignores man for an abstract ideal. There is no doubt that Werfel uses his story to express his disdain for the political activism which he had experienced at the end of the First World War. But one may also consider this text a critique of twentieth-century attempts to establish a utopian state.

The Eternal Road (Der Weg der Verheißung)

As mentioned in the introduction, the biblical drama *Der Weg der Verheißung: Ein Bibelspiel (The Eternal Road: A Drama in Four Parts;* 1935) was written for Max Reinhardt for a specific production at the Manhattan Opera House, where, after many financial difficulties, it was finally performed on 7 January 1937. At the opening performance Sara Delano Roosevelt was present, representing the Christian community, and Rabbi Stephen Samuel Wise represented the Jewish community of New York. The play was well received by critics and played to full houses but, due to the extravagance of the production, it was a financial failure and had to close after five months. It was a gigantic spectacle, written with a specific type of production in mind, and it was skillfully presented, serving to enhance Werfel's reputation as a serious dramatist in America.

The action takes place on five simultaneous stages stacked on each other and connected by stairs. The lowest stage represents a synagogue, the second and third a street, and the fourth and fifth are reserved for sacred and heavenly events. In the prologue we witness a congregation of persecuted Jews in a synagogue at an unspecified point in time. With the rabbi reading from the Torah, important events from the Old Testament are then introduced and interrupted and commented upon by various members of the congregation. The first part, "The Patriarchs," deals with the story of Abraham and Isaac, Jacob and Rachel, and Joseph. The second part contains the story of Moses and the exodus from Egypt to the Promised Land; the third part, "The Kings," reports on Ruth and the Old Testament kings, Saul and David, Goliath, the Philistines, David and Bathsheba, and Solomon; the fourth part, "The Prophets," tells the story of Jeremiah and the blinding of Zedekiah, as well as the servitude in Babel which Werfel would later write about in his novel *Hearken unto the Voice*. At the conclusion, the king's messenger appears in the synagogue announcing to the congregation that they must leave the city by nightfall or face death. The Angel of the End of Days consoles the congregation, and all persecuted Jews in the world:

> God's eternal promise and covenant are
> Immortal beyond ev'n His sun or His star.
> Be grateful for sorrow, your sorrow's cause
> In divine strength rooted still upward draws. (ER 142)

The contemporary persecution of Jews is thus placed into the context of Old Testament persecution and the suffering of the Jewish people through the ages.

In its narrative and enumerative sequence of various biblical events, the play is less dramatic than distinctly epic in quality.[28] The value of the play lies in its skillful interweaving of Old Testament events with the synagogue events to express the concerns and fears of Jews in relation to their persecution in modern times. Here Werfel has introduced various Jewish prototypes some of which would, as individual characters, reappear in his later novel *Cella:* the Adversary, the Rich Man, the Pious Man, the Estranged One. These are timeless incorporations of typical ways Jews have reacted to persecution through the ages. Certainly, author Werfel, director Max Reinhardt, composer Kurt Weill, and producer Meier W. Weisgal all intended to draw attention to the contemporary plight of the Jews in Hitler's Germany, but it is to Werfel's credit that he placed the action of his play in an unnamed kingdom representing modern times in general, rather than into fascist Germany. Thus the element of history and timelessness become part of the representative frame. Given the enormous requirements in terms of stage conditions and an extremely large cast, the play has remained a reading or "closet" drama. With its epically presented Old Testament material it belongs into the series of large-scale film productions of biblical themes of the 1930s and 1940s rather than on stage.

Before Werfel left Austria he wrote an as yet untranslated drama, *In einer Nacht* (During One Night), which in some respects foreshadows the Anschluss of Austria to the Third Reich. The play was first performed on 5 October 1937 in the Vienna Theater an der Josephstadt under the direction of Max Reinhardt. In 1963 Ernst Schönwiese produced a radio play version for Austrian radio.

The main character is Eduard who lives, together with his wife Felizitas, in a castle in the Austrian countryside near Vienna. Eduard is a Nietzschean superman, a man of action and brutal force who has been able to convince Felizitas to marry him, but she is still emotionally bound to Gabriel, a doctor who has returned from Peru and who now visits the couple. When Gabriel wants to leave because he realizes that bad decisions of the past cannot be corrected, Eduard shoots him in the back on the way to the railway station and blames the murder on dangerous political unrest in the area. When he realizes that he has not won over Felizitas for himself, he confesses his crime. Gabriel's "soul figure" which has become alive has suggested this to him without being seen or heard by others. It also tries to reach Felizitas when she wants to drink poison. Ultimately, Gabriel wakes up from his apparent death and is united with Felizitas. The core of the drama is the concept of predestination, of the predestined role of people with others which they must not act against: love conquers all, and it is able to even defeat death. Death itself is a secret, mystical fulfillment—the zenith of life.

Jacobowsky and the Colonel (*Jacobowsky und der Oberst*)

As mentioned in chapter one, Werfel wrote his drama *Jacobowsky and the Colonel: Comedy of a Tragedy in Three Acts* (*Jacobowsky und der Oberst: Komödie einer Tragödie in drei Akten;* 1944) after he had told the story of a Stuttgart banker's flight from the Nazis at a dinner party in Los Angeles. The action of the play is as follows:

In the summer of 1940 the Germans are invading France and the French army is in rapid retreat. Paris is under bombardment, and the Germans are expected to occupy the French capital. At this time in a little hotel two people are introduced who are forced to flee from the Nazis: the former Jewish businessman Jacobowsky and the Polish Colonel Stjerbinsky with his orderly Szabuniewicz. Jacobowsky fears he will be put into a German concentration camp because he is Jewish, Stjerbinsky has fought against the Germans in Poland and in France and has now received orders to take secret papers with addresses of the Polish resistance to London. Jacobowsky buys a beautiful old car but since he cannot drive he agrees that Stjerbinsky join him as the driver. But instead of driving away from the Germans the Polish colonel first drives toward them in order to pick up his beloved Marianne. Time and again the quick-thinking Jacobowsky succeeds in obtaining gasoline, and the group even escapes arrest after being stopped by a German patrol. After a separation they finally meet again in Saint Jean-de-Luz where the Dice Player, a commander of the British navy, has orders to meet Stjerbinsky in order to take him to England. When at the Môle in Saint Jean-de-Luz the dice player gives him only two spaces on the boat that will carry him to safety, Marianne decides to stay behind and wait for Jacobowsky. Stjerbinsky decides to take along Jacobowsky instead. The Dice Player first refuses, but then agrees to take him along. Jacobowsky decides not to take the poison which he carries with him and instead throws it into the sea.

The relationship of the Polish nobleman Stjerbinsky, with his hollow concept of honor and bravery, and the underdog Jacobowsky, who travels on his wits and who is an expert in the art of survival against all odds, may be seen as influenced by the relationship of Don Quixote and Sancho Panza, or, more exactly, an updating of the tradition of the Spanish picaresque novel.[29] Typical for the picaresque situation is the background of social upheaval, of an emergency situation which here is represented by the war, the persecution by the Nazis that threatens the two protagonists. The German picaresque baroque novel by Hans Jakob Christoffel von Grimmelshausen, *Der Abentheurliche Simplicissimus Teutsch* (*The Adventures of a Simpleton;* 1668), is a prime example of such a situation. In modern times Bertolt Brecht again used the background of the Thirty Years' War for his picaresque drama *Mutter Courage und ihre Kinder* (*Mother Courage;* 1941). Just like the Spanish picaro, Jacobowsky succeeds time and again in various dangerous situations in obtaining gasoline, be it from the French brigadier, or even from the enemy himself. Like the Spanish picaro, Jacobowsky is not only someone exposed to a life-threatening situation but he is fleeing for the fifth time in his life and is forced to build a new existence for himself. He is not concerned about acquiring high social position or great wealth for himself but only to survive in a hostile environment. Like the picaro, he never gives up, not even in seemingly hopeless situations: when the British commander refuses to take him along, he does not swallow poison as it first seems, but instead takes pills against seasickness. In contrast to the world view of the Polish colonel which is determined by old-fashioned concepts of gallantry, bravery, and honor without regard for danger, Jacobowsky's worldview is realistic and not pathetic, aimed at a shrewd evaluation of the situation at hand. *Jacobowsky and the Colonel* also contains numerous picaresque satirical elements: Werfel not only satirizes Stjerbinsky's value system but also the arrogance of the Immortal (Member of the Académie Française) and the hollowness of the pronouncements of the Tragic Gentleman. He pokes fun at the French brigadier who wants to arrest Jacobowsky as long as he is on duty, even though the French government has collapsed, but who switches to an attitude of great helpfulness as soon as he is off duty. There is no doubt that this drama contains many elements of the old picaresque tradition which also has inspired many modern German novels and dramas.

Jacobowsky and the Colonel is a play that combines tragic and comic elements. No wonder then that in his groundbreaking work on the German tragicomedy, Karl S. Guthke treated *Jacobowsky and the Colonel* as a tragicomedy.[30] Some critics have criticized Werfel for making the disaster of the French army and the Nazi atrocities in France the basis for a comedy. Most famous in this respect are Eric Bentley's remarks: "Adapted or restored, acted or printed, it is a dreadful play. Only the subtitle—Comedy of a Tragedy—is apt, for one is embarrassed throughout by all this fooling and footling in the midst of death. I never would have thought—till I witnessed it—that an audience could so enjoy the fall of France."[31] This statement has to be countered by the fact that in writing a comedy, Werfel did exactly the same as other German exile writers. We may call upon the Swiss dramatist Friedrich Dürrenmatt as a witness here, having declared time and again that the problems of our age can only be adequately represented by the comedy, that the tragic element should arise from comedy.[32] Brecht also pitted his comic figure Schweyk against the Nazis.[33] Besides, Werfel does not trivialize the Nazi terror; he does not induce his audience to laugh at it, nor do his characters find it funny. The terror is always present as an ever increasing threat, and the characters are often on the verge of desperation. The tragic elements remain tragic but the humor breaks holes into the tragedy. Originally conceived by Werfel as a farce, *Jacobowsky and the Colonel* transcends superficial entertainment and it becomes a multidimensional drama.[34]

It is true that in most cases in reality the outcome of peoples' attempts to flee from the Nazis ended in disaster. In Werfel's drama too, most people in the café Au Père Clairon at Saint Jean-de-Luz are arrested in a raid carried out by the German Gestapo and the French police: the famous conductor Kamnitzer has committed suicide by taking poison—just as Werfel's own friend Walter Hasenclever and the German critic Walter Benjamin did. But then Werfel himself, together with Heinrich Mann, Golo Mann, Lion Feuchtwanger, and others, like the Stuttgart banker Stefan S. Jacobowicz, did succeed in fleeing, together with their wives, under conditions that were very similar to those depicted in Werfel's drama. Historical reality thus testifies to the drama's realism. Werfel points out that not only does the likely occur, but often the unimaginable.

Jacobowsky and the Colonel is an extremely optimistic play. It depicts the ability of the underdog to escape the overwhelming power of the seemingly almighty. His weapons are his intelligence, his wit, and particularly his ability to communicate. Thus the comedy shows the triumph of the intellect, of the mind, and of the word over brutal force.[35] It offers the triumph of independent and free will over environmental or situational determinism.

The proponent of such a view is Jacobowsky himself. Throughout the drama he always sees two possibilities. He is optimistic to the very end, and it is this ultimate optimism in the face of seemingly certain death that earns him the respect of the British commander and thus the place on the boat to freedom. Jacobowsky never gives up, and it is clearly not the colonel's bravery that allows them to escape but Jacobowsky's inventiveness and quickmindedness. But, as with most of the play's characters, Jacobowsky has symbolical significance: as a Jew he is associated with many of the negative qualities common to the anti-Semitic tradition; he appears materialistic, calculating, ingratiating; in short, he is a stereotype. Thus Lionel B. Steiman writes:

> He does appear to embody the less "pleasant" characteristics Werfel regarded as typical "Jewish"—he is calculating and ingratiating, he is materialistic and uncannily lucky without being particularly resourceful in conventionally admirable ways; he is an outsider conscious of being so, shows an awareness and sensitivity to anti-Semitic slights without fighting back, and he accepts implicitly the rules of a society which never lets him forget who he is—but whereas in Werfel's other writings such "Jewish" characters almost function as a justification for anti-Semitism, Jacobowsky is an affirmation and celebration of this stereotype, and is so in a manner that makes him an indispensable element in the salvation both of himself and of the very society that persecutes him.[36]

In a letter to his old Prague friend Max Brod, Werfel justified the way he characterized Jacobowsky by stressing that he consciously intended to portray the Jewish tragedy in an unheroical manner "because he did not wish to have a superhuman hero to stand for the Jewish people in its hour of tragedy":[37] "For that reason I made an average business Jew the hero."[38] All the same, he is careful not to make him an overly skillful businessman. When

Jacobowsky buys the car, for example, he is portrayed as inept, to counter the cliché of a wheeling and dealing Jew.[39] The justification for such a decision is clear: Werfel had intended to portray Jacobowsky as a sympathetic Jew. As such, it would have been a mistake for him to invent a character which would have run counter to the common perception of Jews. It was far more effective to endow his hero with supposedly typical qualities and to show their lovable sides. Indeed, Jacobowsky has such a lovable side, and he owes his greatest success to his quickmindedness and humaneness rather than to his business sense or his logical thinking.[40]

Jacobowsky's opposite is Stjerbinsky, the Polish officer and nobleman who looks down upon Jacobowsky. Stjerbinsky and his more primitive companion, the orderly Szabuniewicz, are unashamedly anti-Semitic. Already in the first scene Szabuniewicz comments upon Jacobowsky's persecution by the Nazis: "Ser-r-rves you right" (JC 15). When Jacobowsky makes it clear that it is only because of his energy and eloquence that they have been able to obtain gasoline, Szabuniewicz comments: "You will have to do it again, Mister-r-r! *After all, it is in the gentleman's blood*" (JC 47).[41] Stjerbinsky increasingly sinks down to the level of his unsophisticated orderly. Jacobowsky's continuous success in the struggle for survival makes Stjerbinsky feel powerless and humiliated. When he becomes afraid of losing Marianne to his traveling companion, Stjerbinsky comments: "Even Colonel Tadeusz Boleslav Stjerbinsky, of the ancient Pupicky-Stjerbinsky, wor-r-rks with his hands. Only the Jacobowskys do not wor-r-rk with their-r-r hands. For-r-r that they ar-r-re too good. . . . What do the Jacobowskys have to do except to clip coupons fr-r-rom bonds, carr-r-rry on long telephone conver-r-rsations with beautiful star-r-rs, and look for-r-r their-r-r names in the paper-r-r ever-r-ry day" (JC 63). And a little later: "But who is the highwayman? Who seduces by sobr-r-riety? Who br-r-ribes by cr-r-rawling meekness? Who ingr-r-ratiates himself by helpfulness? Hitler is r-r-right. Your-r-r whole existence is nothing but gr-r-rabbing, gr-r-rabbing, gr-r-rabbing" (JC 74). Ignoring the fact that it was Jacobowsky who has taken care of him on this flight, Stjerbinsky has assimilated Hitler's anti-Semitic arguments. At the same time he uses anti-Semitism to look down upon Jacobowsky, to treat him with disrespect to assert his waning feeling of superiority and to overcome his fear of losing Marianne to Jacobowsky. Further, despite his old-world grandezza, his feeling of honor, his personal bravery, and his gallantry, Stjerbinsky is clearly a potential Nazi. Thus Jacobowsky says to Stjerbinsky: "I'm no better than anyone else. But I *do* have one advantage over you. I can never be Hitler, never, as long as the world lasts. But you could easily have been Hitler, and you could still be. At any time!'' (JC 49). The irrationally anti-Semitic Stjerbinsky is a potential Nazi. Did Werfel intend to criticize through him the tendency of the old European nobility to flirt with fascism and national socialism? He certainly criticizes the lack of action by the Allies to put an early stop to Hitler's aggression before he had gone too far. In Jacobowsky's and Werfel's opinion the Allied Powers thus bear equal responsibility for the fate of the Jews in Europe. Jacobowsky addresses Stjerbinsky:

> You are a Pole, and I am a Pole, although your people drove me from my home when I was only three years old. And then, in nineteen thirty-three, when this pest and this grief broke out over me in Germany, you Poles rubbed your hands and said: ''Serves him right, this Jacobowsky!'' And later on, when this pest and this grief broke out over me in Austria, you shrugged your shoulders and said: ''What's that to us?'' And not only you said: ''What's it to us?'' but all the rest of them said it too. Englishmen and Americans and Frenchmen and Russians! And then, when this pest and this grief broke out in Prague, you still didn't believe that it was any of your business, and you even used the opportunity to stab the poor Czechs in the back. But when it finally came over you, this pest and this grief, you were very innocently surprised, and you weren't prepared at all, and you were done for in seventeen days. . . . But if you—you, and all the others—had not said at the beginning: ''Serves this Jacobowsky right!'' or, at best ''What's it to us?'' but if you had said: ''This Jacobowsky is a human being, and we can't stand by while human beings are treated like that,'' then you wouldn't have been done for yourselves so miserably and absurdly and disgracefully just a few years later, and the pest would have been exterminated in six weeks, and Hitler would have remained what he really is, a loud-mouthed fool in a stinking Munich beer cellar. And that's why I say that you yourselves, you alone and all the others, *are* Hitler's greatness, his brilliance, his Blitzkrieg, his victory, and his world domination. (JC 49f.)

No wonder that this speech was originally scrapped for the premiere American performance by the Theatre Guild! Only after Werfel loudly protested was it restored. The speech was no less controversial in the German postwar performances, drawing loud applause from the German audiences and anger on the part of the Allies. *Jacobowsky and the Colonel* remains a politically charged play, although, in typical Werfel fashion, a metaphysical element is added later on.

Under different circumstances Stjerbinsky might not have appeared as ridiculous as he does in this drama. He certainly does not lack courage, riding as he does against German tanks with a sword in hand—as Don Quixote fought against windmills. And, like Don Quixote, he remains loyal to his lady, Marianne, retrieves her even under the most dangerous circumstances. But Werfel makes it clear that in the modern world of tanks, war planes, concentration camps, and disregard for individual lives, Stjerbinsky is an anachronism. It is as foolhardy to attack tanks with a sabre as it is ridiculous to serenade your beloved with a violin while German war planes strafe civilians with their machine guns. It is similarly ridiculous when he wants to duel with Jacobowsky over Marianne while the German Gestapo is only minutes away. One rightfully laughs at Stjerbinsky's chivalric behavior, but when he takes himself so seriously that he is unable to comprehend reality he becomes dangerous.

Yet Stjerbinsky is also one of the characters who in the course of the drama undergoes change. When in the face of adversity Jacobowsky becomes ever more audacious and inventive, Stjerbinsky feels increasingly humiliated by his adversary's successes. This is especially the case since his beloved Marianne seems to recognize Jacobowsky's value, and Jacobowsky in turn seems to be wooing her. Jacobowsky is in his proper element, whereas Stjerbinsky's values and mode of behavior do not work under the threatening circumstances. Consequently, at the beginning of Act Two, Stjerbinsky repeatedly admits: "I am ver-r-ry melancholy" (JC 67). In part two of Act Two, Stjerbinsky wants to kill Jacobowsky, and the duel between them is only prevented by the arrival of the German vanguard. In order to avoid arrest by the Germans, Stjerbinsky has to play a lunatic and finally a blind man. In so doing he must deny his very nature, assuming the hunted existence of Jacobowsky, the Jew—hence his transformation by Act Three. Stjerbinsky finally overcomes his egocentric prejudice,[42] and recognizes what Jacobowsky has done for him: "On this flight Mister-r-r Jacobowsky never-r-r once failed. He even saved my life by his quick pr-r-resence of mind. . . . I r-r-regar-r-rd Mister-r-r Jacobowsky just like a comr-r-rade who stood next to me in the battle on the Somme" (JC 114). Ultimately, he even physically attacks the British commander in order to force him to take Jacobowsky along to safety.

Jacobowsky and Stjerbinsky are realistic characters but they are also symbolic representations of opposites who fight a duel to the very end. The symbolic element of the dramatis personae is already apparent in Marianne, who historically represents France. In this drama the symbolic character, St. Francis, addresses her as "Madame la France!" (JC 77). She is thus less of a real person but rather the object of our two heroes' battle, the catalyst for them to prove themselves. In all her actions she represents France with its charm and lack of rational foresight in the face of Nazi aggression. Werfel seems to be ridiculing this lack of realism when he introduces her, as she insists that her dog, cat, and all her luggage accompany their flight. During the journey, however, she shows remarkable objectivity in judging and appreciating Jacobowsky, although she never stops loving Stjerbinsky, not even in his most humiliated state. In Act Three she shows true greatness when she decides to give up her personal happiness, her togetherness with Stjerbinsky, in favor of saving Jacobowsky. By contrast, the religious difference between Jacobowsky and Stjerbinsky is projected onto two unmistakably symbolic characters who appear in part two of Act Two: the Intellectual [the Wandering Jew] and the Monk [St. Francis].[43] They are riding on a tandem bicycle, thus demonstrating that they are working well together. Jacobowsky comments: "I see two opposites who get along very well together." The Intellectual replies: "Oh, we are bosom companions! Just let opposites get old enough and they'll meet, just like parallel lines in infinity" (JC 76). Werfel uses these symbolic characters to stress the mutual dependence and at the same time the close relationship of the two—of Judaism and Catholicism. The author thus injected his drama with one of his favorite ideas from his "Theologumena," namely the interdependence and connectedness of Judaism and Christianity, neither one of which in his opinion can exist without the other. The Wandering Jew and St. Francis are, of course, idealizations of the drama's "earthly" characters, Jacobowsky and Stjerbinsky, representing a possible harmonious relationship between the two who are always just about to fight their duel.

It is this duel to which the two refer at the very end of the drama:

> Colonel Stjerbinsky (*Slapping* Jacobowsky *on his shoulder*): Don't celebrate too soon, Jacobowsky, Our-r-r duel is only postponed.
> Jacobowsky: Our duel is eternal, Stjerbinsky. (JC 119f.)

One may argue, as Helmut Koopmann has, that the spectator knows the duel is finished, that it has taken place in front of the German Gestapo and that it ended with Jacobowsky saving Stjerbinsky's life with his inventiveness and linguistic omnipotence.[44] The long-awaited duel between Stjerbinsky and Jacobowsky will probably not take place—one only slaps a friend on the shoulder, not the man one wishes to kill. It is the eternal duel between Judaism and Christianity to which Werfel refers, the competition between opposites which in his view are not opposites at all. Throughout the drama Jacobowsky always saw two alternatives, two possibilities. By the conclusion he discovers a third one. One could not only be locked up by the French or turned over to the

Nazis for certain death but also be saved by the British. It is Stjerbinsky who does his utmost to make this possible, and thus the two parallel lines do meet in the end.

The play was first performed by the Theatre Guild on Broadway and it became a major success. It was the only play by an exiled German author that not only received the critics' attention but which also became a financial theatrical success. The literal translation of Werfel's original text, however, was freshly adapted for the performances. The Theatre Guild had accepted the play only under the condition that it conform to the taste and expectations of an American audience, and Werfel was horrified when he saw the first adapted versions. Ultimately, the renowned playwright Samuel Behrman was commissioned to produce an adaptation. Behrman's work did not please Werfel either, but the Theatre Guild insisted on the terms of their contract which gave them the final say in all disputes. Werfel complained about all the deviations from his original, about the melodramatic aspects that were added, about the omission of speeches and dialogues, additions of boring and, in his opinion, superfluous scenes, and the loss of dramatic effectiveness.[45]

In the opinion of today's critics, Behrman's version was not necessarily worse, and some of its features even constituted an improvement over Werfel's original.[46] The development of the drama became more logical, thus increasing the plausibility of the action. All miraculous elements were excised, including the surrealistic appearance of the Wandering Jew and St. Francis. On the other hand, Behrman added sentimental dialogues, as well as a Western-style fighting scene between Stjerbinsky and the German vanguard. He smoothed over the blame laid upon the Allies who, after all, at that time were still fighting the Germans. Stjerbinsky is made to appear more positive for fear the superiority of Jacobowsky might give rise to anti-Semitic feelings.

After various test performances in New Haven (27 January 1944), Boston (31 January), and Philadelphia (14 February) the play opened on 14 March 1944 in the Martin Beck Theater in New York City (director: Elia Kazan; set designer: Steward Chaney; Jacobowsky: Oscar Karlweis; Stjerbinsky: Louis Calhern; Marianne: Annabella).

The translation of Werfel's original first appeared in May 1944.[47] Because of the intervention of Behrman's lawyer, the first German edition was an American textbook edition with an introduction and notes for students of German, unique for a major German drama.[48]

The significance of the play lies in Werfel's expression of his theories about the peaceful coexistence between Jews and Christians; in a Broadway success which other great dramatists of the Weimar Republic—Bertolt Brecht and Carl Zuckmayer—were unable to attain in exile; and in its importance as a great German comedy, one of the relatively few in German literary history. More precisely, as a tragicomedy, it was a precursor of the great works in that genre by Friedrich Dürrenmatt, another German language author whose plays, written twenty-five years later, were also successfully performed on Broadway.

NOTES

1. The poem bears similarity to Goethe's poem to Frau von Stein, "Warum gabst du uns die tiefen Blicke" ("Why Did You Give Us Deep Insights").

2. See Annemarie von Puttkamer, *Franz Werfel: Wort und Antwort* (Würzburg: Werkbund, 1952) 34.

3. See Lothar Huber, "Franz Werfel's *Spiegelmensch*: An Interpretation," in *Franz Werfel: An Austrian Writer Reassessed*, ed. Lothar Huber (Oxford: Berg, 1989) 75.

4. For a detailed analysis of Werfel's indebtedness to other dramatists see Huber 65–80.

5. Huber 66.

6. Franz Werfel, *Gesammelte Werke: Die Dramen* vol. 1, ed. Adolf D. Klarmann (Frankfurt am Main: S. Fischer, 1959) 549f.: "Ich weiß nicht, ob ich ein Dramatiker bin, aber ich weiß, daß keiner heute schreibt, der so viel Theater in sich hat wie ich."

7. Frank Lambasa, "Franz Werfel's *Goat Song*," in *Franz Werfel: 1890–1945*, ed. Lore B. Foltin (Pittsburgh: University of Pittsburgh Press, 1961) 71.

8. Harold Lenz: "Franz Werfel's *Schweiger*," *Monatshefte* 28 (1936): 168.

9. Lenz 171.

10. Trans. from Werfel *Gesammelte Werke: Die Dramen* 1:372.

11. Lenz 172.

12. See Hans Vogelsang, *Österreichische Dramatik des 20. Jahrhunderts: Spiel mit Welten, Wesen, Worten* vol. 2 (Vienna: Wilhelm Braumüller, 1981): 147.

13. See Paul Wimmer, *Franz Werfel's dramatische Sendung* (Vienna: Bergland, 1973) 103.

14. Wimmer 101.

15. Trans. from Werfel, *Gesammelte Werke: Die Dramen* 1:383.

16. John Warren, "Franz Werfel's Historical Drama, Continuity and Change," in *Franz Werfel: An Austrian Writer Reassessed*, ed. Lothar Huber (Oxford: Berg, 1989) 154.

17. Axel Schalk, "Franz Werfels Historie *Juarez und Maximilian*: Schicksalsdrama, 'neue Sachlichkeit' oder die Formulierung eines paradoxen Geschichtsbilds?" *Wirkendes Wort* 38 (1988): 79.

18. Warren 156.

19. Werfel, *Gesammelte Werke: Die Dramen* 1:557. Trans. H.W. Not in the American edition.

20. For a detailed list and analysis see Werfel, *Gesammelte Werke: Die Dramen* 1:157ff.

21. Wimmer 110.

22. Wimmer 108.

23. Werfel, *Gesammelte Werke: Die Dramen* 1:404. Not in the American edition.

24. One may, of course argue, as Schalk does (pp. 83ff.), that Werfel wants to demonstrate that history in a world which is determined by radical realism is an automatism that determines the actions of the hero. Schalk is wrong, however, when he says that in a paradoxical reversal the hero's idealism is instrumentalized (p. 84). Maximilian does not make his mistakes because of his idealism but out of moral humiliation.

25. Werfel, *Gesammelte Werke: Die Dramen* 1:559. Trans. H.W.

26. Wimmer 120f.

27. Wimmer 124.

28. Vogelsang 152 even sees in this play a shift of Werfel's work to the epic area of poetry. In view of his later plays "In einer Nacht" (During One Night) and *Jacobowsky and the Colonel* I only see a temporary move in this direction.

29. The following remarks are based on my article "Die Renaissance des Schelms im modernen Drama," in *Der moderne deutsche Schelmenroman: Interpretationen,* ed. Gerhart Hoffmeister, Amsterdamer Beiträge zur Neueren Germanistik, vol. 20 (Amsterdam: Rodopi, 1985/86): 53–76, in particular, 73–75.

30. Karl S. Guthke, *Geschichte und Poetik der deutschen Tragikomödie* (Göttingen: Vandenhoeck & Ruprecht, 1961) 367–72.

31. Eric Bentley, *What Is Theater? Incorporating the Dramatic Event and Other Reviews 1944–1967* (New York: Atheneum, 1968) 358.

32. Friedrich Dürrenmatt, *Theaterprobleme* (Zurich: Arche, 9th ed., 1963) 45, 48.

33. J. M. Ritchie, "The Many Faces of Werfel's *Jacobowsky,*" in Huber 197.

34. Wolfgang Nehring, "Komödie der Flucht ins Exil: Franz Werfels *Jacobowsky und der Oberst,*" in *Franz Werfel im Exil,* ed. Wolfgang Nehring and Hans Wagener (Bonn: Bouvier, 1992) 112.

35. This is the basic tenet of the interpretation by Helmut Koopmann, "Franz Werfel: *Jacobowsky und der Oberst:* Komödie des Exils," in *Drama und Theater im 20. Jahrhundert: Festschrift für Walter Hinck,* ed. Hans Dietrich Irmscher and Werner Keller (Göttingen: Vandenhoeck & Ruprecht, 1983) 259–67.

36. See Lionel B. Steiman, *Franz Werfel: The Faith of an Exile. From Prague to Beverly Hills* (Waterloo, Ontario: Wilfrid Laurier University Press, 1985) 174.

37. Steiman 175.

38. Max Brod, *Streitbares Leben* (Munich: Herbig, 1969) 79.

39. Nehring 127 n. 29.

40. For this rationale see Nehring 120.

41. The italicized anti-Semitic sentence was left out in the American edition. The German reads: "Es liegt dem Herrn ja im Blut." Franz Werfel, *Jacobowsky und der Oberst,* in Franz Werfel, *Gesammelte Werke: Die Dramen vol. 2,* ed. Adolf D. Klarmann (Frankfurt am Main: S. Fischer, 1959) 279.

42. See Nehring 124.

43. In the German original they are only called the Wandering Jew and St. Francis. Werfel, *Gesammelte Werke: Die Dramen* 2:302ff.

44. Koopmann 266.

45. Nehring 115. Behrman's adaptation appeared as *Jacobowsky and the Colonel. Original Play by Franz Werfel. American Play based on same by S. N. Behrman* (New York: Random House, 1944).

46. Nehring 116f.; and Ritchie 198f.

47. This is the first edition from which I am quoting in the text: *Jacobowsky and the Colonel: Comedy of a Tragedy in Three Acts. The Original Play by Franz Werfel,* trans. by Gustave O. Arlt (New York: Viking, 1944).

48. *Jacobowsky und der Oberst: Komödie einer Tragödie in drei Akten,* ed. with introduction, notes, and vocabulary by Gustave O. Arlt (New York: F. S. Crofts, 1944).

CHAPTER FOUR

The Road to Religion: Prose 1918–39

"Not the Murderer" (*Nicht der Mörder, der Ermordete ist schuldig*)

Werfel's first larger piece of prose published in book form, the novella "Not the Murderer" (1920), was written in 1918–19, approximately at the same time he worked on his Expressionist drama *Spiegelmensch*. Thus the prose work and the drama have much in common: the father-son conflict as well as other lesser motifs, such as the protagonist destroying his own image in a mirror.

In *Twilight of a World* Werfel provided an introduction to the novella in which he writes: "The little book was written in a few days; its occasion a crime which was a nine days' wonder in Vienna, its gist a letter addressed to the Prosecuting Attorney. The letter, with minor alterations, was incorporated in the novel; the extraordinary crime, the basis of the tale, is narrated in bold words and according to the actual facts, without further comment" (TW 567). Werfel then goes on to report how, in the spring of 1918, he and his wife had visited the famous Wurstelprater in Vienna, the vast and permanent fairground, where a dingy shooting booth had made a lasting impression on Alma:

> Years before she had gone to the Prater with a group of friends and this same booth had remained her chief memory of the place, for the reason that the dummies were human figures in the round, with most lifelike faces expressive of all the misery in the world. Instead of rifles, large hard balls were used as missiles. A freckled half-grown lad served the clients with balls. In the company that night was an artist with a well-known gift of second sight. He watched for a while the human figures being battered by the balls, then remarked, pointing to the freckled boy: "Some day he will be a murderer." (TW 568)

When, during a visit years later, Alma inquired about the booth she was told that on the preceding night the owner had been murdered by his own son. "This encounter between the mystery of life and its actuality—the inextricable involvement of one sort of wrong with another—moved the writer strangely. With youthful ardour he sat down and wrote to the Prosecutor the letter to which he then felt compelled to add the novel" (TW 568).

The narrator of the novella, as I would prefer to call it, is Karl Duschek, who tells the story of his life: the story of conflict with his father, an officer in the Habsburg army who is insensitive to his son's feelings and musical inclinations. The sole concern of this father, also named Karl, centers on the accomplishments of his son in the military academy to which he has been sent to continue the family's military tradition. When the boy turns thirteen, the father dons civilian clothes and takes him to the fair, where he asks his son to aim hard balls at the figures of a shooting booth. He fails terribly, hitting the father's face instead. Eventually, young Karl becomes a lieutenant in the army but always cuts a poor figure as an officer. Later, when introduced to a group of anarchists, he joins them enthusiastically. Shortly before he can carry out their assignment to assassinate the visiting Russian czar, they are all arrested during a police raid. Karl Duschek resists the arrest and is brought before his father, who humiliates him in front of his entourage by whipping him with a riding crop. Later, Karl hides in his father's home, waking him at night and chasing the naked old man around a billiard table intent on killing him with iron dumbbells. When his father kneels down before him, however, begging him, "Do it quickly!" (TW 672), he resists committing patricide and instead sends his father back to bed.

After one year's confinement Karl takes his leave from the military in order to emigrate to America. On his way to Hamburg, where he plans to board a ship, he visits the old fairgrounds and learns that the owner of the shooting booth had been assassinated by his son the night before. Just as Werfel has done, Karl writes a letter to the public prosecutor, justifying himself and the murderer by pointing out the general nature of the father-son conflict: "in the last resort, it is of no importance whether the father is hard or soft. He is hated, or he is loved, not because he is good or bad, but simply because he is the father" (TW 698). And he quotes an old Albanian proverb: "Not the murderer but the murdered is the guilty one," the title of the original German edition of the novella.

In the American edition of the novella Werfel prefaced it by reprinting part of an older poem of his, "Father and Son" ("Vater und Sohn"), thus pointing out that the theme was one that had occupied him for some time, just as the theme of judgment and the paradoxical reversal of guilt, as expressed in the title, are typical of his work. No doubt the often strained relationship with his own father, very similar to that of Kafka, formed the background for this novella:

> Severed we stay
> Severed, as in a dream

> Dimly we see our gathered loves were serving
> Love's immortal ends by boundless loving . . .
> And pity, like a gentle tide renewing,
> Drowns space away.

The theme of the father-son conflict was a popular one during German Expressionism, the most famous examples being Walter Hasenclever's drama *Der Sohn* ("The Son"; 1913), Arnolt Bronnen's *Vatermord* ("Patricide"; 1915), and Georg Kaiser's subplot in *Die Koralle* ("The Coral"; 1917). Thus Werfel's novella must be seen within the context of this contemporary theme of the Expressionists' conflict between the generations. Usually the father represents the old world, the oppressive power that must be overcome, thus justifying the son's act of patricide. In Werfel's novella, too, the father is only the representative of an overall oppressive system. For this reason Karl is desperately eager to join the anarchists who are fighting "against the patriarchal world-order," against "the rule of the Father, in every sense" (TW 612), wanting to dissolve this system "through the discipline of self-knowledge and love" (TW 613). The problem of the father is seen by the anarchists as a problem of state, society, and military, and as the problem of authority in general: "Religion—for God is Father of us all. The State—for king or president is the father of the citizens. The court—for judge and warder are the fathers of those whom human society calls criminals. The army—for the officer is the father of the soldier. Industry—for the manager is the father of the worker" (TW 613). "The *patria potestas*, the authority, is monstrous, it is the destructive principle itself. It is the source of all murders, wars, evil deeds, crimes and hatreds and damnations, just as sonship is the source of all repressive slavish instinct, the carrion built up in the tomb of all the states that have been founded through time" (TW 614). The anarchists want to bring about an era of self-knowledge and love "through blood and terror" (TW 614).

The fight of the anarchists certainly has to be seen within the framework of the Expressionists' revolutionary outcry against traditional society. But in his characterization of the anarchists it very quickly becomes clear that Werfel does not subscribe to this kind of revolutionary thinking. They are no more than a collection of hoodlums, social misfits, drug addicts, and people who have become criminals in trying to attain their revolutionary goal. The female anarchist Zinaida, for example, suffers from her failed attempt to shoot a Russian grand duke, which resulted in his innocent little daughter's death instead. Werfel thus warns of the effects of revolutionary activity, the possible results of which may differ radically from the ones originally intended. Indeed, Karl Duschek's offer to kill the Russian czar is stimulated more by his love for Zinaida than by his enthusiasm for the anarchists' cause.

Karl's inability to kill his father is mitigated less from the feeling of having accomplished the same by humiliating him spiritually than from the realization that his father is not so much the embodiment of a hated principle but rather just a sick old man who in his nakedness is a human being: "No, that I had not wanted, that my father should kneel before me! He must not do it. No one should. Is that my father? I cannot tell. But I will not kill this ailing old man, because I do not know. Pity, sympathy!" (TW 672) When he chases his father around the billiard table he is under the same hypnotic spell that the puppets in the shooting booth exerted over him when he was a boy. That scene, characterized in negative terms as a "madness of almost insupportable triumph" (TW 673), has a cathartic effect on Karl Duschek, who realizes that he has been under a spell: "Later, on the street I flung away the dumbbell, and with it all my morbid childhood" (TW 673), thus admitting that his hatred of his father was not justified. In his letter to the public prosecutor he still judges his father as the guilty one, but he is guilty too: "Ah, no, I would not absolve myself! I, the murderer, and he, the murdered, we are both guilty. But he—he is a little more guilty than I" (TW 688).

Young Karl thus decides to escape to a different and free world which does not suffer from the paternal tradition: America. In an epilogue to the novella he proclaims what Werfel was to restate time and again a decade later: the value of inwardness in contrast to a world which had violated true humanity through the paternal tradition in every form: "My childhood and youth were spent in a world where, as I verily believe, not a single soul had even a faint notion of true inward life" (TW 690). And he clearly judges his youthful escapades, his association with the anarchists, as dangerous: "Who can say what is productive? But whatever it is, it can be only that which springs direct and immediate from the soul. Then have a care of the dreams of cripples, the downtrodden, perverted, flippant, revengeful, which they present to you in the guise of creative deeds!" (TW 691). In complete contrast to his original hatred he now wants to get married, to have a son himself, and to buy a small farm out west. "I will give back my stock to the earth, the freed, limitless earth, that she may absolve us of all our murders, our vanities, sadisms, the corruptions born of our urban, huddled lives" (TW 692).

It is thus the Expressionist vision of the new man that concludes this novella, the idea that human salvation and atonement can only come from a return to the simple forms of life. Georg Kaiser had seemed to advocate the same in his *Gas* trilogy. But whereas the ideas of Kaiser's heroes fail because of the enmity of a society which is irreversibly dependent on technology, Werfel's hero can realize them in the New World.

Stylistic elements which link this piece to Expressionism abound. Among them the dramatic scenes in which Karl Duschek faces his father and hopelessly shouts "Father!" in order to penetrate the facade of the uniform; the careerist thinking and obedience to the "highest service"; and attempting to realize a human father-son relationship of the kind the son envisions as natural. The anarchists are all stock Expressionist characters as well, resembling the lifeless figures Karl had seen at the shooting booth. He repeatedly points out these similarities. Obvious are also the secret connections between father and son who operate the shooting booth on the one hand and Karl Duschek and his father on the other. The theme of killing the wrong person, already significant in Carl Maria von Weber's opera *Der Freischütz* (*The Freeshooter;* 1821), is skillfully applied to Karl in the shooting booth scene as well as to Zinaida. Repetitions and secret connections of this kind cannot solely be claimed for Expressionism but they are typical for a number of Expressionist dramas. What is inescapable, however, is that in this early work Werfel's later ideas of inwardness versus nihilism or realism were already manifested in Expressionist guise.

Verdi: A Novel of the Opera (Verdi: Roman der Oper)

Given Werfel's enthusiasm for Verdi since his adolescence, it is little wonder that he would eventually write a novel about his hero. And later, by adapting seven Verdi libretti, including *La forza del destino, Simone Boccanegra,* and *Don Carlos,* he helped usher in the Verdi renaissance in Germany. Moreover, in 1926 he published an edition of Verdi's letters.

Verdi: A Novel of the Opera deals with the aging composer who, in the fall of 1882, has come to Venice in order to resume his work on a *King Lear* opera after a dry spell which has lasted a decade. Verdi's fame has been overshadowed by the rising popularity of Richard Wagner who, during the winter of 1882–83, is also in Venice. During the course of the novel, Verdi not only gives up his work on *King Lear*—he tosses the score into the fireplace—but also realizes that he has actually come to Venice to meet his adversary face to face. When, after two accidental, anonymous encounters, he is able to do so and he goes to the Palace Vendramin where Wagner resides, it turns out that Wagner had died a few minutes earlier. Verdi has, however, been able to regain his inner freedom and his artistic forces gradually return to him.

Verdi is written in the same expansive, talkative, and highly realistic style as Werfel's later novels. He describes in detail all the places in Venice with which he himself was intimately familiar, and displays his art of realistic characterization in vividly drawn characters: Verdi's friend, the senator, who is an incarnation of the revolutionary generation of 1848; the grotesque centenarian Marchese Gritti who is obsessed with the idea of living for many more years; the half-mad envious Italian maestro Sassaroli as well as the German modern composer Mathias Fischböck; Italo, the young senator's son; the doctor Carvagno and his wife Bianca; and Mario, the crippled son of Dario the doorkeeper at La Fenice. The only exception is the young opera star Margherita Dezorzi, who is characterized as a scheming woman, obsessed by ambition with elements of vulgarity, whose negative character traits are ultimately traced back to the physiological fact that her reproductive organs are not functional. Adding to the realistic traits are the direct quotes from original Verdi letters and poems or statements of other music theorists and biographers. These serve as mottos for individual subchapters. Somewhat artificial, though, is the contrivance of Verdi's two encounters with Wagner which do not result in a conversation. Wagner is omnipresent in the novel. He is constantly on Verdi's mind though rarely present, a technique that Werfel carried to an extreme in his drama *Juarez and Maximilian* (1924).

Verdi was the first novel Werfel published with the Zsolnay publishing house, and it was also the first publication of that press. Work on the novel was completed in 1923 and it appeared on 1 April 1924. Plans for this, Werfel's first major novel, had been conceived twelve years earlier, but as he spells out in the preface, "the writing of it has always been deferred" (V v). The plan obviously goes back to about 1911, to a time when Werfel's first collection of Expressionist poems, *Der Weltfreund,* was ready for publication. Thus the time between the conception of the idea and the completion of the novel spans Werfel's entire Expressionist period. Apart from the drama, *Das Reich Gottes in Böhmen,* Werfel never allowed this much time to pass between the conception of a work and its execution. There are several reasons for this hesitation, some of which he lists himself in his foreword. On the one hand he gives aesthetic reasons, the necessity "to move at once upon two separate planes—the poetic and the historical. . . . The nearness to our own day of the period in which the story unfolds. . . . [T]he danger of handling a romance dealing with the world of art" (V v). The actual reason supposedly lay in the hero itself, in the discrepancy between the hero of a novel, a romance, and the historical Verdi who was extremely reserved and who shied away from any public appearances. But one additional reason must be mentioned: the self-preoccupation of the young Expressionist Werfel was clearly a hindrance to the execution of a work of such epic proportions as *Verdi* needed to be.[1]

Werfel did not intend to write a historically accurate, realistic biography, nor a historical novel. As he points out in his foreword, he wants to create not a historical, biographical truth, but "the mythical legend of the man, that which is purely and properly his" (V vi). This does not mean that the novel was written without adherence to any historical truth. Werfel paid many visits to the Verdi archives in Busseto and Sant'Agata. Within the novel he constantly refers to his sources. Nevertheless, in many important respects the novel is indeed fictional. The historical Verdi did not spend the winter of 1882–83 in Venice—he was in Genova when Wagner died. Although it is true that Verdi's fame at that time was overshadowed by that of the German, Wagner, the novel's contention that Verdi's long-lasting creative crisis was due to his inability to come to terms with Wagner and his music is Werfel's invention. Also, Verdi's friends and his encounters in Venice are purely fictional. Similarly unhistorical is Werfel's claim that Verdi's art is simply an art of the people. As Walter H. Sokel points out:

> Unlike Werfel's image of him [Verdi] and unlike Werfel himself, Giuseppe Verdi traveled not toward greater and greater simplicity but, on the contrary, toward ever more pronounced sophistication and complexity. *Otello* and *Falstaff*, if not close to modernism, are at any rate far removed from the facile popular style of Verdi's earlier works; they were not the kind of music to be whistled and sung by the masses in the streets. Werfel's image of Verdi (which must be carefully distinguished from the historical reality of Verdi) had been the ideal of his entire Expressionist period. It arose from his craving to be "related to man."[2]

Sokel sees *Verdi* as Werfel's "great epic of his Expressionist period." In his view it "sums up, so to speak, some of the fundamental problems of Expressionism."[3] Obviously it is not the style that makes this work Expressionist in nature, but a number of themes and motives that are characteristic for the Expressionist period and which necessitated the invention of an unhistorical plot and characters, as well as the deviations from character traits of the historical Verdi.

It is primarily the concept of art and the artist that allows Sokel to classify *Verdi* as an Expressionist novel. Verdi is, as is typical for Expressionism, an artist-in-crisis, an artist whose inspiration has faded and who is ready to resign himself to that fact. The problem of the artist's creativeness is approached in *Verdi* from the angle of the failure of creativeness. At a low point of his self-esteem, Verdi is ready to pass a negative judgment upon his entire career as an artist, to condemn his entire life's work as unrelenting drudgery: "His life had been the life of a navvy, a coalheaver. An existence in which there was no time to live. Looking neither to the right nor to the left, asking for nothing but what was convenient and necessary for his work, he had never had the leisure to taste the joy of living. He had never raised his eyes from the cave in which he toiled" (V 364). Only in the rarest moments of his work had he enjoyed inner joy and satisfaction. When he had laid aside his composing, he had devoted time to improving his farm estate. Now exhausted, he questions the usefulness of art for anyone but himself. All his efforts seem to be born out of personal vanity: "And what end had the labor of a lifetime served? Was art of any service to mankind? Unhesitatingly he found the answer: 'Mankind today has not the slightest use for any of the fine arts. The theatre is only a vapid toy of a secure and surfeited class, cut off from all living reality. The art of music like the others has become a babbling repetition of formulas' " (V 365). Werfel's Verdi feels that if his work had never existed it would not make the slightest difference to the world. He castigates himself because he believes he has wasted his life, working not for others but "only out of a self-destroying ambition to be the idol of the people," sacrificing all human interests and personal well-being "in order to be honoured and worshipped as a god, above all other gods, to be immortal" (V 366).

According to Sokel, this idea that "art hath grown too heavy" is typical for Expressionist artists, who often stopped writing (like Gottfried Benn) or did not want to be read (like Franz Kafka). The only way out of such a dilemma, out of such self-hatred as experienced here by Verdi, is the inner change (*Wandlung*), so typical for much of Expressionist literature: "Only if the self-absorbed, narcissistic artist learns: to identify himself with others, share their sufferings, serve and love them, can he save himself, and become a true poet, a seer, and a healer of mankind. The painful feeling of 'unrelatedness,' the sense of one's own inhumanity, was an important reason for the deification of humanity, the demand for embracing all mankind in one grand gesture, which the Expressionist generation postulated."[4] Verdi undergoes such a rebirth, a *Wandlung,* as an artist, renouncing his false concept of personal ambition that had formerly prompted his art. He relinquishes his ambition to outdo Wagner and is thus ready to meet him in person. His inability to do so, because of Wagner's death, is unimportant as far as his own inner change is concerned. All thoughts of rivalry are gone: "if he had a brother among his fellow artists, it was this man" (V 372). He sets out to visit Wagner, ready to offer him his friendship. After having learned of Wagner's death, he decides to leave Venice and retire to his estate, living a simple life as a gentleman farmer. But this inner change allows his powers of inspiration to come forth again and he is able to write *Otello* and *Falstaff,* as well as supposedly several other revolutionary pieces of music which he did not allow to be published.

What kind of art does Werfel advocate? In the course of the novel he introduces a number of musicians in order to personify various kinds of music and, by characterizing some of them more sympathetically than others, suggests where he stands. In one of many flashbacks he introduces Monteverdi, thereby returning to the origins of Italian opera and demonstrating that each style is subject to a fashion and further development:

> The recitative drama of the Florentine Camerata was a scholarly error, and had its roots only in the intellect. . . . Step by step, the poetic drama, in whose psychological fetters music could not be bound, was left behind. Steadily, step by step, opera rose, conquering, as no art form had previously done, the cities, the country and the people. Only in that which can establish itself practically is truth found, not in the protests of the theorists, the intellectuals, whose nerves are unequal to the strain of practical life. (V 283)

In Werfel's opinion Verdi has developed Italian opera to its highest point while at the same time preserving its tradition: "It was Verdi's mission to rescue traditional opera and secure its future development. We see his genius harnessed to the double task of renewing the old, worn-out form and restoring it to human verisimilitude without enslaving it to the music drama of the north" (V 86). In the course of the novel Werfel displays his tremendous knowledge as a music theorist. The work thus becomes a novel about music and musical tastes, a novel about opera. In juxtaposing Verdi, the Italian, and Wagner, the German, the author pits classical Italian opera against the new Wagnerian development: the music drama. In so doing the bel canto of Italian opera is victorious over the Wagnerian *Gesamtkunstwerk,* musical inspiration over the leading idea, independent vocal melody over the orchestral symphony, pure singing style over dramatic declamation, and the aria over the leitmotiv.[5] Since Werfel's love and sympathy belong to the Italian opera, Verdi wins as an artist and as a human being.

Werfel's Verdi is an artist of the people, a popular artist in the best sense of the word. He believes that as soon as his operas are performed the people in the streets will sing and whistle his arias. When Mario, the completely untrained singer, sings an aria, Verdi realizes that the music of Italian opera comes forth naturally from the spirit of the Italian people: "Consequently, the perfect symmetry of the aria, its unity, its proportion, or whatever one might choose to call it, was not a thing willed or governed by any external cause, but was a law of nature. A natural law that had materialised and been brought to light through the genius of Italy" (V 131). Later, when he witnesses the crowds at the carnival parade, he realizes "that his own opera music with its chorale and finale was a thing neither unreal nor superficial, but the expression of his deepest national being" (V 307). Verdi's music, in Werfel's interpretation, is thus the pure expression of the spirit of the people. Verdi is the people's mouthpiece; he never lost touch with humanity. His music is a mirror of Italians and of Italy.

By contrast, Wagner is the composer of the German north, drawn far less sympathetically than Verdi. Consequently, one must ask whether Werfel is not defending his idol Verdi against his wife's predisposition for Wagner. Werfel was one of the few German writers who was able to resist the influence of and fascination with Wagnerian music in favor of Italian opera. He criticizes Wagner's egocentricity, scorning his rejection of tradition and his insistence upon obedience and submission. Werfel understands Wagner as "a paradigm of modernism and a representative of those tendencies he found most deplorable. In Wagner Werfel saw the triumph of the ego, a ruthless genius who imposed his will without compromise, regard or consideration."[6] The spirit of Romanticism had become reality in Wagner, a spirit which Werfel time and again describes in strongly negative terms: "This spirit of madness—mad, in so far as it refuses to face reality—this demon of a narrow, inflamed narration, . . . this idol of the degenerate, worshipped with foolish and forbidden rites, with hypocritical formulas and feverish violence,—the evil-working Romantic spirit is the pest of Europe today, striking to right and left and destroying the vitality of our youth" (V 24). This Romanticism is the background to Wagner's art, which is thus neurotic in its very roots. Its subjectivity leads to the kind of self-centeredness which Werfel's Verdi rejects. When Italo, the senator's son, plays Wagnerian scores on the piano, it has the same emotional effect on him as a night of lovemaking; he feels exhausted having succumbed to the narcotic nature of Wagner's music. For Werfel this kind of modern art is the northern art of Germany, in contrast to the natural, southern art of Italy: "He [Wagner] was a German, and to be German meant—'To you everything is permitted because nothing, no relation and no form can bind you' " (V 87). German art as personified by Wagner is not an art of the people, but of an individual who creates in isolation. Werfel obviously believed that there is something destructive about the art of the Germans.

The basis of Werfel's argument is the fact that Wagner's music has furthered the development toward greater abstraction which, in his view, is the result of the spirituality of Romanticism. Wagner, then, is the link to modernism, to symbolism, and finally to the limits of tonality, manifest particularly in *Tristan und Isolde*. Wagner's hubris, in Werfel's eyes, is his sin.

Modern music, based on abstract theory rather than aesthetic pleasure, is introduced in the character of Mathias Fischböck. There has been much speculation on who may have served as the model for this young composer, presented as a mixture of genius and likable madman. It is possible that Ernst Krenek, who was to marry Alma's daughter Anna Mahler, may have served as the model, but one may also argue in favor of Anton Webern or Joseph Mathias Hauer, whom Werfel may have hinted at by using the same first name.[7] Such attempts at identifying historical models say little about the function of the character within the fabric of the novel. More important is the fact that Fischböck represents the kind of artist who has gone even one step further than Wagner. He has left the laws of classical harmony behind and resembles a precursor to Arnold Schoenberg. He is the modern artist who neither writes for an audience, nor for posterity, but only for himself, attempting to isolate the very essence of music. Werfel does not judge Fischböck harshly. Nor does his Verdi feel threatened by him, although he cannot appreciate this new kind of music. Verdi's attitude is a mixture of pity and respect for this German's commitment to the ideas of modernity, and Fischböck's loneliness is in stark contrast to Wagner's constant desire to be surrounded by admiring friends.

Nevertheless, for Verdi, Fischböck's concept of music is monstrous hubris, the ultimate consequence of Wagnerianism. Verdi could not conceive of such ideas for himself since, for him, artist and audience, art and people belong together. Werfel, the Expressionist artist, sees this unity realized in Italy, not in Germany. In his view absolute art, the way Fischböck wants to create it, has no function. Art must always be art, growing out of the spirit of a people and created for the people. This concept, Werfel feels, is realized only in Verdi and in the Italian people. Artists like Verdi are part of the community of man, creating for the community; thus Verdi embodies the ideal of the Expressionist artist.

In its rejection of modernity, *Verdi* indirectly anticipates the tenor of Werfel's essays from the early 1930s. Werfel has the senator curse the present-day realists, pitting the patriotism and morality of the past against contemporary realism and commercialism. But Werfel's ideas in this respect could not be fully expounded because the novel deals with a period before the modernist tendencies of his own time had come into effect. Therefore, he can only speculate on its forerunners, such as Fischböck, in the area of modern music or project them into the future. He does this in talking about the transitional character of the world: "In the epoch that was coming to an end the city had been completely under the heel of the official burgherdom and the intellectuals. While the soulless modern machine was marching with rigid step over the altered face of the earth, . . . " (V 226f.). As he would point out in his later "An Essay upon the Meaning of Imperial Austria," Prussia is the negative element in Germany. Its type of man is the indistinguishable modern machine man. In Italy this same spirit is personified in the newly found national identity after the establishment of the unified kingdom: "But the old virtue of the men of the provinces has gone out of them, and instead you've got a good average type, plodding and unambitious. We are sharing the fate of Middle Germany. What the Prussian system has done there the Piedmont-Lombardy rule is doing to us" (V 298). One might well ask oneself whether Werfel possibly referred to the contemporary fascists who had established their power in Italy only a few years before he wrote his novel.[8]

There is also an autobiographical element. Werfel reflects his own relationship to Alma in that of the senator's son, Italo, who has a relationship with the more mature Bianca, the wife of the doctor Carvagno. Bianca is nine years older than Italo; Alma was eleven years older than Werfel. Werfel himself felt guilty for his part in Alma's conceiving a child while she was still married to Walter Gropius. This guilt he purged in the novel "by glorifying virginity, maternal love, and woman's love while denigrating the male as a pleasure-seeking egotist."[9]

The Man Who Conquered Death (Der Tod des Kleinbürgers)

The hero of Werfel's perhaps most successful novella, *The Man Who Conquered Death,* is the sixty-four-year-old Karl Fiala. He lives with his wife, his sister-in-law Clara, and his epileptic son Franz in a small Vienna apartment. Originally from Karlowitz in Bohemia, he had been the impressive gatekeeper at the Royal and Imperial Treasury in Vienna until after the First World War, when he was forced to take early retirement and work part-time for a private company. Except for some ostentatious pieces of furniture which are reminders of the "good old times," the furniture of the much larger old apartment has been sold, and Herr Fiala has invested the proceeds in a life insurance policy which his next-door neighbor, the insurance agent Schlesinger, has sold him. The main condition for payment of the insurance benefits is that Fiala survive to his sixty-fifth birthday. Herr Fiala falls deathly ill shortly before that date, but with resolute willpower he manages to fight off death until a few days after his sixty-fifth birthday.

In his preface to the American edition in the collection *Twilight of a World,* Werfel says that the story is set "shortly after the inflation" (TW 441). This would fit with the dates given in the story itself: Fiala is born on 5 January 1860 and he dies a few days after reaching his sixty-fifth birthday, in January 1925. Since the Austrian currency reform took place on 1 January 1925, this means that Fiala's widow probably ended up receiving very little money from the insurance company, a fact which is not referred to in the story itself.

There are several models for this novella. One of them is the actual awe-inspiring gatekeeper of the Royal and Imperial Treasury in Prague whom Werfel and his friends used to admire during their childhood. Werfel's friend Willy Haas talks about him in the afterword of his German edition of the novella.[10] He draws attention to an early Werfel poem, "Der göttliche Portier" (The Divine Gatekeeper), which probably constituted the nucleus of the novella. The first German book edition of the novella was published by Paul Zsolnay in 1927 but, according to Alma, Werfel wrote the story as early as 1925. Alma reports the following about the life models for the story:

> I lost the couple who were taking care of my home on the Semmering. A few days later a married couple applied who carefully concealed their age and who had considerable trouble climbing up our steep mountain. They brought with them a terrible creature who now had to do the work of the old ones. Her name was Klara; she was the sister of the old ones and a real dragon. (In the year 1925 Werfel immortalized all three of them inimitably in his novella *The Man Who Conquered Death*).[11]

To these autobiographical elements three literary influences can be added: first, Franz Kafka had also immortalized the gatekeeper in his short story "Before the Law," with which Werfel was familiar; second, Willy Haas drew attention to certain parallels to Edgar Allan Poe's novella *The Facts in the Case of M. Valdemar;* and third, there are parallels to Tolstoy's story, *The Death of Ivan Ilyich,* particularly regarding the German title.[12]

None of these parallels, however, say anything about the story itself. Attempts to interpret it in terms of the heroic death of a poor man or even as an imitation of the death of Christ—as Karl Tober has attempted to do—miss the ironic, often sarcastic undertone Werfel frequently uses in order to undercut such seriousness, such identification and symbolism.[13]

The German title of the novella is *Der Tod des Kleinbürgers*. The first English language edition which appeared in 1927 accurately translates this title as *The Death of a Poor Man*. [14] This translation, however, gives the title sentimental overtones which the German original does not have. Admittedly, the word *Kleinbürger* is almost impossible to translate into English. "Philistine" or "petit bourgeois" come close, but sound more academic than the German. By referring to Fiala not by his name but rather by his social standing, Werfel makes very clear that he wants to talk not about the death of an individual, Karl Fiala, but about the death of a typical *Kleinbürger*, a paradigmatic death which was determined by Fiala's social affiliation, by his way of thinking. This is confirmed on the first pages of the novella which presents Fiala as a man with an intellectual and emotional makeup which Werfel views as characteristic and typical for the *Kleinbürger*. Fiala creates order in class structures: government officials and officers are "people of much higher position than his" (TW 442). He is thankful for the little he has, he takes pride in a few choice items that represent bourgeois value and refinement to him although they are useless, such as a pipe-rack—he does not smoke—or a blotter and a paperweight. A pretentious sideboard, inherited from his wife's well-to-do parents, symbolizes self-worth: "The owner of a sideboard like that still had something left to live for" (TW 444). The sentiment reveals a feeling of personal honor and responsibility for his and his family's reputation. Bad luck is added to Fiala's world: his son Franz is an epileptic and one of his father's main goals in life is to prevent Franz from being made a ward of the state upon his parents' death. Fiala displays personal pride that he never had to beg and always had enough to eat. Yet Fiala's social decline continues unabated, and he must try to fend off total defeat by poverty. The bright past is always contrasted with the barren present. As a member of the petite bourgeoisie, he is even now concerned with maintaining the appearance of real bourgeois life. This is evident in his presentation of coffee and pastry on a fine tablecloth and on good porcelain, to prove to the visiting neighbor, Schlesinger, that the Fialas come from a respected family. Schlesinger reciprocates this façade. Fiala's concern for security is also typically petit bourgeois, as is the attempt to achieve permanence in the form of photographs and, finally, of cheating death by taking out the insurance policy. In both Fiala's and Schlesinger's eyes this policy has the function of a religious miracle destined to save him and his family from almost certain ruin.

Werfel's contention is that the *Kleinbürger* aims at permanence and security, even beyond his death, and that his security mania forces him to insure everything. Werfel also forces him to accept that he has been disenfranchised by history and will lose out in the end no matter what. In his seemingly heroic refusal to die, to beat death by a few days to make some money for his family, Fiala does not become a Christ-like figure but is instead ridiculed by Werfel. His seemingly heroic effort to continue to live for the insurance money is based on a feeling of duty, a secret order he has given to himself which assumes grotesque proportions. Thus at the end Werfel muses: ''Like a good runner he had run past his goal, and lived two days beyond his self-appointed time'' (TW 496).

Werfel halts his ironic tone only when he talks about Fiala's son, the epileptic Franz, who has a clear sense of the hopelessness of his own situation. He respects the father's superhuman efforts without having to say a word about them. Fiala's wife is depicted as naive; when it dawns on her why her husband refuses to die she feels only terror. Her sister Clara, however, has a petit bourgeois greed for possessions that has taken on psychopathic forms: she steals anything she can get her hands on, even foodstuffs which eventually mold in her corner of the kitchen. All negative elements Werfel sees in this social class are combined in her to such an extreme that she can only be viewed as a grotesque caricature of petit bourgeois life. The insurance agent Schlesinger is interesting as a character because he mirrors Fiala's fate as a Jewish counterpart—like Werfel he smokes too much—who has been baptized because he thought it might be socially advantageous. His decline is just as hopeless as Fiala's, and when they both meet in the same hospital room for patients who are dying, he bursts out in hatred for Fiala because he sees in him a mirror image of his own failed existence: ''For there in the next bed it was not Fiala who was lying, but a failure like himself; it was his own botched and bungled life, the disappointment, the stuffy home to which he had been condemned; it was misery and chains and stupidity, the suffocating senselessness of everyday life'' (TW 479). This is one of the few instances in which the misery of petit bourgeois life is presented without ironic distancing.

Stylistically, the story runs from the naturalistic description of Fiala's environment at the beginning to the almost Expressionist rendition of Fiala's dreams and fever visions. Yet the irony and sarcasm which pervade the story prevent the impression of social pity on the part of the author which would have been so typical for either naturalism or New Objectivity. At the same time there is always the feeling of distance, almost mockery on the part of the author. The irony and sarcasm seem to increase as the story progresses, beginning with the description of the women's pilgrimage to the cemetery on All Soul's Day. Attempts to interpret Fiala's demise as a superhuman feat are subverted when the heart specialist and former student for the ministry,

Professor Cornelius Caldevin—the name is reminiscent of Calvinus—makes an attempt in that direction by preaching to his students: "Gentlemen! There is something in us which is king over the heart," only to be ridiculed by one of his students who jokingly shouts: "The king of hearts" (TW 483).

Another perspective in the death of a typical *Kleinbürger* becomes apparent when two young doctors of the hospital, Dr. Burgstaller and Dr. Kapper, discuss the Fiala case in their favorite café. Kapper talks to Burgstaller about Fiala, calling him the "dead man who won't die":

> "Listen: you know how the proletariat dies. It is most edifying. They are not afraid and they make no demands. Everything is settled, they are calm and submissive—and they all die alike. But the middle class [that is, *Kleinbürger*]—each one has his own way of dying, and of not wanting to die. Because each one of them is afraid of losing something besides life. A bank-account, a greasy savings-bank book, a reputation—even a ramshackle piece of furniture. As a rule, a middle-class man is a man with a secret." (TW 484)

All these criteria fit Fiala perfectly. Here Werfel confirms that he had intended a social criticism of the philistine mentality of the *Kleinbürger* when he wrote his novella.

This element is almost lost in the American edition of *Twilight of a World*. The title alone which had already been used in the first American edition of 1927 makes this clear: *The Man Who Conquered Death* is not the ironic portrayal of a typical *Kleinbürger*, but a hero. In his introduction Werfel does not even once refer to Fiala as a *Kleinbürger*, or to any aspects of the petite bourgeoisie which he might be viewing critically. Rather, he begins: "The reader makes herewith the acquaintance of a genuine hero and symbolic figure" (TW 439); and concludes: "The gatekeeper defended his empire in a memorable struggle, more heroically and religiously than even the Kaiser his." In the entire introduction Werfel portrays Fiala as a heroic figure who parallels and symbolizes the empire and its decline. This aspect is also present in the text itself. Thus when looking at his photograph as the once almighty gatekeeper Fiala wonders: "All in all, the figure suggested a more stately likeness of another and very exalted personage who in the stern and well-regulated days long ago governed the realm" (TW 446). This is but one aspect of the novella which, of course, fits in very well with Werfel's claim that all stories in *Twilight of a World* deal primarily with the lost ideal of the Habsburg Empire. Nevertheless, Martin Dolch's comparison of the German and English texts reveals that the American translation of 1937 has been rewritten in order to suppress other aspects of the story, namely those referring to the death of a typical *Kleinbürger*. Werfel here does not refer to Fiala as a petit bourgeois or a philistine but as a "small man," a "humble man," or a "modest citizen." In addition, Dolch lists the following examples (original German text): "Nur die Spießer sterben differenziert. Die kleinsten selbst. Jeder Spießer hat seine eigene Art, nicht sterben zu wollen."[15] The edition of 1927 translates this passage very literally: "It's only the bourgeois philistines who die differently. Even the most obscure ones. Every philistine has his own method of refusing to die."[16] The new translation by H. T. Lowe-Porter in *Twilight of a World* (1937) mitigates the sentence to the following generalization quoted above: "But the middle class—each one has his own way of dying, and for not wanting to die" (TW 484). A little later one of the hospital doctors cries: "Ein kleiner Spießer! Nichts als ein muffiger kleiner Spießer!"[17] The edition of 1927 follows this wording exactly: "A little philistine—nothing but a dirty little philistine!"[18] The version of *Twilight of a World* completely takes out the originally derogatory flavor as it refers to: "A man of the lower middle class" (TW 485). Dolch even goes so far as to claim that Werfel had changed his views later on, and regretted the anti-*Kleinbürger* aspects of his story. While this accusation may be excessive, Dolch is probably right in assuming that Werfel has tried to take out the biting sarcasm of his story in order to make it conform better to the otherwise melancholic, idealized memories of the Habsburg Empire. Although *The Man Who Conquered Death* takes place after the decline of that realm, Fiala is, as quoted above, a lower-class image of Emperor Franz Joseph himself. Thus Werfel seems to be referring to Fiala when he says in his introductory "An Essay upon the Meaning of Imperial Austria":

> The familiar remoteness of the Emperor's face penetrated the souls of the generations, it stamped itself even upon their dreams. The face became a prototype. The streets were full of Francis Josephs; faces familiar and remote, with white beards parted in the middle, were in all the government offices. Even porters at the doors of stately palaces wore the mask—though in their case the bent and listening head sat atop of furred and braided uniforms much finer than Francis Joseph's full-dress one. (TW 22)

Fiala and Franz Joseph are equated in Werfel's introduction to the novella in *Twilight of a World* when he states: "He belonged afore-time to the fur-trimmed and silver-braided race of imperial gate-keepers, was no unworthy part of the whole, a serviceable member of the Empire, a stone in the structure of the world-order" (TW 439). On the following page Fiala even becomes a ruler in his own, small empire: "For the gate-keeper too had an Empire and was minded to defend it to his last breath. And this he did; defended it to his last breath, with a superhuman deed" (TW 440). Instead of seeing Fiala as a typical *Kleinbürger,* a petit bourgeois whose weaknesses Werfel castigates in this story, he now wants to see him as a mini-emperor who defends his declining realm with a heroic, symbolic death.

This attempt on Werfel's part to change the thrust of his narrative, as is evident in the slant of the new translation as well as in his introduction, can only be explained by the fact that between 1925 and 1937 he had changed his view about the Habsburg Empire. It had gone from sarcastic criticism of the empire's class structure to a melancholy longing for a mythic golden age. Heinz Politzer even claims that Werfel's views on the Austro-Hungarian monarchy changed around 1925, so that *The Man Who Conquered Death* may be considered a testimonial to Werfel's new thinking.[19] This would account for the ever changing perspectives, for the critical, ironic aspects of the novella which contrast, even conflict with the melancholy and grotesque elements.

On 29 January 1974 the public German television (Deutsches Fernsehen/ARD) broadcast a television movie of the novella. The director was Hans Hollmann. The actors were Bruno Hübner, Lotte Lang, Ruth Drexel, Nikolaus Haenel, Kurt Sowinetz, and Elisabeth Neumann-Viertel. The author of the screenplay, Gustav Ströbel, borrowed from Werfel only the characters and the idea and then expanded the story to form the basis for a full-length feature film.

Geheimnis eines Menschen: Novellen(Saverio'sSecret:Novellas)

The following novellas were all published together in one volume, *Geheimnis eines Menschen: Novellen* (Saverio's Secret: Novellas) in 1927. In addition to the "An Essay upon the Meaning of Imperial Austria," *The Man Who Conquered Death,* and *Class Reunion,* their English translations are all contained in *Twilight of a World* (1937).

"Estrangement" ("Die Entfremdung") is the story of Gabriele, a woman whose much older husband had died a few weeks earlier, and who now travels from Salzburg to Berlin to see her brother, Erwin, a successful violinist. Both were very close as children, and Gabriele later supported his training as a violinist; but after his marriage to Judith, a woman from a higher social class, both have become estranged. In Berlin Gabriele receives a cool reception at her brother's house and, in her sorrow at their estrangement, runs in front of a bus. She now reveals her relationship to her brother in dreams while she is anaesthetized and undergoing surgery. In a final conversation between her brother and the doctor which she hears without being able to speak, the "factual" events are stated and she has the feeling that the estrangement is over: "She felt that he held this hand of hers as he always had; that he pressed and squeezed it and consumed it, as though it were a piece of fruit. Gabriele was holding Erwin's hand, too. It had come: the strangeness was melted. The years were dissipated. She had her brother back. It is granted to her to lead him back to the house" (TW 355). These lines confirm that her brother had indeed taken advantage of her financially as suggested earlier. One assumes that Gabriele will die.

The narrative technique of this story, for the most part a form of fever fantasy, is reminiscent of Arthur Schnitzler's novella *Fräulein Else* (1924). In his introduction Werfel characterizes the story as the "age-old fairy-tale: the familiar story of 'Little Brother, Little Sister,' wandering hand in hand through the world" (TW 283) until they meet the wicked witch,—the brother's wife—who takes the brother away into witchland (Berlin). He then contrasts this description with a dry, factual newspaper article which merely reports an accident of "a young woman belonging to the better classes." Werfel supposedly chose the "narcotized state" for his heroine, "not because it would seem original, nor even because it was easier to present the somewhat involved events and emotions as a series of detached dream-pictures. The choice was made out of other considerations than these. Narcosis, artificially induced unconsciousness, is so violent an attack on the personality that for a short time it does, as it were, succeed in separating the soul from the body. The soul anticipates the experience of dying" (TW 284). Thus under narcosis man is able to experience the realm of the beyond. In this state his "naked ego" soars: "The naked ego! The words have more than one meaning; for the soul loses not only its physical husk, but all disguises fall away, its will, its striving, its self-deception. It is for the first time identical with its consciousness of itself. For the first time it is complete, entire, not one dark speck remains behind" (TW 284).

This story probably represents Werfel's most modern piece of prose with regard to narrative technique. It is significant that the author, so skeptical toward Freudian psychology, ultimately engaged in a technique so closely related to psychoanalysis and its foundations.

"Saverio's Secret" ("Geheimnis eines Menschen") reads like a frustrating detective story. At a party somewhere in Italy (probably Venice) the narrator meets a man who claims to be an artist, but who refuses to show any of his paintings. Ultimately, forced by his audience to do so, however, he produces the fleetingly visible portrait of a man. The narrator is just as unsure of having seen it as he is unsure of having seen Saverio's name in an old catalogue of an art exhibition in Paris, which Saverio shows him later on. When he tries to visit Saverio again he learns that the artist has been committed to a mental institution. Finally, when looking at an old painting which an art-dealer—the owner of the house Saverio lived in and possibly his sponsor or employer—shows him, the narrator has the distinct feeling that Saverio's personality is contained in it.

The story reveals two distinctly opposite character types. Werfel makes a distinction between Saverio who, despite his serious psychological problems, is a man favored by the muses and living in a lifelong, but honest inner struggle with himself, and the art historian Mondschein, a critic, a know-it-all, who is an activist in matters of art. Little wonder that the narrator despises Mondschein and feels time and again drawn to Saverio.

The reader's frustration stems from the knowledge that Saverio is an art forger, even though no firm proof is given. But the reader's and narrator's suspicions are augmented by a constant series of hints and allusions. In his introduction to the story in *Twilight of a World,* Werfel talks about the psychology of a great forger who is the focus of the tale, and he defends its ambiguity as follows: ''The teasing ambiguity of the events corresponds to the ambiguity of the forger's character—whose life task it is, indeed, to deceive. So that the obscurity of the narration is both inevitable and intentional. The hero's final secret is not revealed. The honest narrator may not reveal more than he knows himself'' (TW 360). The final sentence should, of course, be ignored because it maintains the fiction that the narrator is simply a reporter of facts, not recognizing the fact that Werfel is, after all, the narrator's creator. The question to be asked then is whether or not the fleeting ambiguity is convincing enough to make for a good story. Or does this ambiguity indeed capture the problem of a forger who, being a great artist, at some point must have switched from being an original creator in favor of merely imitating the art of others? Regretfully, this reviewer has come to a negative conclusion. The whole story remains too nebulous; the lack of more exacting information about Saverio also reflects a lack of statement about the nature of the forger and not the other way round. The story is thus primarily of interest as an addendum to Werfel's interest in the problem of the artist, which had been the focus of his excellent novel *Verdi* just a few years earlier.

The short story ''The Staircase'' (''Die Hoteltreppe''; 1927) is in some respects a continuation of ''Estrangement'': Again a woman, Francine, is expressing her innermost thoughts while she is climbing up the stairs in an elegant hotel. We learn that she has had a brief affair with a man by the name of Guido which, fortunately, led nowhere. Her fiancé, Philip, has written to her from New York, announcing his return with plans for an exciting future together with her in Geneva. All danger seems over; she seems poised to forget her indiscretion but at the top of the stairs she is overcome by the feeling of desolation and jumps off the balcony.

In his introduction Werfel talks about "the fascination of the abyss" (TW 421), and one may agree with him that some people seem to commit suicide without any reason. Werfel attempts to justify Francine's suicide by pointing out that her father was "the one-time Royal and Imperial Minister of the Crown" (TW 424), a man who ignored the present, whereas she has been born into the new times, into the "twilight." The contrast between past and present is certainly mentioned in the story. Francine's father is a man of old-fashioned morals who had to be persuaded by his wife to go on a trip to Sicily and thus leave Francine without parental protection. Does Werfel want to say that the new times are bad, that the old moral standards were correct, and because of her upbringing Francine has lost her inner equilibrium? It seems more likely that Werfel again tries too forcefully to make his framework provide the interpretation for the story. Reading the text one gets the impression of Francine's boredom as she reads the letter of her fiancé. He is a successful man who uses only clichés to express his love for her, a successful but balding man, who promises a traditional life that Francine does not really desire. In her brief encounter with Guido she had experienced an excitement without which she now cannot live. The reason for her suicide is a private one; it comes from the fear of inner emptiness, of boredom:

> But she found only a great desolation, rushing in her ears like mocking water. The sound of this desolation swelled more and more frightfully in her ear. But it did not deaden her consciousness, no, it roused her to an evil keenness of penetration. "Yesterday I possessed something. Fears, conflicts, resolves. I was rich. The liberation has made me poor. I feel as though today I had suffered a great loss. Fortune smirks and shows her teeth. And what I have been, that I shall never be again. (TW 434f.)

It is this desolation that makes her jump. The word used in the German original is "Öde" which also conveys the sense of monotony, dullness, boredom, and tedium. This element is so important that in the German original Werfel italicized the words "*große Öde.*"[20] His own introduction is thus misleading. It testifies to the fact that he tried to direct his readers' interpretation of his stories to conform to the views he expressed in the title of his collection and in its introductory essay. In this case close reading does not confirm the emphasis he tried to suggest.

In *Twilight of a World* the novella "The House of Mourning" ("Das Trauerhaus") follows immediately after *The Man Who Conquered Death*. In his introduction Werfel correctly calls it a satyr play following a tragedy—in modern terms, a comedy. The house of mourning is a brothel in Prague which caters to an upper-class clientele, to businessmen, government officials, and military officers. Werfel introduces us to the personnel of this establishment, to some of the girls, several customers, to the piano player, and to Max Stein, the owner. On the night the Archduke Franz Ferdinand is assassinated in Sarajevo—the news is brought to the house by a messenger, a soldier reporting to his officers—Max Stein also dies. His funeral makes the establishment a "house of mourning."

Unfortunately, the wordplay of the German original does not carry over to the English, as Werfel also points out. In German the opposite of a house of mourning, a house of joy (*Freudenhaus*), is a brothel. It is on this type of wordplay that the novella lives. It derives its humor from the misunderstandings of the educated President Moré, who delivers a funeral oration full of quotes from German classical authors, from one of the uneducated girls who is his conversation partner, and from the questionable business which is being conducted at the establishment.

The brothel is in many respects a model of the Austrian Empire. The girls come from various parts of the empire, now working together. Werfel points out this symbolism himself: "Down to the very last hour before their deliverance, upon the polished parquetry of that most singular salon, these blithe and serviceable handmaids of the empire shrieked and sang and ate and drank and danced and wrangled with the guests of the house, unforced, symbolic. And destiny, in that very hour, found an easy way past the narrow door, narrow though it was; and, equally unforced and symbolic, turned the house of joy into a house of mourning" (TW 501f.). It is interesting that during the final night the social and national origin of the girls becomes important, leading to a public fist fight which is ended by the arrival of the army's messenger. Although one should not draw a parallel between the death of the Austrian crown prince and the death of the owner of the brothel, both do initiate the end of an era; one the end of the Habsburg Empire, the other the closing of the house of ill repute which had similarly endured for centuries. "At all events it had a long and splendid life between the Thirty Years' War and the Great War: a life which deserved a more romantic ending than to ter-

minate with the death of a decadent, half-witted survivor. But do great king-
doms of the earth perish more grandly? They do not survive, they carry on
wars, and before they know it they are dissolved and divided up as booty''
(TW 561). ''The House of Mourning'' is thus a highly entertaining story, full
of humor and irony. Its symbolic elements, especially its relation to the Habsburg Empire, should be taken as interesting parallels without drawing deeper
conclusions about any similarity to historical events that led to the First
World War.

Class Reunion (Der Abituriententag)

Class Reunion (1928) was the first book in which Werfel indirectly dealt
with his own experiences as an adolescent in the schools of Prague. His novel
The Pure in Heart (1929) attempts to continue the journey into his past
by extending his probing through the First World War and the revolution
of 1918.

Werfel began working on *Class Reunion* in the spring of 1927 in Santa
Margherita Ligure and he finished the novel during the summer of the same
year in Breitenstein. The idea for the story was born when the then popular
German writer Hermann Sudermann, also in Santa Margherita Ligure, revealed his own hard boyhood experiences to Werfel. As Peter Stephan Jungk
remarks: ''His Berlin reunion with Willy Haas and Ernst Deutsch in early
1926 may have inspired the story of a group of students in Prague fond of the
same kinds of adventures that Werfel, Haas, Deutsch, Kornfeld, and Janowitz
enjoyed.''[21] There is no doubt that most of the characters are modeled on the
students and instructors of the Prague Stefansgymnasium. Gustave O. Arlt
has identified the secondary figures of the class with actual former classmates of Werfel's. The prototype for Bland, the intellectual, was supposedly
Werfel's friend Willy Haas; the prototype for the actor-director Karl Schulhof
was the actor Ernst Deutsch. Jungk also considers Werfel's first love, tennis
enthusiast Mitzi Glaser, as a model for Marianne. One of the teachers was
based on Werfel's own teacher Karl Kyovsky (Kio) of the Stefansgymnasium[22] who had once thrown a book at Werfel because he was grinning.
Furthermore, Arlt not only pointed out the similarities between Sebastian
and Werfel, but also those between Adler and Werfel.[23] Franz Adler's physical appearance resembles that of Franz Werfel; they both bear the same given
name, and have similar mental and spiritual characteristics.

The reunion of members of a high school class of 1902 in a provincial capital of the Austro-Hungarian Monarchy, probably Prague, after twenty-five

years only forms the narrative framework of the story. Before the examining magistrate, Ernst Sebastian, can attend this meeting, he conducts the hearing of a man named Adler who is accused of murdering a prostitute. He believes he can recognize in Adler his former classmate Franz Adler. This incident, and the following boring evening with his classmates prompt him to write out, in shorthand, what he believes is "the story of his youthful crime" (TW 279). Because of his poor school performance in Vienna, Ernst Sebastian, the son of the presiding officer of the High Court, is sent by his father to a new school in a distant city and lives there with his two aunts who spoil him out of love. At the school he meets the usual group of adventurous boys, ready to engage in pranks of all sorts, and he meets Franz Adler, the son of a sick Jewish widow, who excels as a writer of dramas and poetry. A rivalry between the two ensues, which Sebastian wins by dishonest means: he claims to be a poet by presenting poems he copies from an old book, and he makes the physically awkward Adler the laughingstock of the class, humiliating him in public. He continues his "work of destruction," "a slow and mysterious process of annihilation" (TW 177) over the next year to the point where Adler's grades make it impossible for him to be passed to the next level. When Sebastian, in Adler's presence, intends to change Adler's and his own grades in the class record book they are caught. Sebastian manages to put the sole blame on Adler and persuades him to leave the city for Hamburg and possibly for America. When in the narrative present the examining magistrate Sebastian sees the accused again on the next day, it turns out that it is not his former classmate Adler. Nevertheless, the magistrate concludes: "So then . . . a substitute was sent me . . . in justice" (TW 278), a messenger sent to him by God.

Werfel tells the story with an extraordinary vividness and mastery of language. The satire of the classroom events and the language of the teachers reproduced by Schulhof, an actor, during the class reunion, is masterful. The psychological elements of Sebastian are very convincing, and all his weaknesses seem all too real. Since the narrative perspective is Sebastian's, Franz Adler is less convincing a character by comparison. He is much more theoretical and abstract, even somewhat exaggerated in his one-sidedness.

Werfel borrowed certain characteristics from himself and from other figures of his boyhood days. This, however, says little or nothing about the novel and its meaning. In his introduction to the American edition in *Twilight of a World* Werfel himself points out:

> Not the atmosphere of the school, not the youthful vagaries of its pupils, nor any psychological, still less pedagogical divagations form the actual

theme of the narrative. It ventures to raise a frightful, perhaps the most frightful problem of our life on this earth: the problem of guilt. Can one man actually destroy another—not by murdering, which need involve no metaphysical destruction—but by more refined methods; destroy him in the most delicate and secret places of his soul? Or are limits set to the guilty man's evil instinct, in that he must destroy himself with his victim, more cruelly and more surely even than him whom he would destroy? (TW 109)

Surely there is no simple, clear-cut answer to this problem, but there is evidence in the novel which supports an affirmative answer to the question posed by Werfel: Sebastian, ''a very modern jurist'' (TW 112) has failed in life. He is unwilling to pursue the career he could have, willingly rejecting all attempts to promote him to higher offices. Unconsciously he seems to be punishing himself for his guilt. Being an examining magistrate seems to fulfill the lifelong task which led up to his final hearing in the novel: to conduct a hearing of himself. Sebastian is obsessed with his own guilt; he wants to find himself more guilty than anybody else. One can only surmise that his guilt has made it impossible for him to develop lasting relationships with women.

Werfel continues his interpretation of the story by stating: ''The guilty man in this case is a high official, the victim a Jew. The writer chose a Jew for the role of victim because it is the mysterious destiny of the Jew to make others guilty, to call out in those others all their evil and cruelty'' (TW 110). The story is thus a practical demonstration of Werfel's attitude to the role of Jews: to bring about sin which in turn necessitates redemption. Moreover, Werfel has chosen as a motto for his novel a quote from Goethe's novel *Die Wahlverwandtschaften* (*Elective Affinities;* 1809): ''Against the greater gift of another there is no remedy but love'' (TW 107). The underlying principle of Christianity—love—is thus what he advocates as a reconciling principle to avoid the kind of guilt portrayed here. In the battle for survival between Judaism and Christianity which he allegorically describes in *Class Reunion,* Adler clearly emerges as the moral victor.[24]

One may even take the interpretation one step further in underscoring the conflict between the metaphysical and the ordinary world, of nihilism or realism, as Werfel would call it, and inwardness, spirituality. ''Tonight I have seen Ressl, Schulhof, and Faltin for the first time in years,'' Sebastian reports, ''They are human beings without a future or a present, two-legged blunders on the part of the Deity—just like myself'' (TW 187). Clearly, Adler is the representative not only of intellectuality, but also of spirituality: ''It seems to me,'' Adler says at one point, ''that atheism is a very silly thing'' (TW 195). What Sebastian thus realizes at the end is not only his own guilt but that by recognizing his guilt his relationship with God has also been reinstated. For the first time he has become a human being different from the crowd at the class reunion: "And indeed there had come to Sebastian one of those unique, never-to-be-captured moments of existence when a spark is kindled between God and man" (TW 278). It is uncertain whether Sebastian will actually use this spark to change his life, to live life in harmony with God, to break out of the emptiness which he had experienced so clearly when he met his old classmates again. He locks the story of his youthful crime into a side drawer of his official desk, but he has at least broken the shell which had formerly constrained his life.

In 1974 the public German television station ZDF (Second German Television) aired a TV film made from the novella for the first time. The director was Eberhard Itzenplitz. Because of the many flashbacks, all parts were played by two actors, a younger and an older one: thus Sebastian was played by Hans Jaray and Jan Christian, Adler by Bruno Dallansky and Peter Faerber, and Komarek by Peter Weihs and Hans Reiter.

The Pure in Heart (Barbara oder Die Frömmigkeit)

The Pure in Heart (1929) is another novel in which Werfel continued his description of the old Habsburg Empire, a novel which, although fictitious, is imbued with many autobiographical elements. In tracing the life of its hero from about 1890 to the 1920s, Werfel tries to come to terms with the prewar and wartime empire, with his own behavior during the revolutionary time at the end of the war, and also with current problems, which he judges in terms of the values of the past.

The work is an analytical novel in its design. At the beginning Ferdinand R., the friendly and reserved ship's doctor of a luxury liner cruising the Mediterranean, has left the company of the ship's wealthy and boisterous passengers, the members of a film crew, and is seen on the foredeck, dropping something white into the sea. What follows is a description of Ferdinand's life which culminates with the identical scene in the last chapter—a one and one-half page verbatim repetition of the first chapter—which concludes with the revelation that Ferdinand had dropped a number of gold coins, given to him by his childhood nursery maid Barbara, into the sea.

The novel is subdivided into four "life fragments." The first contains Ferdinand's boyhood as the only child of a high-ranking Austrian officer; he had formed a very close relationship to his nursery maid, Barbara. After an affair with a dragoon officer, his mother accompanies her lover to Argentina where she falls victim to typhoid. His father dies from a stroke not very long thereafter and Ferdinand is placed into the care of his aunt Caroline.

The second life fragment begins with Ferdinand as the student at the archiepiscopal seminary where he is studying to become a priest. His aunt had ceased to care for him at age ten, so Ferdinand, now a ward of the state, had been sent to cadet school. A sensitive child, he did not fit in like his archenemy, Steidler. After a fit of rage directed against a superior, Ferdinand had been dismissed and sent to the seminary instead. His friend, Engländer, the son of a rich Jewish business family, helps him to leave the seminary and supports him financially as a medical student at the University of Vienna. As a result of a quarrel with his brothers, Engländer has been stripped of most of his monthly income from his parents' inheritance, and years of starvation begin for Ferdinand. At the outbreak of the First World War he volunteers and soon becomes a lieutenant. When he is ordered to command the execution squad of three supposed deserters, he does not give the final order and is sent on a suicide mission by his archenemy Steidler who now is a general staff officer. He is severely wounded.

The third life fragment finds Ferdinand in Vienna during the fall of 1918, shortly before the November Revolution. His war buddy, the journalist Ronald Weiss, introduces him to the Pillar Hall, a café, which is the meeting place of all types of anarchists and other would-be revolutionaries. Through them Ferdinand briefly becomes a member of a revolutionary council which, instigated by the Russian revolutionary Elkan, tries to assume power in November 1918. In his heart he remains distant, though.

The short fourth life fragment begins with Ferdinand's graduation as a doctor. He visits his old substitute mother Barbara in her Bohemian village home where she gives him the gold coins she has saved for him.

As the title of the novel suggests, its secret and ever-present focus is Barbara. In this character Werfel has memorialized his own Czech childhood nurse, Babi, who had also been the subject of a number of his earlier poems. It was Babi to whom he was so close in his early childhood days and who, through her natural piety and their visits to mass, had introduced him to Catholicism. Apart from that, Ferdinand and Franz Werfel have very different backgrounds: Ferdinand is the son of an Austrian officer—Werfel was the son of a Jewish businessman. Ferdinand attends a military academy, a seminary, and ultimately medical school—Werfel attended the neighborhood schools and some university lectures, but did not undergo any professional training. The similarities are somewhat more conspicuous again during the war: just like Werfel, Ferdinand is in charge of his unit's telephone post; just like Werfel, he is stationed in Galicia at the Russian front. Like Werfel, he associates with the café literati and would-be revolutionaries in Vienna and even plays a short, ill-fated role in the revolution of 1918.

It is at this point that the novel becomes an autobiographical roman à clef. The Pillar Hall is obviously the Café Central which Werfel and his friends frequented and there is a clear correspondence to actual figures of the time. The editor of a left-wing newspaper, Kolomann Spannweit, is Carl Colbert, the publisher of a Viennese newspaper; Basil, the editor of many books and short-lived literary magazines, is Werfel's old Prague acquaintance Franz Blei; the guru figure of Gebhard is a representation of a certain Otto Groß, and the journalist Ronald Weiss is none other than the journalist Egon Erwin Kisch.[25] The poet Gottried Krasny is, as Werfel himself points out in a note at the end of the first edition of the novel, the Viennese poet O. Krzyzanowski who died in extreme poverty in Vienna in 1918. The poems quoted on pages 383 and 384 of the first American edition are his.

According to Hans Hautmann, Ferdinand R. is "a fictionalized representation of Werfel himself, devised for purposes of self-exculpation—ten years after the event—by an author now embarrassed by his earlier personal association with advocates of insurrection."[26] Indeed, by the late 1920s Werfel had become connected, through Alma and her salon, with the Austrian chancellor Schuschnigg and many other conservative politicians. Moreover, he may have wanted to demonstrate to Alma his metamorphosis from a revolutionary with ideas which he himself referred to as those of the early Christians into someone who had now realized the futility of all revolutionary undertakings. The novel is thus not so much Werfel's attempt to describe objectively the downfall of the Habsburg Empire, but to express his own political opinion which he had formed at the end of the 1920s.

In accordance with such views, the characterization of the coffee-house intellectuals is extremely negative. Werfel takes pains to point out the contradiction of their pronouncements in relation to their actual behavior. Thus the newspaper editor Spannweit publicly denounces war profiteering and associates with the revolutionaries while he himself lives in luxury. Gebhard advocates theories of free love, sexual liberation, and matriarchy but at the same time is totally incapable of taking care of his own child. Basil invents ever new causes and founds new periodicals but at the time of the revolution becomes reactionary and sees prayer as the only solution. Weiss, by contrast, is drawn more sympathetically but, in spite of his self-critical attitude, he ultimately becomes a victim of his own histrionic tendencies. His revolutionary behavior is based on a playful love for melodramatic effects and on allusions to history—his model is Mirabeau—rather than on a truly revolutionary conviction. The same goes for the emissary of the Bolsheviks, Elkan, who is not a proletarian himself but just self-obsessed, vain and sterile, a conceited Napoleon figure. Nowak, a harmless seventy-year-old lawyer's assistant, who suffers from a romantic love for all kinds of revolutionary activity, calls for bloodshed (though not in the American translation).

This negative characterization of the revolutionaries implies a damning judgment about their political activities as well. The revolution they want to carry out is characterized by confusion and lack of planning. Through the eyes of Ferdinand, Werfel describes these characters and their undertaking with irony and mockery. The contrast between this and his early Expressionist poems becomes obvious when, toward the end of the revolutionary period, Werfel says about Ferdinand: "It was hard for a young man whose fate had drawn him into the midst of these events to find in himself the courage for final admissions. Otherwise Ferdinand would have to admit to himself that all hopes for a renewal of the world are based on a juggling trick of the soul which falsifies the feeling of disorderly liberation (as every downfall causes it) into an enthusiastic belief into the future" (PH 496; first German edition 672; last sentence not in the American edition). Ferdinand's inner voice whispers to him that all the revolutionary activity is without a goal, meaningless, accidental, and lacking inner truth. All the ideas these men are trying to realize through revolution are Werfel's hated, meaningless, unrealistic abstractions—the emanations of distorted minds without any historical or spiritual basis. For him the revolution in Central Europe is suffocating from its own spiritual poverty (pages 616, 618 of first German edition; not in the American edition).

Toward the end of the third life fragment, the end of his entanglement in the revolutionary activities, Ferdinand is in a pensive mood, and he develops a theory of individuation that seems to be the basis of all human thriving. "But the will of every atom," Werfel declares, "to persist refuses utterly to allow the human spirit to be merged in anything greater than itself; it has no real desire even to come to terms with a community,—seeks, in fact, to elude it. The whole atomic purpose of being seems nothing else than a desperate struggle to individualize" (PH 530). Since this struggle shows an insatiable craving for beauty or luxury, even a higher living standard for everyone will not satisfy human beings as long as someone possesses more than another. Communism creates no positive happiness but substitutes other forms of discontent. "Then begins a fresh uprush of individualism, or, what is much the same, of capitalism. Nothing will prevent it'' (PH 531). Werfel thus advocates the theory that the urge for individuation, for being special, makes it impossible for people to reach happiness in a classless communist or in a capitalistic society, since discontent of the masses is a given. Without expressly stating so, he again declares the pointlessness of all social reform and thus of political activism, implying that inwardness and religion are the only positive alternatives.

This aversion to revolutionary activity is foreshadowed in Ferdinand's refusal to give the execution order for the three condemned men. Certainly, this refusal to obey a military order is first hailed as an ''authentic revolutionary act'' (PH 278), but shortly thereafter the author editorializes: ''It would certainly not have escaped Ferdinand's notice, had exhaustion left him a thought along that road, that in possibly saving three he had certainly dragged fifteen to death along with him'' (PH 287), a clear expression of the futility of all revolutionary activity. The case is a picture-book illustration of what Werfel pointed out in his early essay ''The Christian Mission'' (1916) where he expressed his disdain for political activism by declaring that every action has two opposite effects—that helping one person at the same time means harming another.

The character of Weiss and of many other would-be revolutionaries of the coffee house can also be understood in terms of the essay ''Snobbism as a Spiritual World Power'' of 1928. They are men who, just as the prototype of Werfel's snob, have no spiritual roots and adhere to pseudo-ideals, not because they believe in them but only because they are fashionable. The only character who is immune to such modish ideas is the poet Krasny: ''With Krasny the sharper felt a sharper, the jobber a jobber, the charlatan a charlatan. . . . Krasny had been the incorruptible virtue, the very Cato of the Pillar Hall'' (PH 524). It is ironic that the poorest of the coffee house literati who, apart from a liking for food, has rejected all material values, is the only one who sees through the superficiality of all revolutionary activism, including Ferdinand's.

It is through the character of Alfred Engländer, however, that Werfel voices most of the other opinions expressed in his essays of the early 1930s. It would be too one-sided to see Engländer only as a self-parody of Werfel,[27] although Engländer is definitely an ironic self-portrait. Just like Werfel, he comes from a rich Jewish business family which first viewed his lack of business spirit with suspicion. Just like Werfel, Engländer hurt his foot whilst a soldier and was admitted to the hospital. He is intimately familiar with dogmatic and patristic theology. The theories he voices in chapter one of the second life fragment are very much Werfel's own as expressed in his essays. The heading, "Alfred Engländer and the Intellect," gives the first hint: in "Realism and Inwardness" (1931) Werfel talks about the deification of the intellect and about radical realism which can be fought only by the muses. He argued out that modern attitudes had brought forth technology with its concomitant suppression of human inwardness and the devaluation of the human spirit. In "Can We Live Without Faith in God" (1932) he points out that man has been severed from his metaphysical ties, that science is responsible for his blindness to God, and that the world can be spiritually healed only if it finds its way back to Christianity. All these ideas are prefigured in *The Pure in Heart*. Engländer represents the type of man who has overcome the belief in progress through modern technology. "Technique—the monstrous futile gyration of cleverness" (PH 121), he cries out. He believes in Christ and calls upon Ferdinand to admire the miraculousness of God's creation. When he says: "It began with the denial of a Sacrament. And where's it going to end? With the metaphysic of drainage!" (PH 123). He warns of such deification of technology. What Werfel a few years later referred to as radical realism and naturalistic nihilism, Engländer calls the "intelligent world view" of his brothers (first German edition 153; not in the American edition). He prophesies that Ferdinand will also have to go through a phase of believing in such modern ideas, but he feels that Ferdinand is still untouched by them and ultimately will come out alright. Even becoming a doctor in his view is part of this development: "A man like you is bound to be let in for all that intelligence stuff. You *have* to go through that phase, it's impossible just to jump over it. And very soon you'll have swallowed every atom of the tosh. You'll be thinking, for example that some kind of economic system is to blame, instead of just ordinary human godlessness, for the fact that most people behave like a lot of swindling apes, and coldly grin and watch each other perish" (PH 129). This describes not only Engländer's own but also Ferdinand's and Werfel's development, their involvement in the revolutionary movement of 1918. It also expresses Werfel's firm belief that only believing in God rather than in an economic system can change man's fate. His conviction accounts for the absence of any discussion of the material forces of history, his rejection of socialist ideas, and the limitation of historical development to the dogmatic nature of religious faith.

As in "Realism and Inwardness," Engländer sees in the muses the hope for overcoming contemporary nihilism. "The thought of God had really become the pivot of his life. . . . [H]e defined God and the Divine as a harmony akin to music" (PH 163) and he thinks of naive Ferdinand as a "musical man" (first German edition 197; not in the American edition) in contrast to an intelligent one. There is no doubt that at this point Engländer is the mouthpiece for Werfel's own ideas. But it stops there—after the war he suffers from hubris.

Later on Engländer has a battlefield vision of the pope reconciling the warring factions, and he ultimately tries to reconcile Christians and Jews—an undertaking that Ferdinand witnesses and in which Engländer is rebuffed not only by the Jews but also by the Christians. He is subsequently committed to an insane asylum. Werfel seems to tell us that any attempts to understand the divine intellectually and to apply religious insights for a reform of the social and political world are misguided.

At this point Engländer is also the mouthpiece for several of Werfel's other pet opinions. He says that "the state of mind of all Israel" is "the denial of our Messiah against our own better judgment" (PH 390). But when he demands a world Sanhedrin and a new trial of Jesus, he forgets that, as Werfel believed, Israel must exist separately through history in order to bear witness to and repent for the rejection of Christ. These are all ideas that Werfel later explained in greater detail in his "Theologumena."

Chapter two of the first life fragment is titled "The Inner Life," referring to Ferdinand's withdrawn inner life, that is, a "life of the memory" (PH 8). This inwardness, which contrasts all ambition, initiative, and activity was advocated by Werfel in his essay "Realism and Inwardness" (1931) as a kind of antidote against the contemporary abstract age. It ignores the hustle and bustle of the outside world in favor of a deep religiosity, a concern about one's soul and creative spirit; elements in the human being which represent values that are in sharp contrast to the creations of intelligence, technology, and political activity. This pious human spirit is most clearly personified in Barbara, the simple maid from Bohemia, whose life was one of worship, service, unwavering love, and human concern for young Ferdinand. Her love accompanied him without fail during his travels through the vicissitudes of life, even though he did not write to her for years. She was always there when he needed her—when he was lonely as an adolescent, or when, as a soldier, he lay wounded in the hospital. Barbara, the title figure, seems to play a very subordinate role in the novel because she does not enter the action of the novel in the second and third life fragments. Yet the moral and experiential values she represents are always the yardstick by which Ferdinand judges his own actions and to which he returns after years of going astray. "Ferdinand belongs to Barbara and Barbara to him. Throughout his life's journey her spiritual presence enables him to be in the world but not of it; across the miles and through the years, her quiet maternal spirit, pure as the Virgin's, sustains him."[28] When he leaves her behind in her Bohemian village, her presence inside of him grows: "As he left the little old woman further and further in the distance, Barbara, within him, grew and grew" (PH 598). She has become the principle of inwardness itself, has been completely internalized as an ideal by Ferdinand so that her physical presence is no longer necessary. The values she represents are symbolized, moreover, in the gold coins she has given to him: "Gold—it had ceased to exist. The war had swallowed it, more greedily even than blood. Gold was not an auctioned foreign value to be had in exchange for a bundle of one's country's banknotes; gold was no longer even quoted. Gold was the unprofaned and sacred relic of a long since desecrated, almost supernaturally stable set of values" (PH 590). Gold is a "relic of supernatural stability" (PH 590), not money. It is also the "rarest essence, the noblest quintessential extract of fallen Imperial Austria" (PH 591). From his later "An Essay upon the Meaning of Imperial Austria" we know that the basis of the old empire in Werfel's opinion was Catholicism and represented his preferred values. Since this gold has symbolic rather than monetary value, Ferdinand touches it only in extreme situations and ultimately entrusts it to the sea in order to protect it from desecration, to preserve the integrity of the coins' symbolic value: "The honey of the sacred laboring bees is eternally shielded and withdrawn from desecration" (PH 610).[29]

Just as Barbara represents the absolute good, Steidler represents absolute evil against which Ferdinand has to fight time and again. When Steidler issues the order that Ferdinand command the execution squad, this represents a kind of temptation for him to yield to evil. In accordance with such an interpretation, Steidler is expressly referred to as "The Eternal Antagonist" (PH 253)—the heading of chapter twelve of the second life fragment. The fight for Ferdinand's soul is thus a religious battle.

With imperial Austria gone, the old values no longer exist. The postimperial world is characterized by nationalism, activity, and sports. The revolution had not been a triumph of the spirit, as technology rules: "God is a change of gear, the externalization of the body's technique" (PH 567). Only Barbara and her gold have "stayed impervious to the cynical depreciation of the times" (PH 591). The only conclusion Ferdinand is therefore able to draw is to flee from the present, and become a ship's doctor. By traveling the seas he can withdraw into his cabin accompanied by his books and thus realize inwardness and spirituality, far from any political involvement, specifically those attitudes that Werfel advocated in his essays in the 1920s and early 1930s.

The Pure in Heart certainly has many elements of the traditional German *Bildungsroman*. Its hero has a number of teachers whom he gradually leaves behind. Early in his youth he experiences values and ideas which are tested vis-à-vis a hostile environment that does not allow their realization. They are ultimately internalized, and the hero realizes these values by removing himself from society and living his inner values in solitude. Thus by employing the means of the German *Bildungsroman,* Werfel has arrived at the opposite conclusion: not finding one's place within society is his goal, but also the contention that contemporary society is adhering to the wrong set of values. Given the idea that all activity, all attempts to change this society are bad, the individual who does uphold absolute values must remove himself from society in order to uphold them.[30] Ferdinand's journey is thus, as Lionel B. Steiman puts it, "not one of self-discovery and self-realization as in the tradition of the *Bildungsroman,* but rather one of discovering the meaninglessness of the 'world' and the futility of attempting to change it."[31] This implies a strong criticism of Werfel's own time and advocates absolute, religious values as embodied in a somewhat glorified past. In *The Pure in Heart* Werfel defends a spirituality and humaneness that are based on intuitive impulses, and he passes negative judgment upon "the principle of rationality, and thus to the rational organisation of political life."[32] It is, therefore, a very conservative novel and a clear expression of Werfel's rejection of modernity.

"Poor People" (*Kleine Verhältnisse*)

The novella "Poor People" (*Kleine Verhältnisse*), which was written in 1927 and first appeared in 1931, once again takes up the theme of the *Kleinbürger* with which Werfel had dealt in *The Man Who Conquered Death*. The main character, Hugo, is the twelve-year-old son of rich parents in Prague who, because of his delicacy and his overanxious parents, is educated at home. Fräulein Erna Tappert is his new governess whom he likes. Erna has affairs, first with Lieutenant Zelnik, and then with Mr. Tittel, a copying clerk in the municipality. When she takes Hugo with her to her family's apartment, he encounters the lower social classes for the first time, including Erna's brother Albert who, as a result of infantile paralysis, is crippled. Erna is now pregnant. Hugo, trying to help her, betrays her to his parents, not quite understanding what he is saying. Erna is forced to leave the home and is replaced by an energetic young man. Eventually, Hugo attends public school.

In his introductory notes to the novella in *Twilight of a World*, Werfel clearly identifies its two main themes: "the awakening [of Hugo] to love and the awakening to social injustice'' (TW 43). He recalls the background of the work, the turn of the century: ''The prevailing airs are still mild; there are flickers of summer lightning but as yet no thunder. The weapons still hang in the armory. Even the social antagonisms are still comfortably padded by usage. When they clash, there are dull thuddings, but no explosion. Even the poor, as yet with almost no knowledge of the curse of mass unemployment, are still as jealously middle-class 'house-proud' as the middle class itself'' (TW 43).

The first theme, Hugo's ''awakening to love,'' continues Werfel's stories about childhood and adolescence. In this respect the story is reminiscent of the first part of *Class Reunion* and of *The Pure in Heart*. Werfel has described the boy's growing affection for his new governess with sensitivity, the high point being the sexual dream he has about Erna close to the end of the novella. Before that, Hugo confesses to Erna that he would even have left his parents in order to be with her and support her.

The second theme is more complex. Werfel characterizes Hugo's rich parents with a great deal of irony, for example, when he says: ''Papa was often away and Mama had a studio and an interest in life'' (TW 50). The German version is even stronger, stating that now her life had meaning (''Sie besaß nun ein Atelier und einen Lebensinhalt'').[33] Instead of taking care of her child, she is going through the motions ''mechanically, more as a resolute performance of maternal duty'' (TW 58).[34] His mother is not naive, however, and she is well aware of the fact that she is not close to her son because she leaves his education to other people. She also feels guilty because of her actions. When Hugo asks her whether Erna's family are poor people and she replies that ''matter[s] of one's mind and heart and the education one has had'' (TW 93) are more important than money, she realizes that she has sounded banal and cowardly and was ''stupid from a pedagogical point of view'' (TW 94). Hugo's mother is obviously a hypersensitive and spoiled lady with a fear of germs that only a woman of her class can afford to have. His father is a man who knows that he must fight in order to preserve what his own father had acquired. Hugo observes his father returning home late at night and the father's role-playing becomes obvious: ''This father now stood a whole minute in the vestibule, brooding, sunk in thought, supposing himself unseen. He seemed to be hoping that after a while his proper nature, distorted by his social activities, would take on its real shape once more. But nothing came; these yellowish features expressed nothing but apathy and disgust, which finally discharged themselves in a peevish yawn'' (TW 60). When Hugo, toward the conclusion of the story, shows concern about Erna, the father has only "patronizing praise: 'A good heart is a very good thing, of course,' " yet he also continues voicing his honest views: "But soft romantic sentimentality is not a virtue which gets one forward very much in these days. . . . You must get yourself a tougher skin, and sharper elbows. Nobody can be certain that good fortune will last for ever" (TW 99). How his own father had been a strong man who had gotten ahead by "main strength, . . . by willpower and hardness and ruthless energy" (TW 99), these are the qualities that the father ultimately wants to instill in his boy who is forever the dreamer.

Real feelings are to be found only among the poor people, as in a driver of a horse-drawn carriage who tries to ease the pain of the animal which has fallen in the street by putting a piece of sacking under its head. Such genuineness is also found in Albert's mockery of the rich boy who does not know what alternating current is. In reality it is not simply social hatred which motivates his anger but more the frustration of being a cripple. In contrast to Hugo's family, religion and death are taken seriously here. Whereas in Hugo's house a crucifix is seen as a priceless object of art, it has religious significance in the apartment of Erna's family. Werfel's sympathy is with the "poor people." Most of the time his irony is directed against the rich. Only when he talks about the pedantic Tittel does he seem to paint a parallel picture of Hugo's health-conscious mother on a different social plane. Tittel is almost a caricature, but the irony here is not biting social criticism, rather it is a mitigated form which is close to humor.

References to the specific period are the strongest in Werfel's introduction. In the novella itself it is manifest primarily in the ironic characterization of the social class to which Hugo and his parents belong:

> Clearly the house and its owners belonged to the chosen few, the people affected by the changing times only to the extent that these were inevitably the subject of earnest conversation. They were so secured against rising tides as to know about them only by hearsay. The gall and wormwood of the times had passed through a hundred sieves, each finer than the last, before reaching the palates of these favoured folk, on whose tongues the bitterness was savoured only as a fine spray and aroma that added spice to their views of life. (TW 46)

It was the seemingly secure time of pre-First World War Austria which was supposed to guarantee everlasting peace and prosperity for its upper classes.

"Poor People" is told from the perspective of the twelve-year-old boy. This offers the advantage that the readers know and understand many things the boy does not, thus adding to our identification with the pleasure of discovery. In many respects the novella is a counterpart of *The Man Who Conquered Death*. Erna's family has a great deal in common with Fiala's family. Here too is a son who is suffering from the effects of a devastating disease.[35] Here too is poverty and memories of a better past when the father was alive and had a good job with the railroad company. In contrast to *The Man Who Conquered Death,* this story is told from the perspective of the rich boy. As a result, Werfel always contrasts the rich and poor families. The focus is not on Albert or Erna, but on Hugo and on his development, which will ultimately be a successful one. No matter what effect his father's ideas will have on him, his childhood impressions will remain strong.

The Pascarella Family (*Die Geschwister von Neapel*)

In *The Pascarella Family* Werfel returned to Italy which had previously been used as the background to his novel *Verdi*. The fact that he did so much of his writing in Italy contributed no doubt to his choice of the topic—he began working on the novel in February 1929 in Santa Margherita Ligure. In this town on the Ligurian coast, Alma met an Italian lady married to an Englishman. She told Alma about her childhood with her brothers and sisters, about her tyrannical father, who went bankrupt, of the help her family had received from an Englishman, and of her brothers' emigration to America. After Alma recounted this story to Franz Werfel, he immediately developed it into the plot of the novel, *The Pascarella Family*.[36]

The widowed Domenico Pascarella, owner of a small banking business in the center of Naples, is the father of six children, three boys and three girls, whom he carefully tries to guard from all influences of the outside world. Like a father from Roman antiquity, he rules his family as a benign dictator, allowing them only the joy of listening to his singing of arias from his favorite operas on Sundays and the annual attendance of an opera in the Teatro San Carlo. The children accept their father's rule as a law of nature—but only up to a point. The first major infringement takes place when Lauro and the beautiful Gracia, without their father's knowledge and approval, attend a ball at the Hotel Bertolini, where Gracia falls in love with the Englishman, Arthur Campbell. The others rebel against their father's rule, as well: Ruggiero secretly plays soccer and joins the youth group of the fascist party; Annunziata, the oldest sister, wants to enter a nunnery; Placido, the student, secretly writes poetry and attends lectures on philosophy.

While Grazia and Lauro are at the ball it is revealed that their father has been cheated by his partner, Battefiori, and that only using his daughters' dowries and all his personal assets will prevent his firm's collapse. He finally must even agree to the emigration of his three sons to Brazil in order to support the family. Except for the practical Ruggiero, the sons fail. Lauro dies from a snake bite; the father's telegram orders the other two home. The youngest daughter, Iride, falls sick with leukemia. Grazia sends a letter to Arthur Campbell who returns to Naples. There he is able to free the father, Don Domenico, imprisoned by the fascist government. The experience has changed Don Domenico's heart. Arthur Campbell saves the family business with his personal fortune and marries Gracia. Iride is healed by a blood transfusion. Except for Lauro, whose place is taken by Arthur Campbell, the family is once again united.

The happy end of the novel indicates that it has much in common with a fairy tale. All trials and tribulations are resolved: the tyrannical father has changed into a loving old man, Iride has regained her health, and Gracia is going to marry her prince. Arthur Campbell acts as the magical hero reminiscent of the tale of Cinderella: he attends the ball where he meets Gracia. Also fairy-tale-like is Gracia's cry for help and the postcard which she purposely addresses inaccurately—but which finds Arthur anyway—reuniting him with his beloved precisely when she is about to commit suicide. He is indeed a "dragon slayer" when he frees her father by skillfully deceiving the representatives of the fascist state. Werfel himself points out these fairy-tale similarities when he calls his novel "a tale of fatherhood and the love between brothers and sisters" (PF 368)—the German original uses the term "Märchen," fairy-tale (the first German edition 421).

As Annemarie von Puttkamer points out, the novel also bears great structural similarities to an opera.[37] In spite of their individual features, all persons are typical operatic characters which can even be equated with the particular voice categories: the rough and stern father (bass); Campbell, the young hero and lover (tenor); Gracia, the young dramatic female (soprano); and Annunziata, the motherly character (alto). There is even a wicked and somewhat ridiculous intriguer, the Pascarellas' servant Guiseppe (falsetto), who spies on the children and reports on them to their father. Even if such exact voice equations may seem somewhat strained, the argument that there are a number of typically operatic scenes nevertheless is convincing: the brothers' and sisters' conspiracy to have Grazia and Lauro attend the ball; the ball itself; the brothers' departure for Brazil in order to help the suddenly impoverished father; Grazia's seduction by Campbell and the ensuing curse of the father; the father's arrest and incarceration; the sons' homecoming and reconciliation with the father; the dramatic discussion between Campbell and the prefect of Naples, which leads to the father's release. The success of Campbell's plot is based not on convincing arguments but is also typically operatic—mistaken identity. Not only does Don Domenico sing arias from his favorite opera, Ponchielli's *La Gioconda,* in the first and last chapters of the novel brothers and sisters are paired off in twos, and apart from chapters that are devoted to one person each (individual arias), chapters ten, eleven, and twelve bear the names of the three brotherly and sisterly couples as subheadings, and thus clearly suggest operatic duets (Lauro and Annunziata, Ruggiero and Iride, Plazido and Grazia).

The operatic interpretation suggests an inner harmony which does not, however, exist. Don Domenico's pain is real, and there is no doubt that the dissolution of the family has Shakespeare's *King Lear* as its model. As in this classic tragedy, everything seems to take place within the family and the simultaneously heroic and pitiable patriarch is its center.[38]

Other attempts toward an interpretation have been based on the names (for example, Grazia means "full of grace"), relating Lauro and Grazia to each other like sacrifice and grace, or on the basis of planetary symbolism. Thus Adolf D. Klarmann draws attention to the fact that the father's first name, Domenico, also means Sunday in Italian, and the last name, Pascarella, relates to Easter. His total name may well refer to the resurrection of the sun which since time immemorial has been the symbol of God the Father and of Christ. "Werfel repeatedly pointed out the planetary symbolism of his book, the symbolism of the planetary children of the sun who in veneration and according to the law revolve around the sun. Even the character of the individual children seems to correspond to the one which is traditionally ascribed to the individual planets. It must be doubted, however, that Werfel would have been satisfied with an exclusively astronomical interpretation."[39] More significant than this kind of speculation, therefore, is an interpretation which is based on content. The novel is to a large extent a romantic love story between Gracia and Arthur Campbell—in itself a rarity in Werfel's works. This, however, does not account for the message of the book. Fatherhood in its various forms constitutes the most important theme: fatherhood of the family and fatherhood of the state. The novel thus assumes a political dimension which in light of the times is important. The action of the novel itself takes place during 1924 in fascist Italy, and the theme of fascism, which was already hinted at in *Verdi,* is now more fully addressed.

From the First World War on, the fascist movement under Benito Mussolini had gained momentum and power in Italy. After his famous march on Rome on 28 October 1921, Mussolini had been asked by the king to form a government with the nationalists, and during the following years the fascists consolidated their grip on the state without formally changing its democratic constitution. Mussolini ruled with dictatorial power: On 6 April 1924 the first elections under strict fascist control were held and the fascists received 65 percent of the votes. After the socialist member of parliament, Matteotti, had been assassinated by the fascists on 10 June 1924, the nonfascist members of parliament vacated their seats, demanding an end to fascist brutality and force. Nevertheless, Mussolini kept all oppositional activity under strict control. The political situation in Italy at the time of the novel found the fascists in power but with opposition secretly active. The fascist dictatorship battled its opposition with imprisonment, exile of opponents, censorship of the press, and, in 1925, with the ban on freemasons. All these elements emerge in the novel, particularly in Don Domenico's arrest, as well as during his interrogations by the representative of the fascist state, and in the conversation between Campbell and the prefect of Naples.

The novel was written in 1929, at a time when fascism in the form of German national socialism was spreading in Germany and several radical groups were fighting against each other in Austria. Werfel was thus not only making a statement about fascist Italy but also about the threat of dictatorships in general.

Don Domenico represents the old ideal of fatherhood based on his understanding of the absolute power of the father in ancient Rome, the paterfamilias. It is also furthermore based on his belief that the family incorporates the only true values in life, that all outside influences are inherently bad. For that reason he does not want his children to mingle with other children, and he does not want Ruggiero to play soccer or to join the youth group of the fascist party. He would also not allow Grazia and Lauro to attend a ball which he considers "a dissolute assembly of 'the hostile world' " (PF 20). Don Domenico even suffers a kind of persecution complex in his belief that this hostile world has conspired to further the decline of the once respected Pascarella family:

He came to the conclusion that a special fatality, a peculiar family fatality, was at work against the Pascarellas. Although the children had never seen a trace of this fatality, they accepted the revelation in good faith. From Papa's statements one might have imagined that the whole world was nothing but the instrument of this hostility of fate. Outside this diningroom there was nothing but false gods, conspirators, creatures filled with mad hatred. Raising his voice, Don Domenico exhorted his children to avoid human kind, not to seek social life, and strenuously to shun so-called pleasures, honours, success and similar "intrusions." Any lapse from this doctrine would inevitably be revenged on them. There was only one way of salvation from the universal hatred of the world, to live inviolable. (PF 26)

Don Domenico does not like to go to restaurants and to socialize with other people. Ironically, this behavior, designed to protect him and his family, backfires. Since he does not invite his partner Battefiori to his home, Battefiori takes revenge by embezzling their firm's money. Since he forbids Ruggiero to be a member of the fascist youth group, Ruggiero gets into trouble with his friends and his teachers, and when Domenico's sons want to emigrate to Brazil, they have serious problems obtaining a passport. The message is clear that man cannot live in isolation, severed from society. In his insistence on his family's isolation, Don Domenico's character is seriously flawed: "The truth is that Pascarella's paternity had withered up all the tendrils which at that earlier time had reached out to other human beings" (PF 41f.). He has become arrogant and overbearing. Domenico does learn his lesson when he is thrown into prison and hit over the head as he feebly attempts to flee. Having always been totally indifferent to politics and having not opposed the fascist party, he now suffers for his noncommittal attitude. Werfel seems to be saying that in the twentieth century one cannot remain isolated or ignore politics. Even noncommitted tolerance will be punished by dictatorial systems.

While the declared goal of fascism is to return to the ancient myth of the Roman family, to reestablish authority, Domenico counters with "One has authority, . . . but one does not establish it" (PF 36). At his sons' departure Domenico is outraged by the behavior of the state which subjects his sons to a body search: "Don Domenico trembled with righteous wrath. Little as he doubted the supreme validity of the *patria potestas,* of his own paternal authority, the highhanded power of the State sorely embittered him" (PF 185). When the state finally intrudes into his banking office demanding to inspect his books, he tries to defend himself with his revolver and is overcome by force. Arthur Campbell becomes his defender in a discussion with the representative of the fascist government, the prefect of Naples, and defends the right of the individual to defend himself against any intrusion into his private sphere: "Any unjustified and illegitimate intrusion into my house or my place of business, whether carried out by the police or anybody else, is in my view assault" (PF 374). This "liberal view of personal freedom" is rejected by the prefect who wants to see the fascist enforcement of discipline and authority based on the model of the Roman State. The British Campbell thinks little of such models and rather relies on his "own sense of justice." Such rights and feelings of the individual, however, mean little to the representative of the fascist state who counters: "I lay far less stress on private feelings than you do. What does a personal sense of justice of this kind signify compared with actual national justice?" (PF 374). The rights of the individual to have a sphere free from the influence of the state clashes with the claims of the fascist and, just a few years later, the national socialist state, to intrude without due cause. The modern dictatorial state assumes an importance which is much greater than that of the individual, preaching that what is good for the state outweighs the rights and welfare of the individual.

Werfel briefly attacked this negation of the individual during the same year in his essay "Realism and Inwardness" (1931), as the expression of what he termed radical realism, and, one year later, in "Can We Live Without Faith in God," he termed it "naturalistic nihilism." This worldview, which in his opinion is held by modern man, is precisely the worldview of the fascists in *The Pascarella Family*. The apotheosis of the state is one of its main criteria.

Werfel characterizes the members of the fascist party, similarly to those of the Young Turks' Ittihad committee in *The Forty Days of Musa Dagh* (1933), as cold, uniform, unindividualistic members of an almost biological order: "The Prefect was certainly no older than thirty-five. He had the trained body and the clear-cut face, in short, was of the handsome, determined type which had been predominant in Italy for some years. These young men form not only a party, but in a sense a biological class. In his own way the *prefetto* resembled the spokesman who had ordered Domenico Pascarella's arrest, only on a higher mental and physical plane of the hierarchy" (PF 371). With prophetic vision Werfel has thus already seen the supposed master race of the SS incorporated in this representative of Italian fascism.

In Domenico Pascarella and his family Werfel has dealt with the crisis of the patriarchal family unit. He continued a theme which was prevalent in his earlier writing, the Expressionist theme of the children's rebellion against the power of the father. Here he expanded it into the political sphere: the family not only threatened by the rebellion of the younger generation against the omnipotence of the father but by the political power of the state, which threatens the rights of the individual. While the paternal principle in "Not the Murderer" or in *The Pure in Heart* was also represented by the state, the state was nevertheless benevolent. The Habsburg Empire, at least in Werfel's opinion, took care of its subjects. In *The Pascarella Family* the state has become absolute, its own aggrandizement and power have become much more important than the welfare of the individual. Whereas Domenico Pascarella is finally able to comprehend his dictatorial misuse of power, the state is not. It was precisely through the state's misuse of power by arresting Pascarella that he learned his lesson. True fatherhood and the care of one's children, the supposed underlying principle of the relationship between man and God and man and the state, has collapsed. That this political theme is much more important than all the operatic features of the novel becomes obvious in the final, prophetic words: "The era of song and statute is at an end! But what era had begun?" (PF 437).

The Pascarella Family has a number of serious flaws. There is, on the one hand, the character of Don Domenico, who seems unlikely in the twentieth century. Even more unlikely is the willingness of his children to tolerate the father's tyranny, not to question it but rather to reward it with love and respect. The happy ending can be explained with the operatic, fairy-tale character of the work, but the novel, it may be argued, is a realistic genre, and happy endings normally do not occur in reality. Here it is brought about by the timely return of Arthur Campbell who, with all his money, is able to save the Pascarellas. At the time of its appearance the novel was received as a happy Italian "tale of fatherhood and the love between brothers and sisters" (PF 368). In hindsight, however, the political aspects seem much more important.

The Forty Days of Musa Dagh (*Die vierzig Tage des Musa Dagh*)

In *The Forty Days of Musa Dagh*, which appeared at the end of 1933, Werfel deals with the fate of a relatively small group of Armenian farmers and craftsmen who are resisting annihilation by the Turks, as well as with the inner changes and the personal fate of their leader, Gabriel Bagradian. The son of a wealthy Armenian family, Gabriel has lived in Paris for twenty-three years as an archeologist, an art historian, and a philosopher who is financially independent due to his family's wealth. He had married a beautiful French lady, Juliette, who bore him one child, Stephan. After his older brother Avetis, who had been in charge of the family business in Istanbul, has fallen seriously ill, he is obliged to return to his homeland and, since his brother has since died, to take care of estate matters. While Gabriel and his family are staying in the family villa outside of the village of Yoghonoluk, the First World War erupts, and the Young Turks as leaders of the Ottoman Empire decide to take the opportunity to ged rid of the hated Armenian people— largely Christian—who are living in the center of the empire. They have remained as a separate people with their own religion and culture, working primarily as scholars and merchants. Under the pretext of relocation to other parts of the empire—necessitated by the exigencies of war—the Armenians living in Anatolia, Cilicia, and northern Syria are rounded up and sent into the deserts. They die in concentration camps, starve, or are beaten to death during the long marches. Between 1915–17, over 1 million men, women, and children thus became the victims of the first genocide in modern history, victims of a government-ordered and -calculated holocaust.

After having been informed about the true intentions of the Turkish government, the inhabitants of seven Armenian villages located at the Mediterranean coast decide to resist annihilation. Under the leadership of one of their priests, Ter Haigasun, and of Gabriel—a former lieutenant in the Turkish army who takes over the military command—they move to the top of the Musa Dagh, the mountain of Moses, taking along their herds of goats and sheep and as many belongings as they can carry. They know full well that there is only a very remote chance of survival but they prefer to resist or at least die with dignity. Under Gabriel's leadership they succeed in repelling several onslaughts by Turkish troups but their ultimate demise seems inevitable. The flour for their bread has been destroyed by a heavy hailstorm, and Gabriel's son Stephan whose daring had led to the conquest of two Turkish howitzers is caught and killed by the Turks. His wife Juliette, unable and unwilling to adapt to the conditions on the mountain, allows herself to be seduced by Gonzague, a man of questionable background. The herds are decimated quickly and a group of deserters from the Turkish army who have joined the villagers attempt a coup d'état against Gabriel and Ter Haigasun. After a last, desperate rebuttal of the superior Turkish forces, the remaining villagers are saved by a fleet of French warships, except for Gabriel who half-consciously misses the last boat and is shot to death by Turkish soldiers at his son's grave.

Several chapters also make note of the attempts of the German protestant minister Johannes Lepsius, a missionary, to save the Armenians or at least to alleviate their misery.

The most conspicuous element in the construction of the novel is its symmetry. It is subdivided into three books, the first and last of which have seven chapters each, while the middle one has only four. This tripartite division is underscored by the title of the third book, which also consists of three parts, "Disaster, Rescue, the End." The three books also divide the content of the novel. Book one, "Coming Events," contains the introduction; book two, "The Struggle of the Weak," reports the three victories of the Armenians over the Turks; and book three contains the solution—the rescue of the villagers and Gabriel's death.

In a prefatory note to the novel which was to be Werfel's first great success in the United States, the author wrote:

This book was conceived in March of 1929, in the course of a stay in Damascus. The miserable sight of some maimed and famished-looking refugee children, working in a carpet factory, gave me the final impulse to snatch from the Hades of all that was, this incomprehensible destiny of the Armenian nation. The writing of the book followed between July 1932 and March 1933. Meanwhile, in November, on a lecture tour through German cities, the author selected Chapter V of Book I for public readings. It was read in its present form, based on the historic records of a conversation between Enver Pasha and Pastor Johannes Lepsius. (FD v)

Certainly the sight of the survivors of the Armenian holocaust provided the impulse to write the book, but it was written with careful research of the historical sources available to Werfel. They include a detailed report by one of the survivors, Rev. Dikran Andreas[s]ian written after the arrival of the refugees in Egypt, "Suedije, eine Episode aus der Zeit der Armenierverfolgungen" ("Suedije, an Episode from the Time of the Persecutions of the Armenians")[40] as well as several publications by the German protestant minister, Johannes Lepsius.[41] We are not concerned here about how faithful Werfel remained to these sources. It may suffice to say that "Suedje" is the chief source of *Musa Dagh*.[42] As he points out in his prefatory remarks, Werfel closely adhered to Lepsius's report for his conversation between Lepsius and Enver Pasha. He used a book edited by Paul Rohrbach[43] to familiarize himself with the country and its people. Werfel's friend, Ernst Polak, researched administrative and jurisdictional matters for him, and sent Milan Dubrovic, a young journalist, to the national library in Vienna to look up geographical records and to find out about the exact weather conditions (such as the amount of precipitation and the direction of the prevailing winds) in Anatolia during the summer of 1915.[44] He took great pains to study the exact administrative structure of the Ottoman Empire in order to ascribe the correct responsibilities to the various Turkish officials. Particularly vivid are his descriptions of the military measures ordered by Gabriel and of the actual battles. Just as in the case of *The Pure in Heart,* Werfel was able to draw on his own wartime experiences, particularly his knowledge as a soldier in an artillery unit, in describing the operation of the howitzers. All these details lend verisimilitude to his picture of life on Musa Dagh. Yet, as George

Schulz-Behrend concludes: "Werfel has transformed the material by representing conditions as being more ideal, more picturesque, or more complicated than the sources indicate,"[45] and "in the utilization of the sources Werfel displays an understandable pro-Armenian bias which is designed to win the reader to the Armenian side."[46] As far as the characters are concerned, Lepsius, Tomasian, Enver Pasha, and a number of minor characters are based on real people, but are often altered; thus Tomasian is considerably different from his historical model, and the character of Iskuhi, an Armenian girl with whom Gabriel falls in love, has evolved from no more than a name. Entirely fictitious is the character of Gabriel as well as his household, including Juliette and his son Stephan. Such numerous fictional contributions transform the book from mere historical account to a novel, and it is here that Werfel has displayed his skill as a writer.

The entire book is narrated in a rich prose that attempts to render the spirit of the area and its people. The most conspicuous stylistic elements, however, are the great conversations in which the friends and foes of the Armenians clash:

1. The German pastor Johannes Lepsius and the Turkish War Minister Enver Pasha (book one, chapter five, "Interlude of the Gods," FD 123ff.);
2. Lepsius and the German privy councillor in Berlin (book three, chapter one, "Interlude of the Gods," FD 529ff.); and
3. Lepsius and the pious Turkish Sheikh Achmed and his friends (book three, chapter one, FD 543ff.).

The importance of these conversations is that they are removed from the action of the Musa Dagh and its people and, instead, the fate of the Armenians is discussed by outside people who fight for or against them. It is here that the surface action gives way to a battle of principles, which were important to Werfel, thus revealing his underlying views. In these conversations it becomes clear that Werfel is not primarily interested in the political history and its implications but rather in the underlying religious and cultural values.

Although Werfel took pains not to make Enver Pasha's arguments totally implausible or ridiculous, they are clearly the arguments of a nationalist who wants to rid himself of a racial minority he perceives as a plague. He simply declares the areas where the Armenians are living to be war zones which must be vacated by potential inner enemies. His arguments are those of a politician who acts purely on the basis of *raisons d'état*. The dreams of a new Turkish empire based on the wrongly perceived concept of racial purity are, in Lepsius's or Werfel's opinion, "such dreams . . . the narcotic of nationalism engenders. Yet at the same time he was moved to pity for this porcelain war god, this childlike Antichrist" (FD 139). In addition to nationalism, it is this antireligious, rationalistic attitude that Werfel sees embodied in the Young Turks: "What Herr Lepsius perceived was that arctic mask of the human being who 'has overcome all sentimentality'—the mask of a human mind which has got beyond guilt and all its qualms, the strange, almost innocent naiveté of utter godlessness" (FD 142).

Atheism, modernism, and nationalism are the evils personified in Enver Pasha. The godlessness of modern man is pitted against the arguments of the man of God, Johannes Lepsius. The actions of the godless Young Turks are directed against a pious Christian people, the Armenians. It is no accident that the leader of the Armenians on the Musa Dagh is a priest, Ter Haigasun, and that the center of their community on the mountain is their altar. The conversation which Lepsius has with Enver Pasha is mirrored in the conversation he has with the German privy councillor. Imperial Germany, under the leadership of the Prussian Hohenzollern dynasty, is the result of nationalism—as Werfel later on pointed out in "An Essay upon the Meaning of Imperial Austria." Germany's imperial title is usurped, its nationalistic power is the cause of the downfall of the author's much admired Austro-Hungarian Monarchy. Little wonder then that imperial Germany is the ally of the Young Turks, and that the privy councillor also conceives several types of *raison d'état*—Werfel, through Lepsius's eyes, talks about him as "the sphinx-like countenance of the State" (FD 529)—to prove that Germany is in no position to do anything for the Armenians for fear of upsetting an important alliance. As Enver Pasha is for Lepsius the embodiment of modern godlessness, the privy councillor who is almost a Prussian caricature quotes Nietzsche, a source of modern anti-Christian thought: "Doesn't Nietzsche say: 'What totters, ought it not to be thrust down?' " (FD 535). When Werfel continues, "But Nietzsche was not the man to disconcert such a child of God as Johannes Lepsius," he makes clear that Lepsius again faces the embodiment of godlessness.

The meeting with the pious Turkish Sheikh Achmed and his friends actually continues a conversation Gabriel had with one of his father's friends, the Agha Rifaat Bereket, in chapter two. The pious Muslim had warned Gabriel about the coming events and saw atheism and nationalism, imported from Europe, as responsible for the war and the problems of modern Turkey. At the meeting with Sheikh Achmed, one of the people present, the *Türbedar* (holder of exalted office, "guardian" of the tombs of sultans and holy men), accuses the Germans of ultimately being responsible for the Turkish malaise by referring to the Berlin Congress of 1878. Lepsius says: "As far as I know, the big massacres did not begin before the last century—after the Berlin Congress." To which the *Türbedar* replies: "At the Congress you Europeans began to meddle in the domestic affairs of the empire. You urged reforms. You wanted to buy Allah and our religion of us" (FD 552). Again modern Europe meeting in Berlin under the aegis of Prussia's Bismarck is blamed for the persecution of the Armenians by the Turks.

It is the pious Muslim group around Sheikh Achmed, including the Agha Rifaat Bereket, which represents the spirit of the old Ottoman Empire. The same fate had befallen the Ottoman Empire as the Austro-Hungarian Monarchy which, in Werfel's opinion, had fallen victim to the modernism and nationalism instigated by Prussia. The old Turkish realm was based in deep religiosity just as the Habsburg Empire was informed by Catholicism. Earlier, in book two, chapter three, Werfel had talked about the caliphate, the Muslim religion, and nationalism of individual peoples in the same terms he would talk about the Austro-Hungarian Monarchy and Catholicism in "An Essay upon the Meaning of Imperial Austria." In this novel the Young Turks are thus analogous to Prussia in relation to Austria:

> Here, as everywhere else in the world, nationalism had set to work to break up the rich, indeed profoundly religious concepts of the state into their paltry biological components. The Caliphate is a divine idea, but Turk, Kurd, Armenian, Arab denote only terrestrial accidents. The pashas of former days knew well enough that their concept of all-embracing spiritual unity—the Caliphate—was nobler than the uneasy itch of pushful entities for "progress." In the indolence and vice of the old empire, its *laissez aller,* there lay concealed a cautious wisdom, a moderating, resigned governing principle, which entirely escaped short-sighted westerners striving after quick results. . . . But the Young Turks managed to destroy the work of centuries in a breath. They did what they, the chiefs of a state comprising several races, never should have done. Their mad jingoism aroused that of subject peoples. (FD 414)

Once again, Werfel analyzes political developments not in political but in cultural and religious terms. He is not interested in economic or political issues or explanations but solely in their deeper, theological significance.

In the Muslim group around Sheikh Achmed, the *Türbedar* becomes the mouthpiece for Werfel's favorite ideas. As in the author's essays, he first speaks out against modern activity: "Don't you know that all which you call activity, advancement, is of the devil? Your whole devilish restlessness shows us plainly that there is no 'progressive activity' not founded in destruction and ruin'' (FD 553). The ultimate reason for these devilish concepts is secular materialism, that is, Werfel's old nihilism: ''You may do hypocritical lip-service to the religion of the prophet Jesus Christ, but in the depths of your hearts you believe in nothing but the forces of matter, and eternal death'' (FD 554). The old sheikh echoes: ''Nationalism fills the burning void which Allah leaves in the hearts of men when they drive Him out of them'' (FD 554).

The subplots involving Lepsius and the pious old Turks have little purpose other than to demonstrate the supposed real reasons behind the genocide of the Armenians. They give Werfel the opportunity to voice his pet ideas about the godlessness of modern man, the evils of nationalism, and the goodness of empires in which the unifying element of religion guaranteed the peaceful co-existence of many different peoples.

In describing the fate of the Armenians, Werfel doubtless also thought of the Jewish people and their persecution for centuries due to their racial and religious differences within predominantly Christian countries. The fact that Musa Dagh means ''mountain of Moses'' is historically accidental, but other parallels to biblical history in the novel are not. In the various historical sources the Armenians spent either fifty-three or thirty-six days respectively on the mountain. By deviating from these reports and changing the time to forty days, Werfel clearly evokes biblical connotations such as the forty days of the Flood, the forty days of Moses's fasting on Mount Sinai, the forty days the Jews wandered through the wilderness, and Christ's time in the desert. Just like Moses, Gabriel Bagradian also became a leader who had been raised and educated abroad and now joins his people again to lead them out of captivity. Like Moses, he does not reach the promised land. The complaints of the Jews against Moses and their preference to stay in Egypt rather than to wander is mirrored in the Armenians, who rebelled against Gabriel and believed that deportation might have been better than resistance against the Turks.[47] But God is on the Armenian side in battle just as he had supported biblical Israel.

It is tempting to make Werfel the prophet of the fate of his own people because the parallels to the fate of the Jews during the Third Reich are so numerous. Armenian stores are looted in *Musa Dagh* as Jewish stores were looted on 9 November 1938 during the Third Reich. Just like the Armenians were made to believe that they were merely being deported for resettlement to other areas of the empire, the Jews in Eastern Europe were also told they were being resettled. In both cases the deadly deportations were carried out with similar bureaucratic orderliness. In both cases the property of the deported became property of the state or of other people who were permitted to enrich themselves. The Armenians who have been forced to build a road are shot to death the same way many Jews were by the German SS.

Yet, despite the fact that these parallels appear in hindsight to be uncanny, we must remember that Werfel finished the manuscript in March 1933, well before the active persecution of Jews in Germany had begun. What was obvious and intentional were the parallels between the Young Turks' nationalistic ideology and that of national socialism. Werfel himself drew attention to these parallels by reading from chapter five of book one, the conversation between Lepsius and Enver Pascha, during his lecture tour through German cities in November 1932. Thus one might well argue that this historical novel was Werfel's contribution to his fight against the rise of national socialism in Germany. Yet, after Hitler had come to power on 30 January 1933, Werfel's actions did not indicate that he was expecting wholesale persecution of Jews in Germany. As Steiman points out:

> there is no indication that he [Werfel] has much empirical evidence for believing European Jewry to be *in extremis* as early as 1932. This is to be inferred from Werfel's own action in the light of the words Pastor Lepsius addressed to Enver Pasha: "If my government . . . behaved unjustly, unlawfully, inhumanly . . . to our fellow countrymen of a different race, a different persuasion, I should clear out of Germany at once and go to America." Werfel did not decide to emigrate until circumstances forced him to, and that was long after the Nazis had given ample evidence that the fate of the Armenians was an indication of what was in store for the Jews.[48]

After having sent a telegraphic request for the appropriate form on 19 March 1933, Werfel signed a declaration of loyalty to the new ruling powers as requested by the German Academy of Arts and Sciences. Most likely he was afraid that, if stripped of his membership in the academy, his antinationalistic *Musa Dagh* would be forbidden altogether. In light of the quickly changing governments during the days of the Weimar Republic, he obviously did not think that the Hitler government would survive very long. In a letter from Santa Margherita Ligure to his parents in Prague he merely wrote about his work on *Musa Dagh*. With reference to the political situation he stated: "What will happen, will happen, probably not all that much." Just like Italy he expected the German variety of fascism slowly to "consolidate itself . . . until nobody talks about it anymore." "After a period of steady advancement, the Jews would now suffer a setback, he could at least see that coming, 'but perhaps it will be only a brief setback.' ''[49]

The Armenians received *Musa Dagh* as an epic on the genocide committed by the Turks against their people and as a testimonial to their heroism. The previous remarks tried to draw attention to Werfel's interpretation of historical events in terms of his view of history. But what has so far been ignored is the development and fate of Werfel's hero, Gabriel Bagradian. The novel is not really a book about a historical event but rather about the inner transformation one person undergoes as a result of his exposure to the events of history. The fate of the Armenians in Turkey and those who retreated to Musa Dagh were well known at the time. Therefore, Werfel's opus was intended more to be the saga of a man who slowly finds the way back to himself and to his people and who, after many years of Europeanization, finds inner fulfillment in serving his people, ultimately willing to die for them.

The Gabriel at the beginning of the novel is introduced as someone who has lost his identity, his inner self. He has become completely assimilated to his life in France: "He was a thinker, an abstract man, an individual. What did the Turks matter, the Armenians? He had thoughts of taking French citizenship" (FD 7). One must remember that the adjective "abstract," in Werfel's view, characterizes a disturbed relationship to one's environment. Gabriel has lost his roots, his people. In the course of the novel he reestablishes these roots, he fights for them, and it is not accidental that this occurs concurrently with a continuing estrangement from his wife Juliette, who can hardly recognize her formerly European-looking husband behind the Armenian face that now looks at her.

Conversely, Gonzague Maris, the man who becomes Juliette's lover, is of Greek and French origin and holds an American passport. In other words, he is a man without a clear identity. Maris is a modern man for whom the meaning of life is "ruthlessly to satisfy our desires and appetites" (FD 421), who loathes the words "for ever" and "always" (FD 502). Continuity and cohesion are, however, elements inherent not only in religion but also in true human connections, such as those between husband and wife, between a person and his people, and between parent and child.

It is particularly this latter connection which Werfel stresses in the novel. Just like Gabriel again becomes aware of his Armenian heritage during his fight for the survival of his people, so does his son Stephan who soon strips off his European clothes and tries hard to win the respect of his Armenian peers. For Werfel the relationship of a father to his son has religious implications; it marks the extension of the individual through the generations to eternity: "Father and son in the East! Their relationship can scarcely be compared with the superficial contact of European parents and children. Whoso sees his father sees God. For that father is the last link in a long, unbroken chain of ancestors, binding all men to Adam, and hence to the origin of creation. And yet whoso sees his son sees God. For this son is the next link, binding humans to the Last Judgment, the end of all things, the consummation" (FD 15). This linkage is broken when Stephan dies. At the end of the novel Stephan is even "identified with Christ and his death is portrayed as a repetition of the crucifixion."[50] Gabriel dies on his son's grave, and when the Turkish bullets hit him, "he clung to the wood, tore it down with him. His son's cross lay upon his heart" (FD 817). His son has thus been reconnected with all the generations preceding him. When Stephan's body was pierced by the knives of the Turkish Saptiehs, he did not suffer the agony of death but had the vision of his father coming toward him at the railway station in Paris where his parents used to collect him.

Gabriel has given his son for his people and he finds fulfillment in his self-sacrifice. At the end he has found himself fully and, after the rescue of his people, he has become the truly free man that he only imagined he was at the beginning of the novel. Thus his fight for his people had also been a means for him to find self-realization and freedom: "He had shared in the destiny of his blood. He had led the struggle of his own villagers. But was not the new Gabriel more than part of a blood-stream? Was he not more than an Armenian? Once he had thought of himself as 'abstract,' as an 'individual.' He had had to pass through the pen-fold of a commune really to become so. That was it, that was why he could feel so incredibly free!" (FD 814). It is the paradox of the novel that this abstraction on a higher plane is a positive one. It succeeds because it signifies an immediate relationship between Gabriel and God, it makes him "more real than all the people or any nation" (FD 814).

Saving the physical Gabriel at this point would have been a regression and so Werfel allows him to die on the mountain. The novel began by Gabriel falling asleep whilst his son looked on. It ends with Gabriel falling asleep, thereby missing the rescuing ships and perishing on his son's grave. In conjunction with the symbolic crucifixion this may be considered pathetic. Within the framework and development of the novel's main character it is, however, an emotionally satisfying conclusion.

Hearken unto the Voice (*Höret die Stimme*)

In April 1936 Werfel was having trouble deciding what to write about. He had been working on some introductory remarks to *Twilight of a World;* and work on two legends was not progressing and they remained incomplete. As he was walking in the streets of Locarno he bought himself a Bible, and began reading the Book Jeremiah, which inspired him to create the character and the plot for his new novel, *Hearken unto the Voice.* He continued working on it in May in Ischl, and during the rest of the year the new novel was his main occupation. The German original, *Höret die Stimme,* appeared in 1937 and the English translation was published in February 1938.

The novel is partially a biography of the prophet Jeremiah. The prophet hears the inner voice of God who orders him to warn Israel of impending danger and doom and, should Israel not fulfill God's will, be faced with defeat and the enslavement of many of its people by Nebuchadnezzar of Babylon. Jeremiah fulfills the order but he is scorned by his brothers, scorned by the young kings, humiliated, beaten and wounded, suspected to be a Babylonian spy, and almost killed several times. Yet he does not relent, continuing to tell the truth to the Jews and to Nebuchadnezzar.

This biography is embedded in a narrative framework which takes place in the author's present, in and around Jerusalem. A half-Jewish British writer, Clayton Reeves, who after the recent death of his young wife in Egypt undergoes an inner crisis, is threatened by an attack of epilepsy. In the temple at Jerusalem he is, seemingly for a moment only, taken back in time, living the life of Jeremiah, and is thereby cured. In the 1956 edition of the novel this narrative framework was excluded by Werfel's widow, Alma, who explained in an afterword that Werfel himself had later considered the parallels between the writer and Jeremiah to be too artificial. In recent editions the frame has once again been restored.

The biblical book Jeremiah tells the story of the prophet in an extremely fragmented form. The various parts of his life are presented out of chronological sequence. Names of kings and many other characters are given with little more information than their place of birth, and their personal relationship to Jeremiah is not always clear. The biblical book contains little description of environment, and only the most important historical events are reported. It is obvious that the author was addressing an audience that was thoroughly familiar with Jewish history and, consequently, that he could assume that they were familiar with the basic events and characters. The book consists of the many warnings and prophecies God tells the Jews through the mouth of Jeremiah. But Werfel reversed the emphasis in his novel by including only the most important visions and commands that God gave Jeremiah and focusing on the characters themselves. Similar to Thomas Mann in his *Joseph* novels, Werfel is highly successful in invoking the biblical past, in making the Egyptian, Babylonian, and Jewish antiquity come to life, and in transporting the reader to the Middle Eastern cultural centers. Looking more closely, however, it is apparent that he conveys very little about the daily life of the people but deals almost exclusively with their religion. After Jeremiah's beloved Egyptian fiancée Zenua has died, he follows the Egyptian priest Kher-heb of Nu-Ptha into the underworld to find her, only to discover that it is populated by shadows. In Babylon Nebuchadnezzar, who believes in the stars, invites him to accompany him on a "Journey through the Starry Sky" (HV 531ff.), which is undertaken to determine the realm's fate. The result is the same. The Babylonian skies are just as empty and shadowy, without reality, as the Egyptian underworld was:

> His immediate feeling was one of disappointment, which changed to uneasy doubt and finally grew into the definite suspicion that this vision of the stars was not a true vision, any more than his journey through the Egyptian realm of the dead had been a true vision. If the revealing thought had crept into his mind in Amenti [the Egyptian underworld] that death was tedious, he was now beset by the no less illuminating thought: "The stars are vanity." . . . Just as the Kas in Amenti were merely masks to hide a clamorous emptiness, so the stars in Babylon's vision were merely masks emitting false and ineffectual rays. (HV 565f.)

The religions of Egypt and Babylon are lacking the reality of the joy of God and the suffering of man. Werfel thus confirms Israel's God as the only true and real one.

It is surprising that Werfel should take up a theme from the history of Israel and not make greater use of the opportunity of expressing his view on the fate of the Jews in general. Only at the beginning of the book, after pointing out that the father of Clayton Reeves is a Jew, does he have Reeves express: "There can be no cure for us, no earthly peace or order, so long as it is His wish that in relation to every human community we should be eternally different" (HV 29f.). When later he states, "But the nations hated Israel with a bitter hatred" (HV 141), he obviously does not only refer to biblical times but to the waves of anti-Semitism throughout history, particularly at the time of the Third Reich.

Werfel's Jeremiah displays a number of parallels to the life of Christ, similar to accounts from the Old Testament. In a letter to the exiles in Babylon he writes: "Seek the peace of the city, whither the Lord has caused you to be carried away captives, and pray for it" (HV 572). Considering this it becomes clear to Jeremiah that he has made many enemies: "Pray for your jailers! Seek the peace of your destroyers! Bless the archenemy who hates you! Had he really written down these words, which upset the order of the world? He was asking the human heart to belie itself. . . . Jeremiah knew that in asking the exiles to pray for Babylon he had issued a wanton challenge to man's nature, and that retribution for these words would surely be demanded'' (HV 572). It is clearly Christ's command, "Love thy enemy!" that Werfel's Jeremiah is preaching in this Old Testament story, and when Jeremiah is apprehended and accused of being a Babylonian spy, Zedekiah gives him up with words reminiscent of the words of the New Testament: '''Behold, he is in your hand! Do with him what you will.' . . . They struck him, spat in his face, defiled his garments'' (HV 684). Just like Christ's suffering, Jeremiah's suffering is a redemptive one, through which he pays off man's future debt to God: "Humbly he [Jeremiah] accepted the most ominous promptings of the Lord as immutable predictions, and by his own sufferings he forestalled those that were to befall Jerusalem. In this way he was making amends for the guilt of the nation even before the account was presented. Perhaps his sufferings would help diminish to some small extent the great affliction through which the land would have to pass'' (HV 589). The prophets of the Old Testament, including Jeremiah, are, of course, precursors of Christ by virtue of the fact that they were the voice of God until he became man. But for Werfel there was no opposition between the spirit of the Old and the New Testament. The golden rule of Christ was for him also the rule that distinguished Israelites from the heathens. As he puts it in his "Theologumena": "Israel's mission from the very beginning has been to force to the attention of the nations the great paradox of the inversion of naive, heathen values, the great demand: live *counter* to your sinful nature. Jesus Christ is also, in addition to everything that He is, the fulfillment of this mission of Israel'' (BHE 196f.)

It is not easy for Jeremiah to understand God's words. Discriminating between one's own wishful thinking and God's words is difficult, and many other prophets fall victim to their wishful misinterpretations, but Jeremiah is relentless and has developed a sense of discrimination. He is able to understand God, who often is silent for a long time until Jeremiah is ready to receive his words. God does not tell him what will happen, but what man ought to do, and threatens man if such commands are not obeyed: " 'The Lord,' said Jeremiah with a heavy tongue, 'declares His will but not His intention' '' (HV 599). Zedekiah, the king, tries to understand God, and Jeremiah tells him, "Do not try to comprehend . . . only listen to His words!" To which the king replies, "The incomprehensible is not the concern of the King, but only that which can be clearly comprehended. . . . It is his duty to calculate and plan and care for the nation and for Jerusalem'' (HV 600). In Jeremiah's view human planning, or self-reliance on reason, is wrong because it does not do justice to God who may steer the events in a totally different direction: ''Men did not change. Their ridiculous self-confidence and assurance were due to their childish overestimation of the empty conjecturing they called reason and foresight'' (HV 660). Thus in this novel Werfel's two opposite worldviews clash yet again: ''realism'' with all the negative connotations Werfel attributed to it—and the spiritual worldview he advocated—which Jeremiah defends in his actions; and the divine revelations for which he serves as a mouthpiece. Through Jeremiah God asks the Jews time and again not to question him but just obey, even though his divine commands may not make sense to the scheming, intellectual mind. In Werfel's view, which can also be found in his biblical model, all of Israel's troubles stem from its disobedience to God, of placing its own will and reasoning above God's commands. This lack of obedience shows itself in the veneration of many other gods, in ignoring ''to cancel all loans and let their bondmen and bondwomen go with their portion'' (HV 184), and when the seventh year of service—the year of emancipation—arrives, in not subjecting oneself to Nebuchadnezzar as God had commanded.

Unquestioned obedience becomes the clear message of the book which ends when Clayton Reeves judges Jeremiah: ''Jeremiah was a sensitive man, who was implacably opposed to his world and his age. Though he was timid, even the evident and potent inequities of this earth could not vanquish him. For he obeyed none other than the voice of God, which spoke to him and within him'' (HV 779). When he continues to speak he compares Jeremiah's absolute obedience to God to the attitude of the modern world:

> It would, indeed, be one of his future tasks to show that greatness is consistent only with running counter to the world and never with acceptance of it; that the eternally defeated are the eternally victorious; and that the Voice is more real than the clamour that seeks to drown it. He was filled with a joy of the spirit, for he knew that the Voice speaks with its primal power unquenched. It spoke to him and within him. Only he must attune his inward ear more keenly that it might listen with incorruptible integrity to the unique Truth. (HV 779)

In this context one must not forget that the book was written in 1936–37 when it was not easy to present the truth in Germany, potentially the land of Werfel's largest readership. Seen in this contemporary political light, the novel is an exhortation to listen to the inner voice, the voice of God and not to political expediency, to stick to the commandments of God and to live against the times—as Jeremiah had done.

Apart from this very general comparison to the author's present, there are a number of other, concrete allusions to contemporary European history. Chapter twenty-seven, "Caught in the Toils of the League," mirrors very clearly what happened at the outbreak of the First World War when, on account of old promises of mutual support in case of attack by a third power, Germany came to the aid of the Habsburg Empire. We are reminded of the remnants of the old Bismarckian system of alliances and treaties when Zedekiah, king of Judah, must rush to the aid of King Itubaal of Tyre who had suddenly refused to pay further tribute to Nebuchadnezzar. The war of destruction against Israel had begun. For Jeremiah it is the result of overreliance on rational planning, of worshipping the human mind instead of listening to the will of God. The reader is reminded of the assassination of the German foreign minister, Walther Rathenau, on 24 June 1922 by rightist assassins when, after the defeat by Nebuchadnezzar, Gedaliah, who wants to save everything possible through negotiation and cooperation with the Babylonian king, is slain.

But such direct allusions and parallels are rare. Werfel certainly did not want to interpret the biblical story of Jeremiah as a direct and exact analogy to contemporary Europe. He was more concerned with a more general correspondence to the manner of dealing with problems in modern life, with the problems of intellectual approach rather than one which tries to understand the will of God. Such a connection between biblical times and the twentieth century is already suggested by the introduction of the narrative frame. Werfel's British writer Reeves *is* the Jeremiah of the main narrative. Already at the beginning of the novel Reeves voices Werfel's oft-repeated lamentation about the twentieth century, its failure of seeing a divine connection in all existence, and its failure to comprehend the relationship of events in this world to man's obedience of God's will. This sort of logic he advocated and demonstrated in the fate of an Israel which did not listen to God's warnings as communicated by Jeremiah. Reeves says,

> I might try to deceive myself a hundred times, but I *do* believe firmly in sense and logic. Perhaps it is because I believe in them that I am unable to work any more. . . . Everything that is being written today is based on the contrary belief, on the conviction that there is no meaning or coherence anywhere, and therefore nothing is related to anything else. The others are

free to think that way, but I am not. Deep down in me there still lives the old causal God, the God of logic. (HV 28)

As such, the novel is probably one of the most conservative works Werfel ever wrote. His dismissal of a rational approach to solving political problems in favor of listening for the voice of God would hardly place the people of the twentieth century in an advantageous position to fight contemporary dictatorships!

NOTES

1. This hypothesis was first advanced by Franz Brunner in "Werfel als Erzähler" (Ph.D. thesis, Zurich, 1958) 21–36.
2. Walter H. Sokel, *The Writer in Extremis: Expressionism in Twentieth-Century Literature* (Stanford, Calif.: Stanford University Press, 1959) 228f.
3. Sokel 134. The following discussion sums up some of Sokel's arguments.
4. Sokel 137.
5. Annemarie von Puttkamer, *Franz Werfel: Wort und Antwort* (Würzburg: Werkbund, 1952) 70.
6. R. S. Furness: "A Discussion of *Verdi: Roman der Oper,*" in *Franz Werfel: An Austrian Writer Reassessed*, ed. Lothar Huber (Oxford: Berg, 1989) 143.
7. Furness 139ff.
8. Von Puttkamer stresses this point as well as the close association between Wagner and national socialism in Germany.
9. Lionel B. Steiman: "Franz Werfel," in *Austrian Fiction Writers: 1985–1913*, ed. James Hardin and Donald G. Daviau, *Dictionary of Literary Biography* vol. 81 (Detroit, Mich.: Gale Research, 1989): 304.
10. Franz Werfel, *Der Tod des Kleinbürgers: Erzählung*, Nachwort von Willy Haas (Stuttgart: Philipp Reclam, 1959).
11. Alma Mahler-Werfel, *Mein Leben* (Frankfurt am Main: S. Fischer, 1960) 84. Quote trans. H.W. Not in the American edition.
12. See Martin Dolch, "Vom 'Kleinbürger' zum 'Übermenschen': Zur Interpretation von Franz Werfel's *Der Tod des Kleinbürgers,*" *Literatur in Wissenschaft und Unterricht* 5 (1972): 127–43. This is by far the most well-reasoned interpretation to date.
13. Karl Tober, "Franz Werfel: *Der Tod des Kleinbürgers,*" *Der Deutschunterricht* 17, 5 (1965): 66–84.
14. For the following discussion see Dolch 128.
15. Franz Werfel, *Gesammelte Werke: Erzählungen aus zwei Welten* vol. 2, ed. Adolf D. Klarmann (Frankfurt am Main: S. Fischer, 1952) 45.
16. Franz Werfel, *The Death of a Poor Man*, trans. Clifton P. Fadiman and William A. Drake (London: Benn, 1927) 151.
17. Werfel, *Gesammelte Werke: Erzählungen aus zwei Welten* 2:46.
18. Werfel, *The Death of a Poor Man* 153.
19. Heinz Politzer, "Prague and the Origins of R. M. Rilke, Franz Kafka and Franz Werfel," *Modern Language Quarterly* 16 (1955): 57.
20. Werfel, *Gesammelte Werke: Erzählungen aus zwei Welten* 2:179.
21. Peter Stephan Jungk, *Franz Werfel: A Life in Prague, Vienna, and Hollywood*, trans. Anselm Hollo (New York: Grove Weidenfeld, 1990) 119.
22. Jungk 119.

23. Introduction to Arlt's edition of Franz Werfel, *Der Abituriententag* (New York: Rinehart, 1948) 8ff.

24. Jungk 119.

25. For a more detailed discussion of the models for the characters of the novel see Hans Hautmann, "Franz Werfel, *Barbara oder Die Frömmigkeit* und die Revolution in Wien 1918," *Österreich in Geschichte und Literatur* 15, 8 (1971): 169–79.

26. David Midgley, "Piety as Protest. *Barbara oder Die Frömmigkeit*," in *Franz Werfel: An Austrian Writer Reassessed* 126.

27. As does, for example, Werner Braselmann, *Franz Werfel* (Wuppertal-Barmen: Müller, 1960) 49f.

28. Lionel B. Steiman, *Franz Werfel: The Faith of an Exile. From Prague to Beverly Hills* (Waterloo, Ontario: Wilfrid Laurier University Press, 1985) 49.

29. The German original uses the singular, *Arbeitsbiene* (laboring bee), which can be thus more easily related to Barbara.

30. A similar internalization of values which are present at the very beginning takes place in Hermann Hesse's novel *Demian* (1919), but the group around Demian, in very Expressionist spirit, still believes in the possibility of creating a new world, a belief that ten years later Werfel has given up.

31. Steiman, *Franz Werfel* 49.

32. Midgley 136.

33. Werfel, *Gesammelte Werke: Erzählungen aus zwei Welten* 2:241.

34. Again the German is much stronger in its criticism: "gleichsam nur um sich selbst ein wenig konventionelle Mütterlichkeit vorzuspielen." Werfel, *Gesammelte Werke: Erzählungen aus zwei Welten* 2248.

35. He also recalls Dario's son Mario in *Verdi*.

36. See Leopold Zahn, *Franz Werfel* (Berlin: Colloquium, 1966) 36.

37. Von Puttkamer 76.

38. See Norbert Abels, *Franz Werfel: Mit Selbstzeugnissen und Bilddokumenten* (Reinbek bei Hamburg: Rowohlt, 1990) 89.

39. Adolf D. Klarmann, introduction to Franz Werfel, *Das Reich der Mitte* (Graz, Vienna: Stiasny, 1961) 27f., trans. H.W.

40. In *Orient: Monatsschrift für die Wiedergeburt des Ostens,* ed. Johannes Lepsius, 4–5 (1919): 67–73; and in *Deutschland und Armenien 1914–1918: Sammlung diplomatischer Aktenstücke* ("Germany and Armenia 1914–1918: Collection of Diplomatic Documents"), ed. Johannes Lepsius (Potsdam: Tempelverlag, 1919) 457–67.

41. Lepsius, ed., *Deutschland und Armenien 1914–1918: Sammlung diplomatischer Aktenstücke;* Johannes Lepsius, *Bericht über die Lage des armenischen Volkes in der Türkei* ("Report on the Situation of the Armenian People in Turkey") (Potsdam: Tempelverlag, 1916); and Johannes Lepsius, "Mein Besuch in Konstantinopel Juli–August 1915" ("My Visit to Constantinople July–August 1915"), in Lepsius, ed., *Orient* 1–3:21–33.

42. See George Schulz-Behrend, "Sources and Background of Werfel's Novel *Die vierzig Tage des Musa Dagh*," *The Germanic Review* 26, 2 (1951): 111–23, particularly p. 114. For a detailed account of what Werfel took over from his sources and what he freely invented see this article.

43. Paul Rohrbach, ed., *Armenien: Beiträge zur armenischen Landes- und Volkskunde* ("Armenia: Contributions Regarding Armenian Area Studies and Folklore") (Stuttgart: J. Engelhorns, 1919). In addition, he was able to gain insight into the documents of the French war ministry concerning the rescue of the Armenians by the allied fleet.

44. Jungk 140.

45. Schulz-Behrend 115.

46. Schulz-Behrend 116.

47. See von Puttkamer 86.

48. Steiman, *Franz Werfel* 83.
49. Jungk 143.
50. Steiman, *Franz Werfel* 85.

CHAPTER FIVE

From Austria to Utopia: Prose 1939–46

Embezzled Heaven (Der veruntreute Himmel)

Embezzled Heaven (1939) is the first novel Werfel published in exile. The main character, the Czech maid Teta Linek, has a lot in common with the maid Barbara in *The Pure in Heart* but, in contrast to her, Teta is the center of attention. She does not just represent some omnipresent principle but rather undergoes an important development herself. *Embezzled Heaven* deals not only extensively with the theme of death, but also with Catholic belief, and thus is a kind of forerunner to *The Song of Bernadette* and *Star of the Unborn*. Just like in *The Pure in Heart* and *The Song of Bernadette*, Werfel has chosen a female hero for his novel.

The theme of death figures prominently and follows from the etiology of the story. In the spring of 1938, while already exiled in Paris, Werfel suffered his first severe heart attack which the doctors wrongly diagnosed as nicotine poisoning. Werfel, however, knew very well how serious his situation was. On the first day he felt well enough to get up, he had lunch with Alma. While they were eating, Alma happened to talk about the Czech cook, Anezka Hvizdová or, as Alma called her, Agnes Hwizd, who had been with her for over twenty-five years. "She used to play the zither at night, in secret, spreading the music before her, although she could read neither sharps nor flats and everything came out wrong. She had once fallen victim to a pious fraud."[1] Werfel was so fascinated by what Alma told him about her that he immediately decided to turn it into a book.

The story is a simple one: Teta Linek serves the Argan family for many years. During this time she saves every penny in order to put her nephew Mojmir, the son of her dead brother, through school so that he may become a priest and thus assure her entrance into heaven. After many years and many delays, her nephew finally announces that he will become a priest in Teta's home village Hustopec. When she tries to visit him there, he is not to be found. She ultimately locates him in Prague where he has become a "specialist for propaganda," a jack-of-all-trades who has bilked her out of her money. Back in Vienna, Teta embarks on a pilgrimage to Rome where she meets the young priest Seydel who hears her confession. During an audience with Pope Pius, Teta suffers a stroke and dies shortly thereafter. The narrator, a personal friend of the Argans, supposedly writes this story in Paris where he as well as Seydel are exiled.

Werfel tells the story with much sympathy for the Czech maid, but also with irony about her goal of buying herself into a heaven which she envisions as a kind of permanent pensioner's existence. This irony is equally strong when he writes about Teta's sisters: Kati Zikan, the widow of a chief ticket collector of the Southern Austrian Railways and of several other husbands, and Mila, the retarded younger sister who is in constant fear of being committed to an institution. These are characters who are related to those of the novellas "Poor People" and *The Man Who Conquered Death*. Ironic is Werfel's characterization of the baptized Jew, Kompert, a typical convert, who organizes the pilgrimage with extreme efficiency, with the hope of adding another medal to those already on his chest. Werfel would elaborate on his misgivings about the conversion of Jews later, in *Between Heaven and Earth*.

Making the narrator Theo, a writer and friend of the Argans, not only justifies the ironic tone but also affords him the possibility to insert commentary on the political and spiritual climate of the time.

Apart from the fact that Teta's story is based on Alma's narration of her Czech cook, several other elements also point back to the Werfels. At the beginning of the novel the Argans, a fairly well-to-do Viennese family, suffer the loss of their son Philipp who dies from a fall, and their daughter Doris suffers from encephalitis for years. There is no doubt that Alma's family in many ways served as a model for the Argans. The death of her daughter Manon Gropius was borrowed by Werfel for the death of Philipp. Their house Grafenegg outside Vienna is obviously Alma's house in Breitenstein. The narrator himself, the writer Theo, is none other than Werfel's alter ego—like Werfel he is exiled, and lives in Paris at the time of his writing.

This, however, is the extent of the parallels. The later fate of the Argans does not mirror that of Alma and Franz. At the conclusion of the story the Argans' daughter Doris makes a miraculous recovery, and her father, Leopold Argan, who had been sent to a concentration camp because of his outspokenness against the Nazi regime, is released. The Argans are expected to be able to leave Austria and live comfortably in exile.[2]

In his characterization of the Argans, Werfel endows them with both positive and negative qualities. He praises their hospitality and generosity, their ability for friendship, their ability to live life being true to themselves, their love of life and their fondness of the arts, and above all their love of music. In Werfel's worldview this last element would make them into people who have a sense for metaphysical values. However, the Argans do not, and this becomes clear when their son Philipp dies. In a conversation with the narrator Doris cannot see any order in the universe. She lost this belief a long time ago, and Leopold cannot tolerate watching over his dead son during the night. Leopold Argan comments: "Do we know why we men of the modern age are such godforsaken, miserable creatures? We are on excellent terms with life, on loathsome excellent terms. . . . But with its opposite in that room upstairs [that is, death] we do not know how to get on at all, my dear Theo, none of us, not one" (EH 117). In spite of their uprightness and resistance against the forces of evil (national socialism) the Argans are found wanting. They are tolerably good Catholics but their rationalism makes them blind to true faith. Thus, despite all good intentions, they are representatives of Werfel's modern alienation.

The contrast between them and a true believer becomes obvious when Teta keeps the night watch with the narrator at Philipp's deathbed. Death has no horror for her. It merely marks the transition between this life and the next, and is part of "an ordered universe, in a radiant cosmic system reaching from the skies above to the earth beneath" (EH 122). Teta is the only one in the Argan household who is "on good terms with death" (EH 121). Certainly, her desire to buy herself a place in heaven by paying for her nephew's religious education is naive, but even this scheme has as its basis her belief that eternal life is more important than life on earth. Thus the narrator who, like the Argans, is the representative of modern man, comments: "The realism of which we [modern authors] are so proud consists in proving over and over again that the miracle of reality isn't a miracle at all. . . . You know, there is an element of greatness in Teta. She not only has faith, but also the inflexible will to immortality and salvation" (EH 72). In contrast to modern man, "Teta was a living example of the great art of not taking the transient things of life too seriously, or at least of not becoming hopelessly absorbed in them" (EH 89). Or, as he concludes after Teta's death: "Her whole life was adjusted solely with regard to that which is permanent" (EH 425f.). She pits intuition against science. The materialism, atheism, and nationalism of the former communist and now Nazi Bichler do not impress her.

The entire Argan story which takes up approximately one-third of the book serves only to demonstrate the spiritual superiority of the seemingly simple-minded maid, Teta, over modern man, no matter how sophisticated and how enlightened, humane, and decent.

In spite of the positive features which Teta's character in Werfel's world-view possesses, she is flawed. She believes that she can ensure her salvation by buying herself a priest, thus literally paying off God for all the sins she may have committed. She does not want to sin and even asks her confessor Seydel whether she might not bear some responsibility for Mojmir's character development. Seydel is able to absolve her of such guilt. But by quoting the apostle Paul ("He speaks—I am sure you are familiar with the words—of faith, love, and hope, and declares that of these three love is the greatest," EH 339) he makes her conscious of the fact "that her chief sin lay in her uncharitableness, her lack of love" (EH 343). It is this love that she finally experiences in her relationship to Seydel, a kind of love which again may be flawed—the infatuated love of a seventeen-year-old in a seventy-year-old body—but it is love nevertheless. In comparison, Teta had never loved her nephew as a person and therefore she had never attempted even to see him. Not seeking but entrusting herself to God's guidance, Teta is ultimately saved after she experiences the high point of her life, the personal encounter with the pope, who blesses her by placing his hand on her head.

Teta's adversary is her nephew Mojmir who, from the very beginning, is portrayed very unsympathetically. At the first meeting the ten-year-old boy looks at her "with his peculiarly puffy, slit-shaped eyes" (EH 38), displaying a "vacant countenance" (EH 40). The "slit-shaped eyes" reoccur as a leitmotiv denoting shiftiness and distrust. Even his penultimate apartment building has windows "like slit-eyes" (EH 205). When Teta finally meets him again in Prague, he has "large soft hands" with "manicured nails" (EH 226) like the *Müdir,* the cold-hearted representative of the Young Turks in *The Forty Days of Musa Dagh.* When he follows Teta after she has left his apartment, trying to tempt her one more time, he is dressed like a dandy in expensive modern clothes with loud colors, wearing canary-colored shoes with white uppers.

Since Goethe's drama *Faust,* the devil has appeared in literature and art as such a cavalier, and Werfel obviously meant to stylize Mojmir as the tempter, as the devil himself. He enforces this by giving the chapter in which he describes Teta's final encounter with him the heading: "A Father of Lies" (EH 202ff.). His concubine Mascha also serves to make this equation clear when she tells Teta, "He's a devil. It's the devil himself from whom you've bought your salvation. . . . You've bought your salvation from the devil himself" (EH 229). His smooth persuasiveness, his sophistic arguments which he uses in order to justify himself, to put the blame for his character development on Teta and to regain her confidence, has much in common with the image of the biblical serpent. In stylizing Mojmir as the devil himself, Werfel has made him a successor of Steidler, Ferdinand's opponent in *The Pure in Heart.*

Other overtones hint at Mojmir's spiritual relationship to the Nazis. His door card reads: "M. Linek—Journalist and Propaganda Expert." Both are titles which apply to Joseph Goebbels, the infamous minister of propaganda during the Third Reich, famous for his smooth persuasiveness and his outright lies. When finally he is compared to the shabby artists who offer their portraits to restaurant guests (in the German, not in the American edition), one is reminded of Hitler himself, who used to sell self-painted postcards before he decided to become a politician.

It is in line with Werfel's essays that Teta encounters the clash between the old and the new during her visit to her native village, Hustopec. Here the benevolent times are the ones before the First World War, and the representative of enlightened modernism and nationalism, the teacher Hvizd, is ridiculed when he prophesies that they will soon all be living in a socialist republic (EH 199). While the mythic past and its firm belief in God are personified in Teta, the spirit of the modern times is incorporated by Mojmir. The modern apartment building he used to live in offends her ("She found a quite new building which combined the most modern type of architecture with suburban shoddiness in a way that was impudently offensive," EH 205). Mojmir now lives in a part of Prague which, although old and run-down, is characteristically called the "New World." His self-defense culminates in the excuse that he is simply the victim of modern science and thought, which has supposedly corrupted his mind: "I came under the stern sway of learning, and of modern thought" (EH 225). Werfel leaves no doubt that modern thinking is responsible for the evils of the present, just as he did in his essays. His first judge is Seydel who, in contrast to Mojmir, has been able to fight off all temptation and became a truly Christian priest. Standing at the gates of St. Peter he wonders about the future:

> Seydel thought of the false and horrible doctrines that prevailed in his own country and elsewhere, doctrines that idolized aspects of life and worshipped the flesh in two forms—as blood and race, or as the masses and economic organization. With the astuteness of feeble minds they recognized only one enemy, and that was the Lord of this Whitsuntide, the spirit of love. Youths of all nations were exulting because the spirit had been eradicated, because their lives had been wholly transferred to the animal plane, because the burden of freedom had been removed from their shoulders, because they were not permitted to think and their inner vacuum had been filled with the voluptuousness of hate and speed. What was to

become of a world where one never saw a young face that was illuminated by the *spiritus sanctus*? (EH 314f.)

Seydel has come to the conviction "that the spirit of the age, even the spirit of our own age, is not necessarily in disagreement with our Christian religion" (EH 335). Only the educated people who are unable to lift themselves up to a truly high plane of thinking are in disagreement.

References to the timely political situation which includes the annexation of Austria by Hitler and exile for many people abound throughout the book although, just as in *Cella*, Hitler's name is never mentioned. The beginning of the novel does make reference to the deluge that is "approaching from all sides, the uncanny leaden light of an intellectual and spiritual eclipse" (EH 7). It is the time of the Spanish Civil War (1936–39), and the rise of national socialism in Austria, as is evidenced by the nationalism and anti-Semitism of Bichler, the gardener and caretaker at Grafenegg. In Seydel's opinion the Catholic Church should have publicly come out against fascism in all its forms—a more dangerous heresy of the rich—than against communism, the understandable heresy of the poor. This value judgment clearly mirror's Werfel's own. In his address to the Austrian pilgrims, Pope Pius XI also sees the threat of fascism only in religious terms: "There [in Austria], as in all countries where the German language was spoken, lurked the treacherous seducer who wished to reverse the values instituted by God and put the lowest in place of the highest, transforming the evangel of love into a discord of hatred and luring weak souls with the bait of arrogance" (EH 391). Again it becomes clear that Werfel sees the onslaught of modern ideologies as a battle between God and Satan.

At the end of the novel, when the exiled Seydel and the narrator talk about Teta and her story in Paris, Seydel questions why the narrator has turned Teta's story into a novel. In his eyes a simple human being "cannot be said to have any interest for the reading public" (EH 420). Coming from Seydel, this lack of understanding does not seem to be justified. It serves only to give the narrator the opportunity to voice all of his—clearly Werfel's own—opinions about the wrongs of modern times. The narrator has thus once again taken over the function of serving as Werfel's mouthpiece which had been Seydel's duty:

I cherish an inexpressible loathing for the general state of mind of our modern world, the religious nihilism which, as the legacy of *elites* that have long since disappeared, has been the common property of the masses for three generations. . . . This loathing, this horror at the denial of a spiritual domain, goes back to my youth and even to my childhood. . . . I recognized at a very early age that the revolt against metaphysics is the cause of all our misery. It began, logically enough, among the protestant nations, puritanism led it to victory by exalting time, work and money to the place of the divine Trinity, and we are now witnessing its most frenzied triumph in our own homeland. . . . Our souls refuse to believe any longer in their indestructibility, and hence in their eternal responsibility. The Heaven of which we have been defrauded is the great deficit of our age. Because of it our accounts cannot be balanced, either in the realm of politics or in that of economics, because everything human springs from the same source. (EH 423)

This long tirade is a sermon which summarizes all of Werfel's criticism of the modern world which he voiced in his essays of the 1930s. Of particular interest to us are the last two sentences from the above quote in which he relates his story of Teta Linek's "embezzled heaven" (the German original uses the same word for "defrauded" as for the title, "embezzled") to his more general contemporary criticism. Again it becomes obvious that for Werfel political and social problems exist only on the surface. Their deeper cause is found in spiritual, metaphysical terms. Teta's story is thus lifted to the level of a parable about the ills of the age, lack of faith, and the loss of metaphysical ties to the divine. Later on Werfel confirmed this symbolic significance in a radio interview by pointing out, "The symbolism of 'Embezzled Heaven' is very simple. Old Teta is nothing but the soul of mankind in its naive desire to become eternal which is cheated by modern intellect out of heaven, that is out of its metaphysical anchoring. Only after a long journey of suffering it regains this heaven."[3]

The novel was made into a movie in Germany in 1958. The director was Ernst Marischka. The main parts were played by Annie Rosar, Viktor de Kowa, Kurt Meisel, and Hans Holt.

Cella, or, The Survivors (Cella oder Die Überwinder) and Eine blaßblaue Frauenschrift (A Pale Blue Woman's Writing)

Cella, or, The Survivors, Werfel's novel which was to remain a fragment, and which did not appear as a book by itself until 1982, was written between September 1938 and March 1939, during the first months of the author's exile in France. Werfel had suffered his first serious heart attack and he was actively involved in a kind of journalistic resistance against the Third Reich, writing and signing all kinds of political appeals, pronouncements, and speeches. It is no wonder then, that at this time Werfel was writing a novel that deals with a person very much like himself—an assimilated Jew in Austria—who witnesses the Anschluss and is forced into exile. This is Werfel's most political novel in which he deals with the concrete present, with actual events and realities rather than with spiritual alternatives to a false reality.

A precursor, in some respects, to *Cella* is the fragment "Pogrom" of 1926. Its narrator is an assimilated Jew by the name of Sonnenfels, whose family for several generations has had the right to add the title of baron to their name. Sonnenfels is a high-ranking Austrian official who, toward the end of the First World War, is sent to an eastern Austrian province to supervise the housing of some 100 refugees, most of them Ruthenian farmers, but he finds some who are orthodox Jews. The atmosphere is very much that of *The Pure in Heart*, in which Engländer and Ferdinand visit a famous orthodox rabbi whom Engländer wants to win over for a reconciliation of Christians and Jews. Even a character named Jakob Elkan is present. The basic problem, however, is the same as in *Cella:* just like the hero of Werfel's later novel, Sonnenfels has forgotten that he is a Jew. He is of Catholic faith and treated by his superiors as a gentile. It is not until Elkan asks him for help ("Because the gentleman himself is a Jew"), that he becomes aware of his Jewishness, his otherness.[4]

The fictional narrator of *Cella* is a lawyer, Dr. Hans Bodenheim, from Eisenstadt, a provincial city in Austria's Burgenland close to the Hungarian border. Though Jewish, Bodenheim is married to a gentile, Gretl, and he has a daughter, Cella, a child prodigy who, with the help of Zsoltan Nagy, a former officer and friend of the family, will soon hone her skills as a pianist in the music academy at the residence of Prince Ernst Esterhazy. Bodenheim believes that this event will set Cella on a course to international fame and recognition. In the meantime the threat to Austria from powerful Nazi Germany increases dramatically. Bodenheim, a former reserve officer in the imperial army who, during the First World War, had distinguished himself, is a member of the Iron Soldiers Ring, an organization of former frontline officers. He helps organize the resistance against a takeover of Austria by Nazi Germany by actively participating in a signature campaign and ultimately by trying to organize armed resistance. But it is all in vain, and Austria is annexed. In Vienna, Bodenheim is forced to scrub propaganda slogans off the sidewalk with insufficient tools; he is arrested and taken to prison. Put on the train to the concentration camp Dachau, he is saved by Nagy, who turns out to be a high-ranking Nazi. Bodenheim is removed from the train and is smuggled across the Swiss border, soon followed by Gretl and Cella.

The action thus takes place within one year of Werfel's writing of the novel. In 1937 there were indeed strong aspirations in Austria to restore the old Habsburg monarchy. The Austrian chancellor, Schuschnigg, seemed to favor such leanings. Since he did not receive any significant outside help for the preservation of his country's independence, he was summoned by Hitler to Berchtesgaden on 12 February 1938 and forced to institute an amnesty for national socialists in Austria, appointing a national socialist minister of the interior, Seyß-Inquart. After national socialist-led unrest began on 1 March, Schuschnigg attempted to organize a referendum in favor of Austria's independence but on 11 March 1938 German troops marched into the country, welcomed by many. On Friday 13 March the Anschluss of Austria to the German Reich was publicly proclaimed.

The model for the character of Cella is, again, Alma's daughter Manon Gropius, an extremely gifted child who grew up with the Werfels and who, as mentioned earlier, died of polio in 1935.

These historical and biographical events form the background to the novel but the actors on the historical stage are not referred to by name. The narrator Bodenheim/Werfel consistently refers to the youthful Nazi groups in Austria as "the white-stockings." About Hitler he says: "I shall never pronounce his name as long as I live. That is a small revenge that I owe to my human dignity" (C 54), referring to him as "the dictator" and later as the antichrist and "the great dragon" (C 85). He never uses the terms "Nazism" or "fascism." He does indeed take "revenge" by not according it the respect that would make it a reality, but thus denies national socialism the well-defined ideological, social, or political reality that it did possess.

There is much to the theory that Werfel wanted to indicate that the conflicts and problems described are of a universal nature. Again, it becomes obvious that he has incorporated ideas he had expressed in his essays. It is Jacques Emanuel Weil, the scholar-industrialist, who sees that the young Nazis have incorporated modern man—who lacks individual traits—like the fascists in *The Pascarella Family,* or the Young Turks in *The Forty Days of Musa Dagh:* "But this is something biological, something physical. Don't they all look alike? These are faces off the assembly line, clichéd faces, a collective of faces that has suddenly formed without our noticing it. *One* single mother could have given birth to this entire generation—an inconceivable mother, to be sure" (C 30). And later:

> Just take a good look at the photographs in all illustrated newspapers, whether in America, Russia, Germany, or even Africa. Always the same

type: slender, handsome, muscular, with blank eyes, a small skull, an activist chin, and glittering cinema teeth. Swimming, jumping, running, boxing, motorized from A to Z! All alike. It is easier to distinguish the faces of horses and dogs than the faces of the white-stockings. The collective drive, the hostility toward individual personality, is not the consequence of this remolding, it is the cause, just like the accompanying politics. (C 31)

Their enemy is "Latin and Greek and mathematics and study and speculation and all the printed paper in the world since Gutenberg. The haughty printed paper is the archenemy for it contains the hardest overexertion of mankind" (C 31). The enemy is thus the educational values of old Europe and its middle class. These are the same ideas which Werfel expressed in "Realism and Inwardness" in 1931. Realism is the enemy of human inwardness and creativity, as represented by the rule of radical realism in the Soviet Union and in the United States. Communism and capitalism alike negate the individual, to which in "Can We Live Without Faith in God" (1932) Werfel added national socialism. Consequently, when Austria has fallen victim to national socialism, Bodenheim/Werfel interprets this as the victory of the mob over the spirit of history, the victory of sports over science: "The illiterate soul of this morning had conquered the arrogance of a culture acquired in the course of centuries; the jungle horde drive had conquered the scrupulous conscience of the free personality" (C 114). The members of the SS that Bodenheim meets correspond exactly to the type described earlier in more abstract terms. They are handsome men, at first glance "astonishingly homogeneous representatives of the new master race. Their faces, however, were . . . virtually faceless. . . . Weil was right. Mother Nature seemed to have been confused by technology and was now bringing forth only types instead of individuals" (C 196). Their faces are characterized by "a grandiose blankness and nonindividuality. They appeared to be nothing but transmissions of someone else's will, which, for them, signified life itself. They were as clean, as exact, as mindless, as conscienceless as engines. . . . Motor-men" (C 196). And henceforth he refers to them as such.

The most intelligent spokesperson of the new type of man is Bodenheim's old friend Zsoltan Nagy, a smart, dynamic opportunist, supposedly a monarchist at heart, but someone who believes that the future belongs to national socialism, to modern man. He eloquently defends his choice in the conversation he has with Bodenheim after he saves him from the train to Dachau.

It is not only the Nazis who are attacked in this novel, but Social Democrats as well. Their representative is the sixty-year-old Franz Stich, one of the inmates of the prison cell to which Bodenheim is sent:

He was the epitome of those devout Social Democrats for whom the world had collapsed several years ago—the world whose future they had figured in a very rudimentary way. Childishly worshiping a scientific approach made up of worn illusions, they believed that nothing could halt the ascent of laboring humanity to a reasonable system. They poignantly called themselves materialists because, with their innocent German efficiency, they believed that the tricky material (rays, currents, waves) of which this life brewed can be sorted and regulated. But they were materialists only to the extent that, with the social envy of all little people, they wanted to strike a blow at the dreaming spirit owned by independent sons of the middle class. In a reality of unpredictable shifts and dodges, these people were convinced by their unerring sense of hard facts and proved to be the visionaries of a linear, fairy tale-like progression from chaos and evil to usefulness and goodness. They had good hearts. (C 142f.)

This is Werfel's reckoning with social democracy and its underlying ideology which developed from Marxist theories, as well as from the philosophical materialism and atheism propounded by the popularizer of Charles Darwin's ideas in Germany, the biologist Ernst Haeckel. Although Werfel grants Social Democrats that they have the best intentions, he must reject the underlying ideology of their politics because of its atheistic bent. Consequently, Franz Stich appears as a man of weak character, as a member of the lower middle class whose atheism quickly collapses under the pressure of the imprisonment: "The vain urge for ceremonies, that petty-bourgeois secret, had erupted in Stich's soul, breaking through the thin veneer of libertarianism" (C 196).

The Habsburg Empire and its supporters are the only defenders left against national socialism. But Werfel, significantly, does not refer to national socialism but instead to Prussia as the actual enemy. In accordance with the ideas he expressed in "An Essay upon the Meaning of Imperial Austria" (1937), he sees a Prussian attempt to establish world supremacy as the driving force behind the rise of national socialism. Thus Grollmüller, the leader of the Iron Soldiers Ring, says that "Prussia was arming herself, in order to make up for the defeat she had suffered and to reach out once again for world domination, this time under better conditions" (C 60). The Nazis and SS men in Austria after the Anschluss are uniformly identified by Werfel as Prussians.

Like many other Jews at this time, Bodenheim defends Austria's independence. For him, the Habsburg Empire is, as for Werfel, the ideal. For both, the old imperial army housed no anti-Semitism—a view which contrasts with

Arthur Schnitzler's intimations in *Leutnant Gustl* (*None But the Brave;* 1901). He also realizes that the Iron Soldiers Ring has a "just, but backward-looking cause" (C 65). This is most obvious in the character of the ancient Field Marshall Baron Dudenovich, the honorary chair of the Iron Soldiers Ring who, during the meeting of the association, suffers an attack of weakness. Bodenheim feels "that a ghost had turned us into ghosts" (C 59). He refers to the old Austrian officials of the chancellory in their abraded black suits as "grieving widowers of a grand idea that lay on its deathbed for decades" (C 117), the grand idea being the concept of the supranational Habsburg Empire.

In spite of his involvement in the activities of the Iron Soldiers Ring, which in his heart he realizes is futile, Bodenheim ignores the signs and events of the time by concentrating all his hopes and aspirations on his beloved daughter, Cella. Through her he hopes to succeed in life, although the novel presents her in a very subordinate role; she hardly ever appears and she has nothing substantial to say. Cella is merely the object of Bodenheim's love and the embodiment of his hopes for further emancipation.

The projection of his wishes onto his daughter's career seems justified because Bodenheim feels that the only major success he ever had in life was during his career as an officer during the First World War, when he was personally addressed by Emperor Charles—Franz Joseph's successor—and his name was mentioned in the daily war bulletin. As is obvious from many "asides," Bodenheim suffers from an inferiority complex. His law practice is not doing very well; only when the rich Jacques Emanuel Weil, a local Jewish industrialist, entrusts him with some important business does it seem to succeed but only when it is too late. How does Bodenheim talk about himself? "I, a nobody, have been gifted with Cella" (C 5); or "I suffer from crestfallen admiration for anyone who is greater than I and enjoys more prestige" (C 66); and "I hope that I can at least manage to depict some of my failings truthfully between the lines" (C 72).

Bodenheim also suffers from the fact that he is Jewish. He has been a brave and highly decorated frontline officer, so that in the company of other former officers he feels recognized and equal. But when it comes to his Jewishness, he lives in a state of denial. He has tried to assimilate and has even married a Christian woman, but he is constantly aware of his otherness when he refers to the Jews as "we, that is, our people" (C 7). Not naming Jews as Jews in this case may be interpreted as observing a taboo. The very act of naming would establish the otherness, draw attention much more than the paraphrase does.

Bodenheim's hope for Cella's great success is designed to continue his assimilation, to continue his father's and grandfather's intent to break out of the ghetto of Eisenstadt. The theme of *Cella* is the fate of the assimilated Jews in Austria, their mistaken belief of being accepted, and their realization in 1938 that they have not made any progress. All their endeavors, compromises, and struggles on behalf of Austria during and after the First World War have been in vain. It is then also in this novel that the exiled, assimilated Jew Franz Werfel comes to terms with his own Jewishness and his mistaken former faith in the brotherhood of mankind.

The theme of Jewishness is the topic of a number of conversations during the novel, for example, between Bodenheim and Jacques Emanuel Weil. Weil tries to invalidate some of the arguments of anti-Semitism which are often advanced against Jews by saying, ''We are accused of being homeless materialists and profiteering nomads, with no relationship to the earth that nourishes us. I consider that one of those half-truths or half-lies on which mankind is choking today, and which are far more dangerous than whole lies or whole truths'' (C 100). Later on Weil is sent to the same prison cell in which Bodenheim is being kept. He, the bachelor, had volunteered to be a Nazi hostage instead of his brothers who have families.

The theme of self-sacrifice, of voluntary suffering for one's brothers, in a very literal sense is a very Christian one, and without doubt Werfel has purposely made a Jew its subject. This theme of representative suffering is also apparent in ''The Priest's Tale of the Righted Cross'' (C 162ff.) where Father Ottokar Felix (the American edition mistakenly calls him Ottakar) talks to his fellow inmates in the manner of Boccaccio's *Decameron* novellas, which are told to pass the time during the plague. The story is of the Rabbi Aladar Fürst from the tiny Burgenland village of Parndorf who, together with his Jewish fellow villagers, is driven out of his home by the Nazis right after the Anschluss. Father Felix accompanies the Jewish exiles. When Fürst is asked by his persecutors to kiss the swastika, which they have created by nailing small pieces of wood on a grave cross taken from a churchyard, he quickly breaks off each piece of wood that had turned the cross into the swastika. When he is then compelled to run for the Hungarian border, he is shot to death. This incident moves the Hungarian border units to advance, drive off the Nazis, and to allow the rest of the exiles to enter the country.

In this story the Jewish rabbi restores the cross of Christ and sacrifices himself for his fellow men. Part of it is a conversation between Felix and Fürst about the relationship between Jews and Christians, which mirrors

Werfel's thoughts on the subject, which go back to Pascal, and which later became part of his "Theologumena." Thus the rabbi says to Felix:

I don't know, Father, . . . why the Church is so intent on converting the Jews. Can it suffice for her to win over perhaps two genuine believers among a thousand overambitious or feeble renegades? And then, what would happen if all the Jews in the world would be baptized? Israel would vanish. And thus the only real witness to the divine revelation would vanish from the face of the earth. The Holy Scriptures would turn from a truth documented by our existence into a limp and empty myth like any Greek myth. Does the Church not see this danger? We belong together, Father, but we are not one. The Epistle of the Romans says, "The community of Christ rests upon Israel." I am convinced that the Church will survive as long as Israel survives, but that the Church must fall if Israel falls. (C 165)

Werfel's pet ideas about the relationship between Jews and Christians are present in this paragraph, including his opposition to the baptism of Jews—already expressed in *The Pure in Heart*—and the perceived necessity to keep Jews separate as witnesses to the divine revelation. When Felix feels that "these happy people have to sin, but these unhappy ones can atone" (C 176), it mirrors Werfel's idea—also expressed in "Theologumena"—that anti-Semitism makes Christians sin so that they may then experience God's grace.

In 1942, long before *Cella* was published, Werfel published "The Priest's Tale of the Righted Cross" separately with a different ending. This version he also read as part of the broadcast series "We Fight Back." Here Father Felix, who in *Cella* is sent to Dachau, has escaped to America where he relates his experiences and tries to alert people of the impending tragedy. Because of this happy end to the story, it has lost much of its impact.

In 1969 the German television station SFB (Broadcasting Station Free Berlin) turned the story into a television movie which was first aired on 9 November 1969, the twenty-fifth anniversary of the so-called *Reichskristallnacht,* which marked the beginning of public acts of violence against Jews in Germany. The director was Tom Toelle; the lead parts were played by Martin Berliner (Fürst) and Peter Putz (Felix).

Apart from Bodenheim, there are two other assimilated Jews in *Cella* who illustrate Werfel's point. A man named Goldbaum, the owner of a silk-goods store, is sent to prison. He does nothing but complain about the money he paid out for war bonds and tries to convince his fellow inmates that he is a law-abiding citizen. The second Jew is a very influential banker called Freudreich—the name, just as Bodenheim's, is almost ironic (in German

Freud[en]reich means "rich in joys" and Bodenheim "ground/land home"). Having been put on the train to Dachau, Freudreich, until he is taken to the commander of the transport, insists that his arrest must be a mistake. He returns, badly beaten up, with part of his formerly well-groomed beard torn out, and the naked flesh showing: "Within half an hour it [his face] had been transformed from the well-kept mask of the bank magnate to the terrifyingly sincere countenance of the Wandering Jew. It gazed at us with eyes that were a thousand years old: they knew the entire truth" (C 214). Bodenheim/ Werfel comments:

> They do not mean you, Freudreich! They do not mean me. Whom do they mean? Israel is not a nation, Israel is an order of the blood, which one enters by birth, involuntarily. There is nothing voluntary in Israel. A prehistoric oath must be honored by the children, generation after generation, whether they wish to or not. This order of blood is bound not by space, but by time, in an eternal debt without the benefit of any statute of limitation. The people of 1938 are not exempted from the payment day of the people who lived under Nebuchadnezzar, Nero or Torquemada. (C 214)

Like Werfel, Bodenheim has thus realized that assimilation is only possible on the surface, that he cannot escape his Jewishness and must bear the consequences of his belonging. *Cella* demonstrates most clearly what Otto Friedrich has called the "pre-Holocaust mentality, the mentality of the myriad German Jews who did not understand what it meant to be Jews," who had tried to assimilate to German culture and society and were denying their origins or "that their origins made them forever different from their neighbors."[5]

The comment is also significant in that it is typical for Werfel's treatment of reality. It shows that he is not interested in either just presenting reality or in providing his readers with a social or political analysis; rather, reality for him only plays a role in terms of its theological or metaphysical significance. Thus it is only in this respect that he can interpret Freudreich's demise and through him the persecution of Jews in Nazi Germany.

The novel fragment ends with Bodenheim's crossing the border to Switzerland. The second volume of the novel which was going to take place in exile and therefore was to be called "The Bread of Exile," exists only as a few chapter headings and notes.[6] Bodenheim and, eventually, his wife and daughter would escape to France and then on to America. In the course of this flight Bodenheim learns that Cella was not really his daughter but that Nagy was her father, a fact hinted at several times in the first volume. Nagy also comes to Paris as a spy and is killed there. In the end Cella plans to give a concert at Carnegie Hall, thus closing the circle: the beginning and the end of the novel both feature preparations for a concert.

In March 1939 Werfel had stopped working on the novel because, as he said, according to Adolf D. Klarmann, "the work had been overtaken by the events of the time."[7] One might very well take issue with this statement. The times had not overtaken the novel; rather, the historical events underlying the novel were incomplete and could not be considered with the hindsight of a completed historical development. As Lionel B. Steiman writes, it "could not be concluded in the social and human political terms in which it was so effectively presented." Or, to be more precise:

> All the hopes of her father and therefore the future of his people are fo-
> cused on the grand recital that is to launch her musical career and thus
> release the power of her spirit. But the structural connection between the
> beginning of the novel, which announces Cella's preparation for the re-
> cital, and the political events that take up most of the succeeding action,
> remained to be worked out. Such a connection could be established only
> after "history" had determined the destiny of the Jews in Nazi Europe,
> and *that*, Werfel must have realized, would render the musical motif either
> grotesquely disproportionate to its function or irrelevant altogether. Rather
> than run these risks, Werfel left the novel a fragment.[8]

After all, "no subject is 'taken over by events' unless it is so predisposed by its own limitations. It was the course of events that disclosed the bankruptcy of *Cella's* vision and rendered further development of the novel pointless."[9] This explanation for Werfel's action, or rather the lack of it, sounds more likely than Leopold Zahn's carefully phrased suspicion that Werfel did not write the second volume of *Cella* because Lion Feuchtwanger published his novel *Paris Gazette* (*Exil*), in which he treated the refugee theme as early as 1940.[10] After all, many other novels dealing with this theme continued to be published.

Most striking in the first volume of *Cella* is Bodenheim's attempt to orga-nize a resistance against the Nazi annexation of Austria, hoping rather for the restoration of the Habsburg monarchy. The representatives of this era, how-ever, are old and decrepit, and the future seems to belong to the modern mo-tormen whom Werfel abhorred. When Bodenheim, as part of a delegation of the Iron Soldiers Ring, walks up the stairs to the Austrian Chancellery, min-istry officials pass them in the opposite direction and proceed to smash plas-ter busts of the Habsburg emperors in the courtyard below. The time of the

Habsburg Empire is over and cannot be resurrected by romantic dreamers. Its memory has been replaced by the reality of the Third Reich. As such, *Cella* appears to be Werfel's acceptance that an era which had represented an ideal for him has come to an end, succeeded by the soulless modern motormen of the SS. The apparent success of the Third Reich in 1938 made it impossible for him to continue his story. He had to realize that there was no future for him in Europe in the foreseeable future and that America was not yet a possibility.

In March 1988 the German public television station ZDF (Second German Television) showed a film version of the novel.

The short novel *Eine blaßblaue Frauenschrift* (A Pale Blue Woman's Writing; 1941) which has never been translated into English, is in many respects a counterpart to *Cella* and, in other respects, to *Class Reunion*. The narrator Leonidas, a high-ranking official in the Austrian Ministry of Public Instruction and the son of a poor Latin instructor, has climbed the social ladder by pure luck. He inherited the tailcoat of his next-door neighbor, a Jew who committed suicide because he could not accept the fact that his idol, Richard Wagner, had passed such harsh judgment on his race. With it Leonidas dazzles a rich young heiress, Amelie, at a ball and subsequently marries her. Eighteen years later he receives a letter from Vera Wormser with whom he had had an affair shortly after his wedding, and whom he had left with child. Vera asks him for help to enable a young man of seventeen to complete his high school in Austria since in Germany Jewish students were not permitted to complete their schooling in public schools. Leonidas assumes that it is his own son and agonizes for a day over his old guilt. He is unable to confess it to his wife who instinctively guesses the truth when she sees the letter. Nevertheless, in a council meeting with his boss, the state secretary for public instruction, he suddenly takes a stand in favor of a Jewish candidate for a professorship in medicine. Next day he meets with Vera to learn that the boy is not her own child but the son of her friend. Vera is on her way into exile in Montevideo and Leonidas is able to continue his former life without confession or embarrassment.

Werfel makes it quite clear that Leonidas has failed. He is a social climber who has succeeded in life through skillful adaptation and imitation of the behavior of the upper classes. He has led a double life and his abandonment of Vera Wormser was a crime which ended in their little boy's death. Time and again Leonidas reveals his not-so-hidden anti-Semitic feelings. The most positive character of the story is Vera Wormser, a self-controlled, realistic, and truly educated woman, who does not reproach Leonidas but is simply concerned for the welfare of her friend's son. In describing the hesitation of the Austrian officials to appoint a Jew to the professorship, Werfel portrays the hidden anti-Semitism in the ranks of the public servants and also the fear in Austria not to offend the Third Reich shortly before the Anschluss by appointing a Jew to a high position.

In 1984 the ORF (Austrian Television), in collaboration with RAI (Italian Radio and Television), produced a two-part television film of the short novel. The director was Axel Corti; the main parts were played by Axel Corti, Friedrich von Thun, Gabriel Barylli, Krystyna Janda, Friederike Kammer, and Rudolf Melichar.

The Song of Bernadette (Das Lied von Bernadette)

In writing his novel The Song of Bernadette (1941), Werfel fulfilled a vow he made when he was stranded in Lourdes, attempting to make his escape from the advancing German troops in June 1940. He reports these autobiographical events in his "Personal Preface" to the novel, concluding: "I vowed that if I escaped from this desperate situation and reached the saving shores of America, I would put off all other tasks and sing, as best I could, the song of Bernadette. This book is the fulfillment of my vow" (SB 8).[11] This statement sounds more clear-cut than the actual events, since on the voyage from Lisbon to New York, Werfel wrote in his notebook: "Almost decided on Bernadette," a statement that appears much less certain than his later preface.[12] Werfel's credibility in claiming he wrote the novel in fulfillment of a vow, however, is underscored by the fact that during his writing he did not believe in any future commercial success. Hagiography—the description of the life of saints—is rarely financially rewarding. Further, while working on the novel Werfel conveyed to Alma several times that he believed that hardly anyone would be interested in Bernadette. He could assume this even more so since the United States is a predominantly Protestant country. Consequently, the enormous success of the novel came as a complete surprise to him.

The novel is the story of the young Bernadette Soubirous who lived in Lourdes in the French Pyrenees. In 1858 she had eighteen apparitions of the madonna in the nearby grotto of Massabielle, where a miraculous spring had appeared, leading to a number of miraculous healings which have occurred ever since. After a scrupulous investigation by Catholic Church authorities, Bernadette was canonized in 1933. The novel not only describes Bernadette's life and her visions but also the victory of her beloved Lady over all doubts from the inhabitants of Lourdes and ultimately over all of France. It follows Bernadette to the end of her life as a nun in the convent of Nevers where she dies with the words: *"J'aime...*I love" (SB 564).

Werfel was not the first to write the story of the young Bernadette Soubirous and her visions. Among others, Emile Zola in his *Lourdes* (1884) and Joris Carl Huysmans in *Les Foules de Lourdes* (*The Crowds of Lourdes;* 1908) had transformed it into literature, although they stressed the commercialization and exploitation of the events and the purely emotional, sultry possibilities inherent in the story. Werfel took a different approach, basing his story on a number of historical sources. He used several simplistic tracts sold then in Lourdes, and probably also read the protocols of the municipal administration and of the commission of Bishop Bertrand Sévère Laurence of Tarbes. His main sources, however, were most likely *Les Apparitions de Lourdes: souvenirs intimes d'un témoin* (The Apparitions of Lourdes: Intimate Memories of a Witness; 1899) by Jean Baptiste Estrade, and *Our Holy Shepherdess Bernadette* by the French canon Joseph Belleney. A German priest, Georg Moenius, who was a fellow exile in California, had provided Werfel with the latter work and he advised him on all theological questions. [13]

The vast majority of the many characters of the novel, listed at the beginning of the American edition (at the end of the German one), are historical persons, although Werfel took the liberty of making some changes. [14] Thus there actually was a nun in charge of the novices by the name of Marie Thérèse Vauzous, but she was not the daughter of a general, nor was she Bernadette's elementary schoolteacher in Lourdes. Bernadette met her for the first time in the monastery in Nevers. The historical Dean Marie Dominique Peyramale of Lourdes, who in *The Song of Bernadette* visits her when she is on her deathbed, had been dead for a number of years by this time. Secondly, Werfel does not mechanically report all the historical events in chronological order but selects the most relevant ones. For example, he describes only ten of the eighteen visions. In the preface he justifies these minor liberties with the aesthetic demands of a work of art: "All the memorable happenings which constitute the substance of this book took place in the world of reality. . . . I exercised my right of creative freedom only where the work, as a work of art, demanded certain chronological condensations or where there was a need of striking the spark of life from the hardened substance" (SB 8f.). Although Werfel made minor factual changes he preserved the inner truth, while also keeping much closer to historical truth than, for example, in his *Verdi*. Consequently, *The Song of Bernadette* is a truly historical novel.

The structure of the novel follows the organization of the rosary, an important theme in the story. It is subdivided into five "divisions" (the German original talks about "rows") of ten chapters each. The fiftieth and last chapter bears the heading "The Fiftieth Ave," pointing at the underlying structure—a rosary containing fifty "Ave Marias."

Structurally, the novel can also be considered a repetition of the close examination the Catholic Church conducted to ascertain the validity of the claims that miracles had indeed taken place in Lourdes and that Bernadette was speaking the truth. Thus, in the course of the novel, not only is the truthfulness of Bernadette confirmed time and again, but all her adversaries are similarly disproved and converted. In the process of convincing them the reservations of the skeptical reader are also laid to rest. Seemingly, without taking a stand, Werfel disarms "the Lady's" enemies one by one and thus conducts a kind of retrial of Bernadette Soubirous in which her innocence is proven.

The conservative style and approach to narration complements the plot of the book and its underlying belief structure. It is straightforward, often from the viewpoint of the person the author is describing, in an unusual mixture of third-person narrative and *erlebte Rede*. As so often in his books, Werfel adds a considerable portion of irony, particularly when he talks about the adversaries of Bernadette or, rather, the enemies of the Lady. Nowhere else is Werfel so antimodern in his presentation. He even explicitly disavows modern tendencies in art. He ironically characterizes the enlightened poet, Hyacinthe de Lafite who wants to reawaken the classical alexandrine verse to renewed life by writing an epic, "The Founding of Tarbes"; but this is, to a certain extent, self-irony because in many instances Lafite becomes the mouthpiece of Werfel's own ideas, as in his tirade against modernism. Although the words "naturalism" or "Zolaism" are not mentioned, the references to various novels by Zola are obvious, and one can only surmise that Werfel indirectly wanted to attack Zola's treatment of the Bernadette theme:

It had become the aim of literature to catch up with man's development. Realism was in breathless haste. Writers delineated the lives of locomotive engineers, stokers on ships, factory workers, coal-miners. The least and least striking formed the subject matter of fiction. Analyses were offered of the sexual conflicts of small-town women and the emotional confusions of commercial travellers. To Lafite's deep discomfort the noble tongue of France was spending its time in suburban markets, shops, and bars, intent in servile fashion on catching the precise accent of the most vulgar slang. And all these trivial attempts were still made in the name of the worn and dated metaphysics of progress and science. (SB 530f.)

This attack on naturalism fits in well with the novel because naturalism was the style that tried to apply scientific principals to art. However, since it is the scientific spirit of the nineteenth century that Werfel attacks in *The Song of Bernadette*, he must logically also attack the photographic realism of naturalism. Conversely, two pages later Werfel also attacks modern art because it has a tendency toward abstraction, a concept which, as his essays show, was anathema to him.

The religious and antimodern tone in Werfel's works of the late 1930s and 1940s go hand in hand. Steiman gives as a reason that "this increasingly antirational, antimodern, and antiintellectual tone in Werfel's later work was partly due to his lack of empirical orientation to or understanding of the world in political or sociological terms, and this tendency was accelerated by the natural beauty and political security Werfel enjoyed in his new home."[15] Steiman reproaches Werfel for not being in touch with the actual political events of his time and for writing politically escapist literature by dealing with a nineteenth-century visionary while millions were dying on battlefields. His increased security in the beautiful Californian environment is then, paradoxically, concomitant to an acceleration of spiritualism, which culminated in the novel *Star of the Unborn*.

This tendency toward increasingly spiritual themes is certainly present, but Werfel must be defended against another reproach that with *The Song of Bernadette* he had written a sweetish religious novel, the purpose of which is to further the belief in mystical visions and miracles. This is simply not the case. At no point does Werfel state that he believes in the apparitions of the Virgin Mary to the Soubirous girl. He reports in a seemingly factual, often ironic, manner, leaving it up to the reader to draw conclusions. His implied conclusion is that, even if no miracles happened, if no healings of actual diseases happen today, Lourdes gives hope to many people who have so far lived in utter desperation.

Bernadette Soubirous is presented as a rather normal child who lives in poverty because her father, a former miller, has a weak character and is a poor manager of his affairs. She is a poor student in school who does not even have the most rudimentary knowledge about religious matters. Werfel stresses, however, her utmost honesty and her ability to disarm adversaries with her quick-mindedness and her honest responses. She does not try to advance her own social standing in the world with her visions and wants nothing more than to be a normal girl, to become a maid, and have a husband and children. Bernadette is thus the victim of her visions, thrown into the limelight of local and, ultimately, state politics against her will. Later, in the convent at

Nevers, she is the victim of the cruel disbelief of her spiritual adviser, Marie Thérèse Vauzous. Bernadette's claims about her vision are convincing because she does not ever claim to have seen the madonna. She simply talks about the "Lady." Her descriptions are those of encounters between a loving child and a beloved lady, whose strict orders are followed and nothing more.

It must be emphasized, however, that Werfel is not concerned about proving the validity of the miracles; he does not want to demonstrate or convince the reader that they really happened. What is at stake for him is the truthfulness of Bernadette, the genuineness of her faith and belief. Thus he does not use the word miracle, just as Bernadette never claims to have seen the madonna. He wants to demonstrate the victory of faith over science, of the spiritual worldview over intellectual reasoning. Bernadette is merely the innocent victim of heavenly grace (or curse?). What distinguishes her is the ability to allow the visions to happen to her, to obey absolutely and give witness absolutely truthfully and without ever doubting. Using the example of Marie Thérèse Vauzous, whose good works do not result in the divine grace, Werfel demonstrates that one cannot force God's grace. She cannot believe in Bernadette until she sees that the young nun is suffering from tuberculosis of the bones, also having been graced with suffering in imitation of Christ.

The novel describes at length the reactions of various people in town who are faced with the events at the grotto of Massabielle: the parents who are embarrassed at first and view the events as just one more trouble they are encountering in life; the seamstress Peyret who, with the mind of a detective, would like to convict Bernadette of trying to mislead the public; Madame Millet, a rich, bigoted widow who is eager to be one of the first to witness a series of miracles and who first wants to believe that the lady is none other than her deceased niece. Then there is the group of city dignitaries who meet at the Café Français, or, as some people call it more appropriately, Café Progrès. As this popular name indicates, most of the clientele are representatives of the modern scientific, enlightened age: Ducan, the proprietor of the café who echoes the enlightened wisdom he has gained from the many newspapers to which he subscribes; the poet Hyacinthe Lafite who would prefer to believe in the apparition of some mythical nymph rather than in the madonna; the doctor Dozous, a municipal physician, who takes a scientific approach and who, on that basis, cannot but attest to the sanity and truthfulness of Bernadette; the revenue officer Estrade, a rational man who nevertheless allows himself to be convinced. Then there is the imperial prosecutor, Vital Dutour, and the city's mayor, Adolphe Lacadé, who wants Lourdes to become a modern spa. "Lacadé's motive, on the other hand, was the most sincere and strongest of the whole age, namely, good business'' (SB 330). His plans for modernization and for the economic prosperity of the city seem thwarted when it turns out that the water from the spring in the grotto of Massabielle is, in chemical terms, nothing but tap water; but as a shrewd politician and a representative of the age of progress he quickly adapts, developing Lourdes into a modern place of pilgrimage.

A third group are the representatives of the Catholic Church who are, without any exception, sympathetically drawn. The fact that Werfel characterizes them as extremely critical and even more distrustful than the representatives of reason makes Bernadette's ultimate victory even more convincing. There is Marie Dominique Peyramale, the choleric local priest, whose irritable and overbearing personality makes it so hard for Bernadette to assert herself. Even harder to convince is his bishop, Bertrand Sévère Laurence of Tarbes. These representatives of the Church turn out to be much more human and likable than the representatives of the state. Thus the bishop of Tarbes easily wins any argument over the Baron Massy, the prefect of the Hautes-Pyrénées. All attempts by the state representatives to discredit Bernadette and to brush her visions aside fail because of their ineptitude. Hence, representatives of the local gendarmerie, particularly the chief of police, Jacomet, as well as the imperial prosecutor, Vital Dutour, both make fools of themselves. Emperor Napoleon III is easily defeated by his emotional dependency on his bigoted wife, Empress Eugénie. Werfel displays the same ironic stance toward them as he does vis-à-vis the simplistic representatives of the Enlightenment in the Café Progrès. But readers identify more easily with the sympathetically drawn representatives of the Church and reasonable men such as the revenue officer Estrade. Thus the reader who begins with a very skeptical attitude at the beginning is gradually convinced together with these persons.

It is through these characterizations alone that Werfel succeeds in making Bernadette's case convincing. Also obvious, however, is that in *The Song of Bernadette* two forces are facing each other representing Werfel's pet ideas: belief versus modern science. Already in his preface Werfel states: ''Even in the days when I wrote my first verses I vowed that I would evermore and everywhere in all I wrote magnify the divine mystery and the holiness of man—careless of a period which has turned away with scorn and rage and indifference from these ultimate values of our mortal lot'' (SB 9).

Werfel's sympathies lie with those people who are ready to accept the existence of the metaphysical on this earth: for example, the many simple and poor people who come to the grotto hoping for a miracle to happen. For them the miracle has an important and very real function: ''All these heavy-handed peasants, shepherds, cottars, road-menders, lumbermen, slate-miners seemed suddenly overwhelmed by the dread-fraught recognition of man's ship-wrecked and outcast estate upon this earth. For once they refused to accept the curse of suffering and torment like oxen at the plough. Like the literally shipwrecked, their souls demanded to see amid the endless fogs of mortality a heavenly flag of rescue—a miracle, the February blooming of the rose" (SB 225); or: "By virtue of an unaccountable intoxication thousands had hoped that here in Lourdes a thing would come to pass that would lend meaning to the meaninglessness of life and demonstrate their undemonstrable faith" (SB 235). Inherent in such a statement is Werfel's idea that this world does not make sense unless it is more than a well-functioning mechanical apparatus. It gains meaning only if it is part of the divine plan, is able to connect earthly existence with God: "Belief in the divine is nothing other than the substantially convinced recognition of the fact that the world is meaningful, that is to say, a spiritual world" (SB 306). By contrast, he refers to "modern nihilistic tendencies" of the modern age which is ruled by "the disciples of Voltaire" (SB 168), to the "official deism and non-official nihilism of the age" (SB 420), the regnant philosophy to which "the miracle of Massabielle give[s] the lie" (SB 430).

In his essay, "Writing *Bernadette*," Werfel even makes an attempt to see the novel as part of the contemporary struggle between good and evil so obvious in the ongoing Second World War. Upon further reflection, however, it seems a bit farfetched to classify *The Song of Bernadette* in this manner. After all, the majority of Americans did not believe that they were fighting against rationalism but against fascism. Yet the author's remarks are interesting because they most clearly place the novel into Werfel's old theoretical framework, that is, the fight between religion and "radical nihilism":

> Not a material but a spiritual principle is at stake in this, the only genuine world war. Today the fronts are still confused and the further developments are not to be foreseen. On the one side stands radical nihilism which no longer regards the human being as the image of God but as an amoral machine in a completely meaningless world. On the other side, on our side, stands the metaphysical, the religious concept of life, the conviction that this Cosmos was created by the spirit and that a spiritual meaning lives and breathes in every atom. It is indeed a war between the principles of spiritual life and death.

In this general war between the two principles, which he addressed and identified more explicitly in *Cella, or, The Survivors, The Song of Bernadette* sets out to justify this "metaphysical, the religious concept of life" by demonstrating the existence of the divine, of its presence in this world:

"The Song of Bernadette" is a jubilant hymn to the spiritual meaning of the universe. Through the medium of this simple and charming personality, we see how, even in our age of skepticism, divine powers are at work and how they raise an ignorant creature, favored by grace, beyond her own natural limits. Although the story takes place in a Catholic milieu it is not only bound to the Catholic form of life but concerns equally all men—Protestants and Jews—all men whose hearts intuitively recognize the divine powers which in rare moments gloriously transfigure our daily reality.[16]

It is the poet Lafite who, toward the end of the novel, explains what Bernadette's visions accomplished and proved. Believing that he will soon fall victim to cancer, he looks back on his own life and sees its emptiness. At this honest moment of self-examination, he expresses Werfel's ideas by saying that he believes "the past forms of thought will some day be the future forms and may look down with a smile upon our entire critical period" (SB 549). He does not believe any more "in a heaven on earth to be provided by better laws and machines" (SB 549). When in his speech of 1933, canonizing Bernadette, Pope Pius XI talks about "the fever of maniacal false doctrines . . . threatening to plunge the human spirit into bloody madness" (SB 574), he is talking precisely about these doctrines, fascism and communism, which, according to Werfel, are the outgrowth of radical nihilism: "In the battle against this, which man must win, not only did Lourdes stand like a very rock, but the life of Bernadette Soubirous retained its prophetic activity within time" (SB 574). In these lines Werfel explains the relationship between the story of the simple girl from the Pyrenees and modern times, and points out her symbolic significance in the eternal fight between the two worldviews as Werfel saw it. At the end of the penultimate paragraph of the novel Werfel writes: "Under the heaven of Rome, where the saints were gathered to welcome their new comrade, flew a military plane" (SB 575). Thus even in the heavens the dangers of contemporary Italian fascism clash with the powers of religion.

The novel was turned into an extremely successful movie in the United States in 1943. The young Jennifer Jones played Bernadette Soubirous. The director was Henry King. In 1990 a French remake under the title *Bernadette* was released with Sidney Penny playing the title heroine and Jean Delannoy directing. Werfel's name, however, does not even appear among the credits.

Star of the Unborn (*Stern der Ungeborenen*)

Werfel's voluminous novel *Star of the Unborn* (1946) is in many respects the sum total of his religious and humanistic thinking. Similar to Hermann Hesse's *Das Glasperlenspiel* (*Magister Ludi;* 1943), it is also a projection of his ideas into a distant future. It was composed in several stages: a draft of the first five chapters was written during May 1943 in Santa Barbara; in spring 1944 the final version of the first three chapters was completed. In the fall of 1944 the second part of the novel was written and in August 1945 the third and last part. The thirteenth chapter appeared separately in the June issue of the periodical *Neue Rundschau* with the dedication, "The following chapter of my new, unpublished book I am dedicating to the great poet of the Germans and of mankind, Thomas Mann, in unwavering admiration at the occasion of his seventieth birthday." Twenty-four of the twenty-six chapters of the novel originated almost simultaneously with the translation by Werfel's American friend, the Germanist Gustave O. Arlt. The last two chapters were translated immediately after Werfel's death. Writing the novel was indeed a race against death—a private doctor was often at his side. Since death was before Werfel's eyes, it is not surprising that the theme is omnipresent in the novel.

The book opens with a motto from the classical writer Diodorus's book *Famous Burial Places* (ca. 350 B.C.): "If it is the concern of politicians and rhetoricians to interpret the intrigues of everyday life, it is the business of poets and story-tellers to visit the creatures of myth and fable on their islands, the dead in Hades, and the unborn on their star" (SU 1). Following this advice, which is well in line with all the classical allusions the novel contains, Werfel does just that, visiting the unborn on their star: as a result of a seance, F.W., as he calls himself, is brought to life by his old friend B.H. (Willy Haas) in the year 101,943. His appearance, in formal evening attire, is a present to the couple Io-Do and Io-La, who are soon to be married. F.W. spends a total of three days, each constituting one part of the novel, in this world experiencing its form of life and ultimately the destruction of its culture. His first impression is one of complete harmony; all problems of the twentieth century seem to have been overcome. The Astromentals, as the inhabitants call themselves, have no material needs; they receive all their food and clothing from the Worker and his many offspring who produce them by conjuring them out of the universe. They live in the underground dwellings of a megalopolis in a world with one state and one language. There has been no war in many thousands of years. They travel effortlessly on earth, not by moving their bodies to their destinations but by moving the destinations to them. Since all material and technical problems have been solved, the sole purpose of life seems to have been reduced to playfulness. They are able to travel far into the universe and their rulers are nameless wise men who are selected because of their lack of interest in power. But the problems are the same as those of the twentieth century: the younger generation rebels against the older one. A shot from an ancient revolver is fired, and starts a war between the young men and the inhabitants of the outlying jungles (which are reminiscent of nineteenth-century society) and the Astromental world is destroyed. F.W. accompanies his new friends to the Wintergarden deep inside the earth where people, instead of dying, regress to the state of babies and finally become daisies. F.W. manages to escape back to the surface of the earth and finally to his own time, 1943.

Instead of writing in a matter-of-fact style, dryly reporting what his character F.W. supposedly saw and experienced in the future world of the Astromentals, Werfel tries to introduce a number of playful stylistic elements to loosen up the often theoretical, theological-mystical discussion. At least one critic has argued that one of the chief attractions of the novel is the contrast between its deep, philosophical, and theological content and the consciously applied style of a naive travelogue.[17] Thus, Werfel supposedly includes his first chapter only "because it seemed inappropriate to begin this opuscule with a Second Chapter" (SU 3), an illogical statement since the second chapter would then be the first one. It is a kind of toying with the reader which reminds us of certain works by German Romanticists such as E. T. A. Hoffmann's *Kater Murr* ("The Educated Cat"; 1820–22). When right under the chapter heading Werfel always briefly summarizes the content of the chapter, he adapts a practice that goes back to older times too; for example, to the baroque and picaresque tradition of Grimmelshausen's *The Adventures of a Simpleton* (1668). His playful attitude becomes most obvious in his conversations with the supposed reader whom he implores, for example, not to spoil his reading pleasure by jumping ahead to the last pages of the book; whom he includes as sitting with him in the park of the Worker; and whom he finally considers "a magnanimous friend who shares my intellectual curiosity as well as my disdain for journalistic nonsense" (SU 247). The novel is also filled with humor, both successful and unsuccessful, the latter in the scene when F.W. encounters Sur, the talking dog of his Astromental hosts. He displays humor when he explains the anatomical absurdity of the notion that angels do not have wings. Humorous also are scenes such as the one in which F.W. rejects the advances of the beautiful Lala until it is too late. The most humorous, satirical, and stylistically successful scene is the exorcism that F.W. is subjected to before he is allowed to talk to the Grand Bishop. In the satirical speech by an exorcising monk, Werfel adapts a style typical for many utopias by going through the entire history of heresies, striking out against rationalism, Marxism, positivism, psychoanalysis, vitalism, and even the poet Stefan George and his circle. This satirical diatribe is directed against all those philosophers and scientists whom, in *Between Heaven and Earth,* he characterized as representatives of "radical realism" and "naturalistic nihilism"; in short: against "modernism in all its forms."[18] Later on he continues his satire of twentieth-century literary schools when he describes the Sympaian, the Astromental version of opera, lashing out against naturalism, symbolism, futurism, expressionism, and surrealism, against the literary avant-garde and the Bohème.

Even his allusions to Hitler, on whose unsuccessful bid for world domination B.H. reports, are satirical. But no humor is present in the parallels to other twentieth-century events and phenomena. Thus the shot that the young bridegroom Io-Do "accidentally" fires during the festive Sympaian, killing the Mutarian and triggering the war that leads to the destruction of Astromental culture is likened to the shots at Sarajevo which set off the First World War: "That war too had been precipitated by a shot fired by a fanatical and irresponsible youth" (SU 596). F.W. says of Io-Do even earlier: "In its time this widely prevalent type was called fascist" (SU 435).

Among the many other parallels Werfel draws between Astromental civilization and the twentieth century, the most important one is the Wintergarden. It is not what the Astromentals want to believe it to be, namely a kind of institution that gives man death with dignity but an institution that has as its historical model the national socialist program for euthanasia. Moreover, the parallels to the annihilation camps of the Third Reich where millions of Jews were being murdered at the time of writing are specifically mentioned by Werfel. It cannot be accidental that bath attendants are taking care of the newcomers to the Wintergarden—Jews were led to their death under the pretense of having to take showers. When he talks about the victims of unsuccessful retrogenesis, the Catabolites, Werfel specifically mentions the parallel to national socialist concentration camps: "I shall not claim that the sight of the Catabolites was worse or even half as bad as the sights that many of my contemporaries attested in the horror camps of Buchenwald or Maidanek" (SU 561).

One of the most marked stylistic elements is often humorous recourse to the ancient Greek and classical mythology. Thus most of the terms used for "new" Astromental phenomena use Greek words or word stems. Not only does the motto point to the world of classical antiquity, the visit to the Wintergarden in particular is referred to as a "Tartarophania, a sightseeing tour of the Underworld, such as even the authors of the 'Odyssey' and the 'Aeneid' had not described" (SU 548). F.W. uses an Ariadne's thread to find his way back, encountering everywhere "mythological realities" (SU 566). After its destruction, the center of the Astromental world, the Djebel, is finally revealed as Gaea's eye.

B.H. represents Willy Haas, who was also exiled in northern India (B.H. even becomes acquainted with the teachings of reincarnation in Tibet). Franz Werfel had not seen him since 1939 and was never to see him again. In the same vein it is Werfel who is hiding behind the character F.W., although one should remember that the first-person narrator F.W. is also Franz Werfel's creation. Thus the author can make fun of F.W.'s reactions, of his reluctance with Lala, of his embarrassment because of his dress. F.W. supposedly has died around 1943. He is resurrected in full evening dress—Werfel had decreed that he wanted to be buried in his tailcoat, together with an extra pair of glasses. The Astromental world where F.W. comes back to life is supposedly California, where Werfel was similarly at home. Indeed, it is to precisely Werfel's own address at the time of his writing the novel (610 North Bedford Drive in Beverly Hills, close to a church) to where he is transported back at the very end of the book. There are references to Werfel's youth in Prague, to the agony he suffered when his and Alma's son was born, to his time and rank in the military, to his exile, and to the Order of Merit for Art and Science that the Austrian government had bestowed upon him in 1937 and which the resurrected F.W. is wearing. Willy Haas "was astonished to find many of the long conversations he had had with Werfel in their youth in Prague reproduced verbatim in the book."[19] Introducing himself as F.W. is a skillful narrative trick which allows Werfel to make his own self the subject and the object of cognition at the same time. Since he is not just an uninvolved spectator but also a participant in the affairs of the Astromental world, his story is vivid, and his trip is a final reckoning with himself and his own time in the face of death.[20]

In the subtitle to the German edition—the American edition does not have one—Werfel calls his novel a "Reiseroman" (travel novel) or, as he contemplates on the first page of the book, "a kind of travelogue" (SU 3). At the beginning of the thirteenth chapter he takes up his discussion of genre again, contemplating: "This is not only an account of an exploration. If I call it a travel novel I am not falsifying truth just to keep the reader's interest. While an account of an exploration is a simple circle, a travel novel is an ellipse with two foci. The second focus is the traveler's ego'' (SU 267). But he stresses again that he has written his novel not in order to tell thrilling adventures but ''to acquaint his readers with an unknown world, with a completely blank spot on the map of the most distant future'' (SU 267). Yet, as he points out later on in the same chapter, unlike Jules Verne, he deals with an Astromental world and not with a technically materialistic one (SU 291). In this brave new world all technical problems, all material ills have been solved, and the question is whether people are happy after they have had time and opportunity to solve all other problems, including those of life and death. Since Werfel's answer, as we shall see, is clearly a negative one, his novel does not describe a positive counterworld, a wishful world, but a negative one, a dystopia rather than a utopia.

As preparation for the novel, Werfel consulted scientific works from astronomy, astrology, geology, history, mathematics, philosophy, and physics. In addition, he read a number of other, older utopias from the Anglo-American tradition, particularly H. G. Wells's *The Time Machine* (1895), Aldous Huxley's *Brave New World* (1932), and Olaf Stapledon's *Last and First Men: A Story of the Near and Far Future* (1930). As James L. Rolleston has pointed out, Stapledon's novel

> is especially relevant because the basic motif of Werfel's book is prefigured here, the conception of twentieth-century people as ''first men'' and the possibility of interaction between the beginning and the end of human time. Very many of the more ''science-fictional'' components of *Star of the Unborn* can be found in Stapledon's work: telepathy, mental travel, advanced cosmology including mountain-like buildings like the Djebel, sudden astronomical occurrences like the transparency of the sun which alter the premises of human existence; further, the various extreme effects of a social or anthropological kind, the oscillation between refinement and animality, the pursuit of perfection and the unceasing debate about death and immortality.[21]

In an interview with the *Santa Barbara News-Press,* Werfel pointed out the relationship to *Gulliver's Travels* and Dante's *Divine Comedy*[22]—B.H., for example, is repeatedly mentioned as F.W.'s Vergil. In contrast to other German utopias of the time, including Hermann Hesse's *Magister Ludi* and Ernst Jünger's *Heliopolis* (1949), *Star of the Unborn* is more concrete, not only because of the contrast between the Astromental and the real world, but also because of the detailed description of the utopia.[23] But, as Steiman points out: "Unlike the utopian visions of Orwell and Huxley, in which the horrors found in the future have evolved directly from the antihuman consequences of institutions and technologies of the present, Werfel's utopia is one in which the opposite has taken place. Institutions and technologies have developed to their logical extremes, but always under human control and with a progressive human end in view."[24] The Astromental world is not a nightmare of twentieth-century civilization, the epitome of the total reign of technology in which man has become totally dehumanized but rather, in line with Werfel's worldview, the focus is man himself. Yet here too Werfel's idea is that all progress requires some loss so that the sum total remains the same—no true progress is possible. Even the planet itself is changed: the oceans have shrunk, mountains and valleys have almost disappeared, everything is covered by a kind of grey lawn. The variety of plants and animals has been drastically reduced to a few species which, moreover, look artificial. Man himself has been reduced in number with pronounced biological changes: he has hardly any growth of hair, and the insides of his hands are without lines. His life has been extended to almost two hundred years and there are no diseases, but fertility is low; one child per couple has become the norm. Drinking liquids of various colors in small quantities has supplanted opulent meals, also not necessarily a positive development.

Not only has the abolition of material needs and problems created an impoverishment of life but the mental problems of humanity persist. Such problems, in Werfel's view, are not those of material well-being but of finding the right relationship to God. Thus, in his view, twentieth-century communism and nationalism both asked the wrong questions and consequently had to give the wrong answers to the problems of mankind. It is not surprising that in this respect Werfel also makes the grand bishop the mouthpiece of his judgments when he declares: "The world without economics is a paradise. But what's the use when man isn't paradisiac. He is the content which he pours into every form" (SU 636).

Star of the Unborn presents a world devoid of material problems and one in which nationalism with its attendant crises has been overcome. The world has been unified into one large state and there is no more power struggle. However, the eternal questions remain unsolved: for example, the question whether God's existence can be proven. The answers given by two Astromental professors whom F.W. is called upon to judge are just as trite or sophistic as those answers given by the twentieth-century philosophers. Taken one step further, the Astromental world demonstrates that the seemingly perfect solution to man's material problems moves man farther away from God rather than closer to him. Thus the head of the Catholic Church, the grand bishop, who is the most eminent figure of the entire Astromental world, says to F.W.: "We are agreed, therefore, that all human history is the history of the consequences of the fall of man, that is, the history of progressive alienation from God. No matter how pitiful the conditions in the nineteenth and twentieth centuries may have been, they were still better by a hundred abysses, by a hundred millennia than those of today" (SU 245). The sin of the Astromentals is that they have tried to invalidate God's curse. They do not toil to take care of their own well-being; most of them have only one child, and their basic fatelessness is indicated by the fact that their hands do not show lines. Worse still, they have tried to defeat death—a word that they no longer use— by deciding when they wish to enter the program of retrogenesis in the Wintergarden. In the opinion of the grand bishop, this is their "central sin" (SU 238). According to the teaching of the Christian churches it is clear why: life is a gift to man from God and it is up to God to take it away when he chooses. Furthermore, death is part of the curse resulting from the Fall and to circumvent it would actually imply a defiance of God's will, a rebellion against God. Thus the grand bishop says to F.W.: "The old civilization of which you spoke, my son . . . at least bore suffering and death and thus accepted the curse of the archangel. Today's civilization, however, . . . which calls itself Astromental, is a deceitful and tricky attempt to escape that curse by insidious intrigue—the curse that enjoins us to eat the bread of the earth in the sweat of our brow and in sorrow, and to return humbly to the dust whence we came" (SU 246f.). It is F.W. himself who, after the escape from the Wintergarden, draws a similar conclusion in a conversation with B.H.: "But you mustn't forget that for me and my time death was a holy ordinance of God, and man has no business meddling with it. I certainly don't minimize the idea and the practice of your detour around death, but its blasphemous character can't be denied any more than its abstruseness and unnaturalness" (SU 608).

Any redemption of the Astromental world, any new beginning that could result in its renewal or salvation must, therefore, begin with the acceptance of death as part of the life ordained by God. This is precisely what happens toward the end of the novel: Io-Runt, the young star dancer in whom F.W. much earlier had recognized the reincarnation of his own dead child, has saved the Isochronion (a sort of Astromental Holy Grail) out of the burning Djebel. Since his space suit was not sealed properly he has suffered severe burns and knows that he will die from them. His father has a bathtub full of retrogenetic humus brought to him and the Animator, as he is called, asks him to take the bath to alleviate his pain. But Io-Runt rejects this temptation and opts for pain and a natural death. F.W. comments: "In the reacceptance of natural death and pain by the little star dancer a new future had taken the place of the old future" (SU 632). There is no doubt that the dying of Io-Runt imitates the exemplary, redemptive death of Christ, which will give the world another chance with a new relationship to God. The text points out this parallel when an attendant friar reports Io-Runt's death to the grand bishop and F.W. uses Christ's words: "It is finished" (SU 641). The final judgment of the grand bishop about the future of man in the Astromental world is therefore a hopeful one: "we are not only alienated from God through the lapse of time but are also brought nearer to God through the lapse of time. That is because we are moving farther and farther away from the beginning of all things and closer and closer to the end of all things" (SU 642). Thus in his two conversations with the grand bishop, F.W. receives first a warning and finally consolation from him.[25] The Christian worldview stands at the end of the novel as its—that is, Werfel's—message.

Not only Christianity has survived the next 100,000 years, Judaism has too. When, at the end of the novel, the grand bishop asks F.W. what—after his return to his twentieth century—contemporaries will find hardest to believe regarding the Astromental world, he replies: "They will definitely *not* believe . . . that Your Lordship and the Jew of the Era exist" (SU 638). And when he is asked why they shouldn't believe "this most modest of all facts" he replies: "Simply because this most modest of all facts cannot be believed without belief in the supernatural. Unless you believe in the first, last, and final revelation of immutable truth through the Old and New Testament, the assumption that the Church of Christ and Israel have survived through the decamillennia is not only an old wives' tale but an offensive idea" (SU 639). Just like in his "Theologumena" which, after all, were written at about the same time as the novel, Werfel insists that the Jews should not cease to exist as a separate entity in order to fulfill the divine plan of salvation. Conversely, in the opinion of the Jews, the Catholic Church will exist just as long as the Jews do. As the Jew of the Era puts it: "The Church will live as long as we live . . . to testify for Abraham, Isaac, and Jacob, who first acknowledged the true God" (SU 256f.). Or, as the Church says: "Israel will live as long as the Church, that is, to the end of things, to testify for the Messiah" (SU 257). Werfel has thus projected his ideas concerning the fate and the task of the Jews into the future.

Werfel repeats his ideas about different types of Jews—already discussed in *The Pure in Heart*. The Jews of the Astromental age are subdivided into two characteristic groups: doctors and political activists. "The attention of both groups was continually centered on human suffering; the more inoffensive of these was concerned with the cure of curable suffering, the other, the more dangerous, with the restitution of incurably injured injustice" (SU 624). Whereas Minioman, the Jew of the Era, tries his skill as a doctor to help the injured star dancer, his son, Jo-Joel, has joined the inhabitants of the jungle, acting as an interpreter and would-be revolutionary. Werfel makes him a Jew whose strained attempt at assimilation is ill-fated. It leads neither to his personal recognition nor to his happiness, and its result—the destruction of the civilization of the Astromentals—is questionable. Once again Werfel has painted a critical picture of the young revolutionaries of the 1920s. Since man has remained the same, the same types of man will be encountered in this Astromental world too.

Werfel uses this new world to demonstrate his thesis of the "spiritual destiny of this world" (SU 110). Thus the geocentric philosophy has been confirmed. When he and B.H. join a class of young boys to travel to other planets, F.W. even encounters real angels. This may be half tongue in cheek, but the message is clear: the spiritual reveals itself in the progression of time. It is fitting then that the most spiritualized human being of the Astromental world, the all-knowing High Floater reveals to F.W. that "the angels in heaven are communications of that which is outside the world with that which is inside the world" (SU 360) and that "the whole has the shape of man" (SU 361) which is neither male nor female but is "wedded to itself" (SU 362). Man is the measure of all things, and there is harmony between the universe and man, the divine and the human; or: "whatever may become of a given society, the spiritual man-centeredness of the universe persists, a challenge for all future societies as they strive to achieve reciprocity and give to man the shape of the whole."[26]

The grand bishop's answer may also be turned around to signify that man is a universe on a small scale. Important is the correspondence between man and the universe: the universe as man and man as the universe.[27] This correspondence is also made clear when, during his excursion into the universe, the teacher tricks his class by sending them into an atom instead. What is above the earth is also on the earth and is present in man. Only such correspondence enables man to travel through the universe and to adapt to its conditions. All the travels F.W. and B.H. undertake in the Astromental world are thus only possible because of the symbolic correspondence between the microcosm and the macrocosm.

In contrast to the "so-called realistic eras that stubbornly refuse to acknowledge the divine duality of reality—as, for example, the twentieth century'' (SU 135), the Astromental age tries to demonstrate the divine meaning behind even everyday things. The people who have traveled the farthest into space are the ones who marvel the most about God's creation.

Would it not be for the new developments of the jungle—seemingly old-fashioned civilizations which, in the eyes of the Astromentals, constitute a return to long-overcome forms of primitive civilization and, in the eyes of the young Jo-Joel, centers of renewal—the Astromental world would seem to have reached a plateau at which there is no historical development any more. But the Young Turks of the Astromental world have become sick and tired of the artificiality of the Astromental culture. Even the young brides are defecting to the jungle, out of a deep-seated longing for nature. After the destruction of the Astromental civilization a new cycle of history will begin. In addition to this hint at a cyclical development of history, Werfel uses B.H. to elaborate his view of history. B.H., F.W.'s friend who has been reincarnated many times, is able to report the course which history has taken after F.W.'s death: the second half of the twentieth century supposedly "witnessed a temporary victory of the metaphysical tendency over skepticism, and that can very well be regarded as a victory of the Counter Reformation" (SU 184). When Werfel states: "The Christian revival began in America" (SU 187) he indirectly repeats the argument he advanced in conjunction with the publication of *The Song of Bernadette*, namely that the novel should be seen as the fight between a spiritual worldview and the godlessness of national socialism. But a final victory of the spiritual principle over the "great naturalistic stupidity and its consequences" (SU 184) was not possible as "both principles have their eras of expansion and contraction, and that's all. A spiritual principle is never more powerful than when it is powerless, and never more powerless than when it is powerful" (SU 184). Not only did a phobia against fast motion, which led to the Astromental mode of traveling, originate in America but also an aversion to the world of capitalism, a plutophobia, and finally the idea of pure, meaningless play as a purpose in life. In Werfel's view America is thus the cradle of the future.

In the foregoing characterization of the novel little weight has been placed on Werfel's many "asides" in which he informs the Astromentals about his own age, criticizing it as a time in which crude technology, materialism, "radical realism" and "naturalistic nihilism" ruled. By contrast, his Astromental world is one in which all these elements have changed. What remains unchanged, however, is man, whose character is the same and whose hubris has carried him farther away from God. To demonstrate man's need for redemption, his need to get closer to God, was perhaps the most important message for Werfel.

NOTES

1. Alma Mahler-Werfel, *And the Bridge Is Love* (New York: Harcourt, Brace, 1958) 245.
2. As Lionel B. Steiman, *Franz Werfel: The Faith of an Exile. From Prague to Beverly Hills* (Waterloo, Ontario: Wilfrid Laurier University Press, 1985) 120, points out: "The rendering of their [the Argans'] account at the end has the ring of an 'all's well that ends well' report. . . . Since the substance of the novel, the story of Teta, had nothing to do with the tale of Argans, its integrity is not violated by according them this gratuitous good fortune at the end. Everyone feels good."
3. Radio interview, "I am an American," on station KECA Los Angeles (NBC) on 16 March 1941. Quoted, in German, by Steiman, *Franz Werfel* 214.
4. Franz Werfel, *Gesammelte Werke: Erzählungen aus zwei Welten* vol. 2, ed. Adolf D. Klarmann (Frankfurt am Main: S. Fischer, 1952) 368, trans. H.W.
5. Otto Friedrich, "Foreword," in Franz Werfel, *Cella, or, The Survivors* (New York: Holt, 1989) viii.
6. Franz Werfel, *Gesammelte Werke: Erzählungen aus zwei Welten* vol. 3, ed. Adolf D. Klarmann (Frankfurt am Main: S. Fischer, 1952) 460.
7. Werfel, *Gesammelte Werke: Erzählungen aus zwei Welten* 3:460.
8. Steiman, *Franz Werfel* 114f.
9. Steiman, *Franz Werfel* 104.
10. Leopold Zahn, *Franz Werfel* (Berlin: Colloquium, 1966) 51.
11. Werfel confirms this view in his short essay "Writing *Bernadette,*" *The Commonweal* (29 May 1942) 125f.
12. See Peter Stephan Jungk, *Franz Werfel: A Life in Prague, Vienna, and Hollywood,* trans. Anselm Hollo (New York: Grove Weidenfeld, 1990) 198.
13. Jungk 198.
14. See Lore B. Foltin, *Franz Werfel* (Stuttgart: Metzler, 1972) 101.
15. Steiman, *Franz Werfel* 144.
16. Werfel, "Writing *Bernadette*" 126.
17. Annemarie von Puttkamer, *Franz Werfel: Wort und Antwort* (Würzburg: Werkbund, 1952) 116.
18. Steiman, *Franz Werfel* 158.
19. Steiman, *Franz Werfel* 159.
20. Von Puttkamer 120f.
21. James L. Rolleston, "The Usable Future: Franz Werfel's *Star of the Unborn* as Exile Literature," in *Protest—Form—Tradition: Essays on German Exile Literature,* ed. Joseph P. Strelka, Robert F. Bell, and Eugene Dobson (University: University of Alabama Press, 1979) 57–80.
22. Foltin, *Franz Werfel* 107.
23. See Joseph P. Strelka, "Die politischen, sozialen und religiösen Utopien in Franz Werfel's 'Stern der Ungeborenen,' " in *Franz Werfel im Exil,* ed. Wolfgang Nehring and Hans Wagener (Bonn: Bouvier, 1992) 175.
24. Steiman, *Franz Werfel* 153.
25. Von Puttkamer 129.
26. Rolleston 74.
27. See von Puttkamer 137.

CONCLUSION: A FINAL ASSESSMENT

When Franz Werfel published his first collection of poetry, *Der Welt-freund,* he became the spokesperson overnight for the young generation which we now call Expressionists. In this first and in the following collections of poetry, he voiced a gospel of brotherhood, of love of one's fellow human beings that soon became one of the main characteristics of this movement in German-speaking countries. *Wir sind* and *Einander* confirmed and intensified this message of the young poet from Prague, and it was not until, under the influence of the experiences of the First World War, *Der Gerichtstag* was published that Werfel's optimism had clearly given way to increasing resignation, a resignation that was confirmed in his later collections of poetry.

Typically Expressionist were also his early dramas, in particular, the metaphysically oriented trilogy *Spiegelmensch,* the Faustian drama about guilt and ultimate self-finding of man; *Goat Song,* the drama about the intrusion of mythical forces into a rural society, about revolution and the ultimate restoration of human togetherness; and *Schweiger,* the drama about madness and guilt and the ultimate victory of humanity through self-sacrifice. In all these dramas a spirit of sacrifice and human closeness, of hubris and ultimate admission of guilt prevails, thus echoing the spirit of the author's poetry. The message of Werfel's first novel, "Not the Murderer," is close to these, taking up the theme of patricide, of the father-son conflict prevalent in so many Expressionist dramas. Werfel wrote his own version, at the same time castigating the spirit of discipline and militarism that stifled all human closeness between the generations, ending with pity for the father who is finally revealed in his naked humanity as an old man.

In his late twenties Werfel wrote his first essay, "The Christian Mission," in which he defended Christianity and rejected the political activism in which he was to engage for a very short period in 1918. He castigated what he called "abstraction," and what later on in his essay "Realism and Inwardness," reappeared as "radical realism" and in the essay "Can We Live Without Faith in God," as "naturalistic nihilism," stating that the modern world was on the road to soullessness, with technology and modern psychology to blame. In "Of Man's True Happiness" he deals with the role art plays in helping man find his true self, and in his collection of aphorisms entitled

"Theologumena," written between 1942–44, he expresses his religious views, his sympathy for Christianity on the one hand, and on the other his conviction that the mission of Israel as negative witness to Christ on earth was manifest in the suffering of persecution and dispersal of the Jews.

It may seem methodically wrong to summarize all these essays in one stroke, but in principle they all say the same thing, merely elaborating on what the young Werfel had said already. Werfel's work is one giant confession: he never changed his basic views. In his essays he appears as a man hostile to modernity, who defends his religious and artistic inclinations. Looking back, he found an ideal in the multinational Habsburg Empire and sang its praises in "An Essay upon the Meaning of Imperial Austria," strangely idealizing reality. Time and again it becomes clear that he rejected any type of revolution, political activism, technology, and any force which estranged man from himself and from his identity as a religious being. Werfel made it clear that he was a *homo religiosus* who would not stop singing the praises of man as a human being and as God's creature.

Consequently, it is irrelevant that he soon gave up the hymnic and ecstatic style of Expressionism in favor of a more factual, more sober style close to New Objectivity. The message of brotherhood may have been toned down, resignation may have set in, but the inner spirit of Werfel's work remained the same.

In *Verdi,* perhaps his last work with Expressionist elements, he describes how the composer can regain his creativity only after he has given up his inner struggle with Wagner and after he has discovered that Wagner is actually his "brother." In the drama *Juarez and Maximilian* he contrasts the well-meaning Maximilian with the calculating political activist Juarez, again showing the struggle of humanity against the political forces of the day. By giving in to seeming political necessities, Maximilian becomes guilty and falls victim to the forces he unleashed. Similarly, in "The Kingdom of God in Bohemia" Werfel depicts the fate of a political and religious reformer who falls victim to hubris and who, again, is taken over by the momentum of the forces he has created.

Just as he was later on to praise the Habsburg Empire in his essay, he mourned its demise in its most insignificant representatives in *The Man Who Conquered Death,* the gripping though ironic story about the dying of a petit bourgeois. In its satirical counterpart, "The House of Mourning," a brothel in Prague is representative of the entire old Habsburg monarchy just before the outbreak of the First World War. Here again Werfel looks back and idealizes a premodern past, a time before the advent of "naturalistic nihilism."

His voluminous novel *The Pure in Heart* was nothing but just such a reckoning with the past. The Great War had set modern forces free against humanity. It had resulted in the activism of Werfel and his friends at the end of the First World War, and it had allowed the timeless spirit of Barbara, the old maid, to counter all these negative forces. In her piety she remained the same through the years, guiding her protégé through the turmoil of his youth until he became a doctor and left the life of "the world" to work on a ship. It is an educational novel about a hero who is guided by his "secret society," Barbara, to find himself and to realize Werfel's ideal of piety and of what humans ought to be.

The conflict between the generations was taken up again in Werfel's "Italian novel," *The Pascarella Family,* but even more it is a novel about the end of an era, about the fascist state which wants to control all its citizens' activities and their feelings. This state does not exercise fatherly benevolence but rather brutal force. But whereas its hero learns what his fatherly limits are, and whereas the forces of love seem successful, the modern reader knows that fascism and the powers of godlessness and evil triumphed, and that any happy ending is merely a fairy tale.

The powers of godless modernity and of traditional belief in God are also contrasted in *The Forty Days of Musa Dagh.* It is not so much a historical novel about a few Armenians under their heroic leader Gabriel fighting against an overwhelming Turkish force, and it is not as much a parallel to the contemporary beginning of the Jewish persecution in Germany, but rather it is a novel about the old, traditional world of belief against the cold, modern one of the Young Turks. Gabriel himself had been in danger of turning into a modern man, but he found his roots again, his true identity as a member and leader of his people. Old, pious Turks, a German minister, and the faithful, innocent Armenians are Werfel's positive examples of what man ought to be and, when he talks about the Ottoman Empire, there is no doubt that he means the Habsburg Empire and the violation of its spirit by militarism and modernism.

An apostasy takes place when the Young Turks form an alliance with the militaristic Wilhelminian Germany, which is not dissimilar to the falling away from God, described by Werfel in *Hearken unto the Voice,* his novel about the prophet Jeremiah and the kings of Israel. Here obedience to God's commands administered through the mouth of the true prophet determines the well-being of God's people, their survival, and their humanity.

Man's relationship to God—the correct relationship to God—was time and again Werfel's theme and, as he became older, the religious character of his works became more pronounced. That heaven cannot be bought is demonstrated by the maid Teta, who believes that financing the theological studies of her seemingly gifted nephew can buy her an intermediary to God and thus a place in heaven. After learning about the deceit of her nephew, Teta accidentally meets a true intermediary—a young priest—and dies in Rome. Again Werfel has contrasted modern man in the person of the nephew and true piety in the old maid.

In many ways this novel is the precursor to *The Song of Bernadette* in which the young Bernadette Soubirous proves the absolute nature of her trust in the Lady she has seen in the grotto of Massabielle, by carrying out her orders against the will of all the elders. The modern spirit, modern science, and deism, represented by the small-town dignitaries in the Café Français, are pitted against the simple belief of the country people in the French Pyrenees. Again, humility and obedience win out over arrogant enlightenment and skepticism.

Even in his posthumously published utopian-dystopian novel *Star of the Unborn* these two forces are opposed to each other. The world of the Astromentals which F.W. visits in the year 101,943 is a world which celebrates the wonders of technology, a time when all basic needs of man have been met, and yet a time when the perfection of technology and hygiene is negative and undesirable. The epitome of human hubris is embodied in the Wintergarden where people are retrogenerated into the state of babies and finally into marguerites. For Werfel this conquest of death is the highest form of hubris, the escape from what God has ordained for man. In spite of its mental sophistication, the utopian world has been unsuccessful in suppressing human aggressiveness so that a war with the outlying jungles results, that is, those areas in which humanity in all its primitiveness has survived. *Star of the Unborn* is Werfel's final statement against the spirit of modernity, against technology, against the attempt of man to escape from or to rival God. It may seem strange that the two forces that are still alive after 100,000 years are Judaism and Catholicism but, according to Werfel's "Theologumena," these are the two complementary forces and institutions that both need each other and must exist separately. They are two parallel lines which intersect at infinity, as Werfel expresses it in his exile drama *Jacobowsky and the Colonel*, where he again pits Jacobowsky, the Jew, against the Polish Colonel Stjerbinsky: both need each other in order to reach their goal—freedom in exile.

Werfel died while exiled in Beverly Hills. Although he was financially wealthy and was one of the few German exile writers who was open to and had adapted very well to his new American environment, he nonetheless suffered the same inner pains as they did. He wrote about persecution and isolation in his poetry and in his novel *Cella,* a fragment which goes back to his years in Sanary-sur-Mer. Nowhere else did he describe the persecution of the Jews and the contemporary forces of evil as graphically. For him the Nazis are the machine men, the embodiments of "radical nihilism" against whom the Austrian representatives of tradition are powerless; the machine men, whose threat their Jewish countrymen realized only when it was too late. More serious than the exile comedy *Jacobowsky and the Colonel,* this realistic novel also deals with those forces and types of modern man against whom Werfel has fought throughout his life.

The case of Franz Werfel is unique. In many ways his work is an integrated whole. Its forte comes from the author's unwavering plea for humanity, for the reestablishment of man's relationship to God, his plea not to succumb to the powers of godlessness, the powers of the modern machine age, the powers of secularism. It is the strength of his religious conviction which unifies his work and fills it with an inner spirit of humanity. At the same time his work fails to deal with the reality of the modern age. Little is gained by longing for an empire of the type old Austria represented. While the development of modern technology cannot be turned back, his diatribes against radical realism and naturalistic nihilism are justified warnings against the loss of metaphysical perspective from which the modern world suffers.

BIBLIOGRAPHY

WORKS BY FRANZ WERFEL

ESSAYS AND APHORISMS

Realismus und Innerlichkeit ("Realism and Inwardness"). Vienna: Paul Zsolnay, 1931.

Können wir ohne Gottesglauben leben ("Can We Live Without Faith in God"). Vienna: Paul Zsolnay, 1932.

Von der reinsten Glückseligkeit des Menschen ("Of Man's True Happiness"). Stockholm: Bermann-Fischer, 1938.

Between Heaven and Earth. Trans. Maxim Newmark. New York: Philosophical Library, 1944. (German version published as *Zwischen oben und unten*. Stockholm: Bermann-Fischer, 1946.)

POETRY

Der Weltfreund: Erste Gedichte (The Philanthropist: First Poems). Leipzig: Axel Juncker, 1911.

Wir sind: Neue Gedichte (We Are: New Poems). Leipzig: Kurt Wolff, 1913.

Einander: Oden, Lieder, Gestalten (Each Other: Odes, Poems, Characters). Leipzig: Kurt Wolff, 1915.

Gesänge aus den drei Reichen: Ausgewählte Gedichte (Songs from the Three Realms: Selected Poems). Leipzig: Kurt Wolff, 1915.

Der Gerichtstag, in fünf Büchern (The Judgment Day, in Five Books). Leipzig: Kurt Wolff, 1919.

Arien (Arias). Munich: Kurt Wolff, 1923.

Beschwörungen (Conjurations). Munich: Kurt Wolff, 1923.

Gedichte (Poems). Berlin: Paul Zsolnay, 1927.

Neue Gedichte (New Poems). Berlin: Paul Zsolnay, 1928.

Schlaf und Erwachen: Neue Gedichte (Sleep and Awakening: New Poems). Vienna: Paul Zsolnay, 1937.

Gedichte aus dreißig Jahren (Poems from Thirty Years). Stockholm: Bermann-Fischer, 1939.

Poems. Trans. Edith Abercrombie Snow. Princeton: Princeton University Press, 1945.

Gedichte aus den Jahren 1908–1945 (Poems from the Years 1908–1945). Ed. Ernst Gottlieb and Felix Guggenheim. Frankfurt am Main: S. Fischer, 1946; Los Angeles: Pazifische Presse, 1946.

DRAMA

Die Versuchung: Ein Gespräch des Dichters mit dem Erzengel und Luzifer (The Temptation: A Conversation of the Poet with the Archangel and Lucifer). Leipzig: Kurt Wolff, 1913.

Die Troerinnen des Euripides: In deutscher Bearbeitung von Franz Werfel (Euripides' *The Trojan Women*. Edited by Franz Werfel). Leipzig: Kurt Wolff, 1915.

Der Besuch aus dem Elysium: Romantisches Drama in einem Aufzug (The Visit from Elysium: Romantic Drama in One Act). Munich: Kurt Wolff, 1920.

Spiegelmensch: Magische Trilogie (Mirror Man: Magical Trilogy). Munich: Kurt Wolff, 1920.

Bocksgesang: In fünf Akten. Munich: Kurt Wolff, 1921. (*Goat Song [Bocksgesang]: A Drama in Five Acts.* Trans. Ruth Langner. Garden City, N.Y.: Doubleday, Page, 1926.)

Schweiger: Ein Trauerspiel in drei Akten (Schweiger: A Tragedy in Three Acts). Munich: Kurt Wolff, 1923.

Juarez und Maximilian: Dramatische Historie in 3 Phasen und 13 Bildern. Vienna: Paul Zsolnay, 1924. (*Juarez and Maximilian: A Dramatic History in Three Phases and Thirteen Pictures.* Trans. Ruth Langner. New York: Simon and Schuster, 1926.)

Paulus unter den Juden: Dramatische Legende in sechs Bildern. Berlin: Paul Zsolnay, 1926. (*Paul among the Jews [A Tragedy].* Trans. Paul P. Levertoff. Milwaukee: Morehouse, 1928; London: Diocesan House, 1928.)

Das Reich Gottes in Böhmen: Tragödie eines Führers (The Kingdom of God in Bohemia: Tragedy of a Leader). Vienna: Paul Zsolnay, 1930.

Der Weg der Verheißung: Ein Bibelspiel. Vienna: Paul Zsolnay, 1935. (*The Eternal Road: A Drama in Four Parts.* Trans. Ludwig Lewisohn. New York: Viking, 1936.)

In einer Nacht: Ein Schauspiel (During One Night: A Drama). Vienna: Paul Zsolnay, 1937.

Jacobowsky und der Oberst: Komödie einer Tragödie in drei Akten. Stockholm: Bermann-Fischer, 1944. (*Jacobowsky and the Colonel: Comedy of a Tragedy in Three Acts.* Trans. Gustave O. Arlt. New York: Viking, 1944. German version edited by Arlt. New York: Crofts, 1944.)

PROSE

Der Dschin: Ein Märchen. Gedichte aus Der Gerichtstag. Blasphemie eines Irren. Fragmente (The Jinn: A Fairy Tale. Poems from The Judgment Day. Blasphemy of a Madman. Fragments). Vienna: Genossenschaftsverlag, 1919.

Nicht der Mörder, der Ermordete ist schuldig: Eine Novelle. (''Not the Murderer.'' Trans. H. T. Lowe-Porter, in Franz Werfel, *Twilight of a World.* New York: Viking, 1937.)

Spielhof: Eine Phantasie (Spielhof: A Phantasy). Munich: Kurt Wolff, 1920.

Verdi: Roman der Oper. Vienna: Paul Zsolnay, 1924. (*Verdi: A Novel of the Opera.* Trans. Helen Jessiman. New York: Simon and Schuster, 1925; London: Jarrolds, 1926.)

Der Tod des Kleinbürgers: Novelle. Vienna: Paul Zsolnay, 1927. (*The Man Who Conquered Death.* Trans. Clifton P. Fadiman and William A. Drake. New York: Simon & Schuster, 1927; trans. republished as *The Death of a Poor Man.* London: Benn, 1927.)

Geheimnis eines Menschen: Novellen (Saverio's Secret: Novellas; contains "Die Entfremdung" ["Estrangement"], "Geheimnis eines Menschen" ["Saverio's Secret"], "Die Hoteltreppe" ["The Staircase"], "Das Trauerhaus" ["The House of Mourning"]). Berlin: Paul Zsolnay, 1927. (Trans. H. T. Lowe-Porter, in Franz Werfel, *Twilight of a World.* New York: Viking, 1937.)

Der Abituriententag: Geschichte einer Jugendschuld. Vienna: Paul Zsolnay, 1928. (*Class Reunion.* Trans. Whittaker Chambers. New York: Simon & Schuster, 1929.)

Barbara oder Die Frömmigkeit. Vienna: Paul Zsolnay, 1929. (*The Pure in Heart.* Trans. Geoffrey Dunlop. New York: Simon & Schuster, 1931; trans. republished as *The Hidden Child.* London: Jarrolds, 1931.)

Kleine Verhältnisse: Novelle. Vienna: Paul Zsolnay, 1931. ("Poor People." Trans. H. T. Lowe-Porter, in Franz Werfel, *Twilight of a World.* New York: Viking, 1937.)

Die Geschwister von Neapel: Roman. Vienna: Paul Zsolnay, 1931. (*The Pascarella Family: A Novel.* Trans. Dorothy F. Tait-Price. New York: Simon & Schuster, 1932; London: Jarrolds, 1932.)

Die vierzig Tage des Musa Dagh. 2 vols. Vienna: Paul Zsolnay, 1933. (*The Forty Days of Musa Dagh.* Trans. Geoffrey Dunlop. New York: Viking, 1934; trans. republished as *The Forty Days.* London: Jarrolds, 1934.)

Höret die Stimme. Vienna: Paul Zsolnay, 1937. (*Hearken unto the Voice.* Trans. Moray Firth. New York: Viking, 1938.)

Twilight of a World. Trans. H. T. Lowe-Porter. New York: Viking, 1937. (Contains "An Essay upon the Meaning of Imperial Austria," "Poor People," "Not the Murderer," "The House of Mourning," "The Estrangement," "The Staircase," "Saverio's Secret," "The Man Who Conquered Death," "Class Reunion.")

Der veruntreute Himmel: Die Geschichte einer Magd. Stockholm: Bermann-Fischer, 1939. (*Embezzled Heaven.* Trans. Moray Firth. New York: Viking, 1940; London: Hamish Hamilton, 1940.)

Eine blaßblaue Frauenschrift (A Pale Blue Woman's Writing). Buenos Aires: Editorial Estrellas, 1941.

Das Lied von Bernadette. Stockholm: Bermann-Fischer, 1941. (*The Song of Bernadette.* Trans. Ludwig Lewisohn. New York: Viking, 1942; London: Hamish Hamilton, 1942.)

Die wahre Geschichte vom wiederhergestellten Kreuz ("The Priest's Tale of the Righted Cross"). Los Angeles: Pazifische Presse, 1942.

Stern der Ungeborenen: Ein Reiseroman. Stockholm: Bermann-Fischer, 1946. (*Star of the Unborn.* Trans. Gustave O. Arlt. New York: Viking, 1946.)

Cella oder Die Überwinder. Frankfurt am Main: S. Fischer, 1982. (*Cella, or, The Survivors.* Trans. Joachim Neugroschel. New York: Holt, 1989.)

COLLECTED WORKS

Gesammelte Werke (Collected Works). Ed. Adolf D. Klarmann. 8 [unnumbered] vols. Vol. 1, Stockholm: Bermann-Fischer, 1948; vols. 2–7, Frankfurt am Main: S. Fischer. 1948–1974; vol. 8, Munich: Langen-Müller, 1975.

Das Franz Werfel Buch (The Franz Werfel Book). Ed. Peter Stephan Jungk. Frankfurt am Main: S. Fischer, 1975.

Gesammelte Werke in Einzelbänden (Collected Works in Individual Volumes). Ed. Knut Beck. Frankfurt am Main: S. Fischer, 1989ff.

CRITICAL WORKS

BIBLIOGRAPHIES

Foltin, Lore B., and John M. Spalek. "Franz Werfel's Essays: A Survey." In *The German Quarterly* 42 (1969): 172–203. Contains a complete bibliography of Werfel's essays.

Foltin, Lore B. *Franz Werfel.* Stuttgart: Metzler, 1972. Contains detailed bibliographical information on primary and secondary material up to that date.

McGowan, Frank. "Works Published 1911–1950." In Lore B. Foltin, ed., *Franz Werfel. 1890–1945.* Pittsburgh: University of Pittsburgh Press, 1961, pp. 96–102. Includes all monographs and separately published works, but not works published in periodicals. English translations included.

Steiman, Lionel B. "Franz Werfel." In James Hardin and Donald G. Daviau, eds., *Austrian Fiction Writers: 1875–1913. Dictionary of Literary Biography,* vol. 81. Detroit, Mich.: Gale Research, 1989, pp. 300–312. Bibliography of all of Werfel's book publications, including English translations.

BOOKS

Abels, Norbert. *Franz Werfel: Mit Selbstzeugnissen und Bilddokumenten* (with documents from his own hand and pictorial documents). Reinbek bei Hamburg: Rowohlt, 1990. Well-researched short biography on the basis of archival materials, diaries, letters, etc.

Braselmann, Werner. *Franz Werfel.* Wuppertal-Barmen: Müller, 1960. Outdated introduction, in German, to Werfel and his works.

Foltin, Lore B. *Franz Werfel.* Stuttgart: Metzler, 1972. The best older introduction to Franz Werfel, concentrating on facts such as biographical and bibliographical data rather than interpretations of individual works.

Foltin, Lore B., ed. *Franz Werfel: 1890–1945*. Pittsburgh: University of Pittsburgh Press, 1961. A collection of nine scholarly essays and a bibliography (see above) on Werfel and his work.

Huber, Lothar, ed. *Franz Werfel:. An Austrian Writer Reassessed*. Oxford: Berg, 1989. A collection of 13 scholarly essays on Werfel and his work.

Jungk, Peter Stephan. *Franz Werfel: Eine Lebensgeschichte*. Frankfurt am Main: S. Fischer, 1987. English edition, *Franz Werfel: A Life in Prague, Vienna, and Hollywood*. Trans. Anselm Hollo. New York: Grove Weidenfeld, 1990. A comprehensive biography with pictures and interviews.

Lunzer, Heinz, and Victoria Lunzer-Talos. *Franz Werfel: 1890–1945. Katalog*. Vienna: Zirkular, 1990. Catalogue of a Werfel exhibition organized by the Austrian Foreign Office in collaboration with the Dokumentationsstelle für Neuere Österreichische Literatur, Vienna, containing many photos and biographical details.

Mahler-Werfel, Alma. *Mein Leben*. Frankfurt am Main: S. Fischer 1960. (English version, *And the Bridge Is Love*. New York: Harcourt, Brace, 1958.) The memoirs of Werfel's widow, reporting many details about her life with Franz Werfel and her other husbands, Gustav Mahler and Walter Gropius.

Nehring, Wolfgang, and Hans Wagener, eds. *Franz Werfel im Exil*. Bonn: Bouvier, 1992. A collection of 11 scholarly essays on Werfel and his work.

Puttkamer, Annemarie von. *Franz Werfel: Wort und Antwort* (Word and Answer). Würzburg: Werkbund, 1952. A treatment of Werfel's work, concentrating on his religious thinking from a sympathetic point of view.

Specht, Richard. *Franz Werfel: Versuch einer Zeitspiegelung* (Attempt to Reflect His Time). Berlin: Paul Zsolnay, 1926. An outdated, panegyric first biography and interpretation of Werfel's works.

Steiman, Lionel B. *Franz Werfel: The Faith of an Exile. From Prague to Beverly Hills*. Waterloo, Ontario: Wilfrid Laurier University Press, 1985. A critical and insightful investigation of the development of Werfel's philosophical and theological thinking.

Wimmer, Paul. *Franz Werfel's dramatische Sendung*. Vienna: Bergland, 1973. An enthusiastic treatment of Werfel's dramas, including detailed plot summaries.

Zahn, Leopold. *Franz Werfel*. Berlin: Colloquium, 1966. A cursory short German introduction to Franz Werfel's life and works.

ARCHIVES

Most of Werfel's personal papers, letters, manuscripts, and reviews of his works are at two archives: the University of California, Los Angeles, Department of Special Collections, and the University of Pennsylvania, Philadelphia. Many other letters, especially those written to Gertrud Spirk, are at the Deutsches Literaturarchiv, Marbach, Neckar. For an account of other archival holdings see Lore B. Foltin.

Franz Werfel. Stuttgart: Metzler, 1972, pp. 1–6; and John M. Spalek. *A Guide to the Archival Materials of the German-speaking Emigration to the United States after 1933*. Charlottesville: University of Virginia Press, 1978.

INDEX